IN THE THROE OF WONDER

By the same author

The Way of Suffering: A Geography of Crisis

IN THE THROE OF WONDER

Intimations of the Sacred in a Post-Modern World

JEROME A. MILLER

State University
of New York
Press

Published by
State University of New York Press, Albany

© 1992 State University of New York

For information, address State University of New York
Press, State University Plaza, Albany, N.Y., 12246

Library of Congress Cataloging-in-Publication Data

Miller, Jerome A., 1946–
    In the throe of wonder : intimations of the sacred in a post-
modern world / Jerome A. Miller.
        p.   .cm.
    Includes bibliographical references and index.
    ISBN 0-7914-0953-8 (alk. paper) : $44.50 — ISBN 0-7914-0954-6
(pbk. : alk. paper) : $14.95
        1. Experience.   2. Ontology.   3. Religion—Philosophy.   I. Title.
B105.E9M54   1992
128′.4—dc20   91-12723
                                                                    CIP

10 9 8 7 6 5 4 3 2 1

This book is dedicated to
James Devereux, S. J., Joseph Feeney, S. J., and Lucien
Longtin, S. J.,

Teachers of the highest order

. . . the son is a debtor, and must repay his debt, and as,
whatever he does, it is not adequate to his obligation, he is a
perpetual debtor.

–Aristotle, *Nicomachean Ethics*

. . . the expression of wonder is worship. And wonder is an ambiguous state of mind which comprises fear and bliss. Worship therefore is mingled fear and bliss all at once.

—Soren Kierkegaard,
"Three Discourses on Imagined Occasions"

CONTENTS

PREFACE

While the subtitle of this book gives the prospective reader some inkling of its content, it does little to help her locate it in the current philosophical landscape. And since there are so many books we would like to read, and so mortally short a time to read them, it would be inconsiderate not to provide some information to help the reader decide whether to become engaged with this one.

Let me begin by saying something about the thinkers who have opened up the territory I try to explore here. Heidegger should be mentioned first because this book, like its predecessor, is part of my continuing agon with his thought. Readers familiar with Derrida, Rorty, Levinas, Freud, and Eliade will be quick to realize that I am also responding to their influence and addressing issues they raise. But one of the characteristics of this book about which the reader should be alerted is that it is not exegetical and is not principally about other texts. The single exception to this is the third chapter, in which I try to understand the connections and disjunctions between Heidegger and Bernard Lonergan, whose work, much less known and, thus far, less philosophically influential than Heidegger's, has decisively affected my way of thinking. While it could never have been written had it not been for the thinkers I have mentioned, this book is reflective in character and exploratory in purpose, rather than scholarly in the ordinary sense. It does not presuppose mastery of, or even familiarity with, the texts which have had the most impact on it, and, with a few exceptions, it does not employ the technical terminology often used to discuss the themes it treats.

It is not as easy to say in a few words what this book is about or to what field it belongs. Perhaps the best way to describe it simply would be to say that it is an attempt to understand certain matters of the heart—certain experiences which have a profoundly

transformative impact on us because they affect us in the core of
our beings. Wonder and horror are such experiences, as are the
experiences of anguish and awe to which they lead. Our culture has
prejudiced us into thinking that these experiences are subjective,
emotive responses to events in the world that can be objectively
described. I explore here a very different possibility—that such
experiences are disclosive in character and open up to us realities
which are not accessible to us as long as we are governed by everyday practical concerns. Indeed, when we try to plumb the meaning
of these experiences, we find that they are charged with ontological
significance. Consequently, this book is as much about being and
nothingness as it is about wonder and horror, but I try to make
sure that my discussion of these topics, which can so easily become
abstract and obscure, remains grounded in the sometimes wonderful, sometimes upsetting human experiences which first give us
access to them. Indeed, I am concerned throughout with how such
experiences transform our knowledge of what is by awakening us
to realities of which we would otherwise be oblivious.

I find it as impossible to separate these themes from each other
as I find it inappropriate to impose a systematic order on them.
Each, I discover, has a way of exploding outward toward the others,
and all of them are bound together by a dialectical grace which I
think it would be both fruitless and wrong to try to control. Because of the range of these themes, and the necessity of letting them
influence each other, it would be misleading to identify the territory of the book with one particular field of philosophical inquiry,
but I hope it will prove engaging to those interested in hermeneutics and ontology, in philosophy of religion and the phenomenology of religious experience, and to those whose thinking
has been affected by the post-modern crisis of philosophy itself.

To say anything here about the conclusions to which I am led
would change this from a preface to an afterword. But perhaps I
should say that the conclusions of the book do not form a closure,
but an opening. It is being published in the hope that the process of
getting to it will be for the reader, as it has been for me, the way to
a small beginning.

ACKNOWLEDGMENTS

Chapter 2 of this book, "Wonder as Hinge," originally appeared in slightly different form in *International Philosophical Quarterly*, March, 1989, pp. 53–66. An earlier version of chapter 3, "On the Way Between Heidegger and Lonergan," appeared in *The Journal of Speculative Philosophy*, Vol. II. No. 2, pp. 63–88 (copyright 1988 by The Pennsylvania State University). "Horror and the Deconstruction of the Self," the original from which chapter 6 has been developed, appeared in *Philosophy Today*, Winter, 1988, pp. 286–298. I am grateful to the publishers of these journals for their generosity in allowing me to bring these essays into the present text.

ACKNOWLEDGMENTS

PROLOGUE

It can be difficult for those of us who have become what Thoreau called "professors of philosophy"[1] to remember what it was like to be seized by philosophical wonder for the first time. But I think that implicit within that wonder was the discovery of all possible worlds, and the realization that there is a way to ask a question about everything at once. The experience of asking such a question is especially liberating because of the fact that it releases amazement from all restraints and enables us to become total wonderers. Socrates's accusers were right in suspecting that this experience would have a revolutionary impact, if its promise of an unrestricted inquiry were taken to heart. For the very act of asking an un-restricted question shatters our ordinary world and gives us access to a literally unlimited horizon.[2] In doing so, it awakens an inex-haustible longing which might otherwise have remained dormant but which, once ignited, has a potential for effacing every compet-ing passion. What makes a question philosophical is precisely its ability to express wonder in a completely uninhibited way, and its power to bring wonder into focus without abridging its scope or moderating the eros which it inspires in us. Realizing that there *are* such questions, experiencing for the first time their power to pene-trate all the way through us to that mysterious source in us from which all wonder springs, is a radically transformative event, com-parable only to our experiences of love and death. It changes the world we live in forever.

But like romantic love and the encounter with nothingness, the experience of wonder is not something we can cause to happen to us. It is true that we can prevent it from happening, just as we can prevent ourselves from falling in love, by refusing to allow it to disrupt our ordinary world. We make the event of wonder possible insofar as it cannot occur unless we at least momentarily let down our guard and respond receptively to it. But while wonder cannot happen without our consent, we cannot bring it about through our own causal efforts. Why is this the case? What is it about the very nature of wonder that prevents our being able to initiate it in ourselves?

These questions belong to a large and inexhaustible problematic—the nature of wonder and its import for philosophy as a whole. This book is devoted to an exploration of that problematic; it is an exercise in wondering about wonder. To explain ahead of time where this exploration leads and what destination it reaches would require putting the whole book in the introduction I am trying to write to it. It would necessitate my making available here at the beginning of the book what becomes accessible in it and through it. It is understandable that a reader would like to know beforehand what a book is about and whether its conclusions are important and justified; the writer would also like to possess a guarantee for the success of his enterprise before beginning it. But such a guarantee, if it were provided to either reader or writer, would make the act of reading or writing itself superfluous. We wish we could have a warranty so we could know ahead of time whether our time with a book is going to be well spent. But we could only know that if we could begin with the conclusion, start with the end, have the future fully available in the present. We would like to save time by abolishing it. We would like to already know what we are about to explore.

If such a guarantee is unavailable, we would at least like to make sure that we get off on the right foot by taking our first step in the right direction. But as Socrates told us, the beginning is the hardest and the most dreadful part of an action. If only we knew enough to make our first sentence infallible, we could use it as a bridge to cross over the abyss which seems to separate us as knowers from the unknown we are about to explore. Such a bridge would be especially helpful to the philosopher, for whom the dread of a misstep at the very beginning of inquiry is especially acute.[3] For because of the fact that philosophical wonder is unlimited in scope, it pulls the ground out from under one and throws absolutely everything open to question. In such a situation we would dearly love to be able to cling to some saving surety, some clear and certain truth about which no doubts or suspicions could be raised. But to protect any truth from the disruptive impact of one's questioning would restrict the scope of one's wonder and thus deprive it of that uninhibited character which makes it philosophical. To be philosophical means, therefore, precisely to let go of all one already knows and to surrender oneself wholly and without reserve to the throe of questioning itself.

But as soon as we realize that to be fully engaged by a philosophical question we must relinquish everything we consider to be obvious, we recoil from it as from the edge of an abyss. A question which makes everything questionable takes the known away from us and makes us aware of the whole of being as wholly unknown. By uprooting us from the given, and taking away from us the obviousness of the obvious, a philosophical question removes us from our familiar surroundings and puts us down, without maps or compass, in the middle of nowhere. The fact that everything is included in its questioning prevents philosophy from beginning in any other way. It cannot gradually assimilate the unknown to the known by slowly exploring the territory which lies just outside the parameters of the familiar; for philosophy requires us to recognize as unknown precisely the familiar which we thought we knew. *At the very beginning it situates us in the middle of a whole which we know only as wholly unknown.* To philosophize is to not know where one is; to ask a philosophical question means to become aware of oneself as radically lost.

Because the unknown is not assimilatable into the given, we can become aware of it as unknown only by acknowledging its difference, and the impossibility of homologizing its otherness with what we have heretofore thought of as the already known. The fact that we can ask a question and the fact that in the very act of asking it we break through the known to the unknown, the given to the transcendent, may at first seem to prove that the mind has the power to penetrate what is beyond it, the capacity to surpass the limits which reality tries to impose on it. But such an interpretation flies in the face of the experience of wonder itself. For, as wonderers, we do make a breakthrough to the beyond, but we do so by becoming aware of it in its very character *as* beyond us—as transcending what is given to us in a way that will forever prevent our equating it with what is given to us. Precisely because the unknown is given to us as radically unknown, we lack the kind of control over it which we would have if it were wholly given to us and thus immediately knowable.

This begins to explain why the breakthrough which occurs when we become questioners is not something which we ourselves can cause to happen. In order to cause myself to become a questioner, I would have to have the unknown at my disposal, since an awareness of the unknown is the indispensable prerequisite for questioning; but if the unknown were at my disposal, it would not transcend me and would therefore be incapable of operating as the catalyst for questioning. Having no control over the unknown, we can have no control over the process of questioning it awakens in us. It is not we who break through to the unknown. It is the unknown which breaks through to us, ignites in us the eros of the desire to know, and so transforms us into questioners. To philosophize is to realize that everything is unknown, and to surrender to the throe of questioning which that realization sets in motion. This, as Socrates himself warned us, is a kind of divine madness.[4]

Socrates could compare the experience of being caught in the sway of philosophical eros to the experience of contracting an incurable and deadly disease, because of the fact that this eros leads us to question relentlessly, even to the point of jeopardizing the apparently self-evident principles which lie at the basis of our common-sense rationality. To ask what these principles mean and whether they are really true must seem like madness to anyone who takes it for granted that they define the parameters of sense and the boundaries of being itself. But common-sense rationality, by taking its own principles for granted, treats meaning and truth as givens which are simply to be accepted in their givenness. This leads common sense to criticize as irrational the whole process of being seized by wonder, being driven to question, being caught up in the eros of inquiry, unless that eros remains confined inside the presuppositions of everyday practice.[5] But when common sense tries to restrict the scope of wonder by appealing to the given, it is really encouraging us to betray intelligence itself. For how can it be intelligent to impose restrictions on rational inquiry? And how are we to become fully engaged by the spirit of inquiry if we repress without question the drive to wonder which animates and sustains it?

To be fully rational requires surrendering unconditionally to the throe of wonder instead of clinging to the given; it means allowing oneself to be cast into the abyss of the unknown instead of trying to find a way to secure oneself from that vertiginous possibility. But if this is true, being rational has little in common with the drive to plan and control, the desire to manage and organize, the effort to program and systematize, which have led, over the past four centuries, to the "rationalization" of human life in all its facets. Ordinarily, the attempt to "rationalize" human life is motivated by the hope of achieving precisely the kind of control over the unknown which we do not enjoy when we experience it as unknown and so are aware that it transcends us. It is true that to be rational in this managerial sense we are required to be inquirers, but such inquiry is limited to figuring out how to bring the unknown inside the parameters of the known, how to disarm its difference, how to remove its transcendent dimension so as to reduce it to something manageable. Every method which sets up knowledge as a goal to be achieved by means of its methodical procedures conceives of knowing, whether it knows it or not, as the process of gaining control over what is to be known.[6] For in construing knowledge as a goal to be achieved, we make the search for it a practical project which we are to accomplish by making the object of our search yield to our grasp of it. Inquiry is thus transformed into a way of mastering the unknown. What makes the achievement of such mastery so attractive is precisely the fact that it promises to provide us a way to escape the inferior position in which wonder places us when it makes us aware of the unknown which transcends us.

But for any method to deliver on its promise of mastery, it must provide us a way to reach out and take possession of the unknown without exposing our own weaknesses and vulnerabilities. A method would defeat its own purpose if, in order to use it, we had to give up our secure position, and venture forth defenselessly into the unfamiliar territory of the radically other. For the whole reason for having a method in the goal-oriented sense of the term is to use it as a paved highway by means of which we can travel from the known to the unknown without running the risk of getting lost. But the dilemma which confronts everyone who tries to invent such a method is how to secure the unknown without jeopardizing one's hold on the known, how to explore without letting go, how to cross over from the familiar to the utterly foreign without leaving everything familiar behind. The only way to resolve this dilemma is to practice inquiry as a process of colonization by means of which the unknown is incorporated, assimilated, appropriated into one's native country without ever allowing its *difference* from the familiar to emerge. Method, by virtue of its very goal-oriented character, introduces an imperialist politic into the life of the mind. For in order to succeed in its ambition to master the other, method must, from the very beginning, from the very first step it takes in approaching the other, repress the heterogeneity of its difference since its emergence would jeopardize the security we enjoy by knowing the known and having it given to us. Method, in short, methodicalizes the destruction of the other.[7]

To allow the other to be, on the other hand, requires the relinquishing of all goal-oriented method. But to allow the other to be does not mean to remain separate from it, to keep our distance from it, to never cross over the boundary line separating it as unknown from what we think we already know. Such indifference, such detachment, though it might on the surface seem to be compatible with being aware of difference and respectful of it, inevitably leads us to reduce the other to the status of an observed object whose difference poses no threat to our world. Such an observational attitude involves looking at the other as something given— even if it is only given to us at some distance from us. When we "objectively observe" the other, its very difference from us has already been repressed. The alternative to such repression is to let the other be not in the sense of being indifferent to it but in the sense of allowing oneself to be vulnerable to its difference, and overcome by it. Thus, to enter the unknown as unknown instead of trying to colonize it requires our approaching it in a spirit of meekness and voluntary poverty. And we embrace such poverty intellectually only by surrendering fully to that throe of questioning which requires our leaving the given behind and accepting ignorance as our destitute condition.

There is no way to rehearse this spirit or plan ahead of time how one is going to practice it. All one can do is surrender to the throe of the unknown and let it transport one wherever it will. There are no royal roads, no freeways, not even any maps or compass by means of which we might render ourselves less vulnerable to the possibility of getting lost. But that does not necessarily mean one must travel without a direction; it only means that the direction cannot be known ahead of time because it does not come from us. To be an inquirer without a method means that one takes the unknown so seriously that, instead of setting out to master it, one gives up all one thinks one knows and becomes its servant. To make that turn, to undergo that conversion, seems, to those who look at it from the perspective of what it leaves behind, like a kind of death—like the death of thought itself. To the one who undergoes it, who awakens in wonder to the other in its otherness, it seems like the birth of genuine thinking. To one who is in the very throe of this turn, it is like dying and being born at the same time.

In writing this book, I have tried to surrender my thought to the influence of that throe and to let it turn my thinking inside out. I do not begin by announcing a goal or proceed by taking the steps that promise to lead to a preconceived destination. Indeed, I do not set out to "prove" anything if this is taken to mean the process of paving the way for the adoption of specific propositions. The chapters of this book are not related to each other as successive links in a chain of reasoning, each of which is expected to add an increment of truth to an accumulating argument on behalf of a particular thesis. Rather, they are successive efforts to explore the unknown itself in its radical otherness as it becomes accessible to us in the experience of wonder; my purpose is not to enclose the unknown within a chain of reasoning but to allow its difference to breach my thinking, even though, in doing so, I run the risk of losing my bearings and falling into error. To think the other as other requires the primal risk of entrusting one's thought to it and following wherever it leads. We have a terrible fear of losing control of our thought, which is intimately related to the experience of dread in the face of death; we especially dread what we will be led to realize if we surrender to our most threatening intimations instead of deflecting or repressing them. For thought to be courageous in the face of such dread does not mean trying to overcome the unknown but precisely the opposite—trying to be open to it and even willing to be devastated by it.

Such vulnerability to the unknown, such openness to the other in its otherness, is the distinguishing characteristic of every inquiry which is animated by wonder and governed by its exigencies. In its obligation to be faithful to those exigencies, philosophy does not differ from other disciplines. But unlike those disciplines which respond to the beckoning of a particular kind of other and provide us a way of access to its particular world, philosophy would have us marvel at all our worlds, and realize that we are beckoned by the endless array of others into a pleroma of universes. Our capacity for unrestricted wonder does not make us the center around which all these universes revolve; but it does make us a nexus where they intersect, a meeting place for their differences, an agora where every one of their appeals can be heard. If philosophy cannot keep from using terms of unlimited generality like "being" to describe what it addresses, it is not because it has a weakness for vague abstractions but because it wants its receptivity to otherness to be as all inclusive as wonder and as unrestricted as the eros of the mind which wonder provokes.

This link between wonder and being, this intimate bond between our experience of amazement and the unknown other which becomes accessible to us in and through our amazement, this fertile but fragile rapport which inspires the eros of questioning, is the point of departure, the jumping-off place, for all the explorations I attempt here. What makes wondering about wonder so liberating, what makes it evocative of so many themes and suggestive of so many insights, is the fact that wonder is the opening through which we gain access to literally all our insights. This book as a whole is an attempt to enter that opening. Each of its chapters opens onto the others, is a way of access to the others, insofar as each breaches themes which its neighbors address, similar to the way in which the different movements of a symphony play upon recurring motifs without ever pretending to exhaust their possibilities. The cumulative result of this process is not that, at the end of it, I get through the opening to what lies on the other side of it. For in wondering about wonder, as in wonder itself, there is no closure.

Indeed, the whole point is not to close the opening but to open it, to live in that openness, to be the unconditional questioner. But one's questioning is unconditional only if one surrenders without reserve to that which makes our questioning possible by breaking through to us in its otherness: the other itself. If this book can be said to be a whole, it is not because its chapters constitute a closed system of meaning but because taken together they form an opening which cannot be closed off, like a painting which, both in spite of and because of its frame, gives us a way of access to an inexhaustible space which we can enter in no other way. We can enter such a whole only through the rupture it creates in our world.

Here I have anticipated the motifs but not rehearsed the meaning which the progress of inquiry itself alone permits to emerge. That we cannot know anything ahead of time, that we know only by trusting that throe of temporality in which we are irretrievably caught by virtue of being wonderers—even this cannot be known ahead of time but only in time and through it, only inside the throe of the book.

CHAPTER 1

The Love of Wisdom and the Consolations of Fallibility

In a revolutionary shift made possible by unmasking the myth of the given and undermining the metaphysics of presence, philosophers have come to recognize during the last few decades the inescapability of interpretation and the centrality of its role in the constitution of meaning. Whether we speak of alternative conceptual frameworks or hermeneutical circles, we are now very much aware of the fact that we operate in different universes, are governed by different paradigms, play different language games; we know our thoughts have been shaped by different myths, and are grounded in different presuppositions. Difference is now the starting point of philosophical discussion, and the pluralism it entails promises to remain our more or less permanent condition. This sense of living in the midst of a multiplicity of worlds, indeed an endlessly multipliable number of different universes, is characteristic not just of philosophy but of post-modern culture in general; philosophy has simply helped us become self-conscious of it so that we can now recognize ourselves *as* post-moderns, cut loose from the roots of the given, and traveling (more like tourists than pilgrims) from one universe of meaning to another.

The question I seek to address directly in this chapter, and at least indirectly in all the chapters of this book, is what it might mean to seek philosophical wisdom when one is situated in the midst of such a world—or rather such a multiplicity of worlds. If philosophers do not say much about wisdom these days, if it is not often taken seriously as an ideal to be sought or even as a theme to be examined, perhaps that is because the pluralism of post-modern culture makes this cardinal virtue of our intellectual tradition seem

11

impossible to achieve and therefore irrelevant to us. Why would we seek to know "not only . . . what follows from the first principles, but . . . the first principles"[1] themselves, when so many of us are convinced that there are no such originary truths, only presuppositions that govern different universes of discourse? As Richard Rorty has helped us to realize, the philosopher who thinks there is no knowledge to be had outside our conceptual frameworks and hermeneutical circles cannot continue to conceive of himself as a philosopher in the traditional sense; for, lacking any originary wisdom, all he can offer is advice about which conceptual framework best suits our practical purposes.[2]

And yet might it not be precisely now, in this pluralistic situation, when we no longer hope to ground our interpretations in the immediately given, that we have an opportunity to rediscover wisdom as an intellectual virtue because we are in a unique position to appreciate how lost we are without it? Like the sophist of old, the pragmatist would have us believe that, having given up on the given as an arche on which to build a universe of meaning, we have no basis in terms of which to evaluate the rival paradigms, the alternative frameworks of interpretation, which we find at our disposal. This is to presume that the given gave us the only access we ever had to wisdom, and that, having lost that access, we have no other open to us. But to the degree that it jumps to this conclusion, a pragmatism like Rorty's still remains profoundly under the sway of the myth of the given which it purports to have demythologized. For it still looks back to the lost myth as the one and only chance we ever had to be wise. In this book I will be trying to explore the opposite possibility—the possibility that by no longer looking to the given as its source, we might be able to take wisdom more seriously than we once did, since we will no longer mistakenly presume that the given can give us a basis from which wisdom can be derived. The demythologizing (deconstruction) of the given, I suggest, does not finally prove that philosophical wisdom is unachievable, as Rorty has claimed; the end of the myth is less like closing a door than it is like opening one. My purpose here is to put my hand on the latch to it, not to claim wisdom but to suggest that it is still possible—and profoundly wise—to aspire to it.

TRADITIONAL WISDOM AND ITS
POST-MODERN UNMASKING

I did not mean to imply by quoting it that Aristotle's description of the wise person in the *Nicomachean Ethics* lays down the unrevisable parameters in terms of which any fruitful inquiry into the nature of philosophical wisdom must be carried out. In fact, we can understand the apparent impossibility of such wisdom in post-modern culture only by appreciating how profoundly this culture calls into question the parameters in terms of which Aristotle framed his description.

Philosophical wisdom, Aristotle argues, "must be intuitive reason combined with scientific knowledge."[3] We do not consider the specialist in a particular technical or theoretical field to be wise in the philosophical sense, for such specialized expertise is compatible with ignorance concerning everything outside its purview.[4] We consider a person to have such wisdom only if he[5] has an understanding of the whole *as* a whole, and that requires an understanding of the principles that govern everything—indeed, an understanding of the principles of being as such. Such principles provide scientific knowledge with a rational ground and thus enable it to justify its claim to be scientific; but precisely because they constitute the basis of science itself, such principles cannot be scientifically demonstrated themselves. They can only be grasped by "intuitive reason." These originary truths provide the Archimedian basis on which the infrastructure of meaning is reared, and for that reason they are located neither inside nor outside the system they ground; they constitute, as it were, the very baseline where system and ground meet.[6] (If the first principles were located *within* the parameters of the conceptual framework which they are meant to ground, they would be conditional on and therefore relative to the framework instead of providing it the unconditional, absolute basis it needs, if its truth claims are to be justified. If the first principles were *external* to and detached from the conceptual framework they are meant to ground, the latter would have no firm and secure foundation on which to rest.)

From this Aristotlean point of view, the philosophically wise person is distinguished from his common-sensical counterpart by the fact that the former grasps the first principles which govern the universe of meaning inside which the latter moves unknowingly. The philosophically wise person possesses a masterful hold on the whole by virtue of the fact that he possesses an intuitive knowledge of its guiding principles. It might be mentioned here parenthetically that the privileged status of these grounding principles as the foundation of knowledge was transferred, in our Western educational tradition, to those classical texts which were thought to be their primary locus. To be philosophically wise thus came to be associated with being not just a reader but a master of these privileged texts, the most privileged of which were the texts of metaphysics since the intuitions contained therein made accessible the principles of being itself.

If the contemporary debate about the privileged status of these texts is often acrimonious, it is because losing them uproots our tradition at its source, removes its Archimedian principle, creates an-arche, deconstructs the whole universe of (our privileged) culture. Losing them seems like a betrayal of the whole purpose of "higher" education as traditionally understood—the pursuit of wisdom itself. But to make that traditional center hold, or even to shore up its ruins, one would have to deny that our culture is only one among many and affirm that our primal intuitions are superior to those that ground universes of meaning other than our own. And how could one go about making a case for such superiority when the very principle whose superiority one intends to prove would have to be intuited at the beginning because it alone could provide a basis for one's argument? The more one reflects on that paradox, the more one is led to suspect that the real but repressed purpose of every universe of meaning is to construct a system of defenses around a primal prejudice which is treated as an absolute principle so that its ungrounded character can be disguised. How wise is someone who masters a whole universe of meaning but does not question its basis, so that he accepts as immediately given whatever its primal intuitions present to him as obvious?

Now if it is true that what lies at the basis of every universe of meaning, every "culture" in the classical sense of the term, is a prejudice disguised as an intuition, only a person able to unmask such disguises will have the wisdom not to be taken in by them. To learn how to unmask, how to deconstruct conceptual frameworks, how to undermine the privileged position of their founding principles, one must free one's thinking from their confining parameters. That, I take it, is the purpose of what Ricoeur calls the hermeneutic of suspicion[7] which, far from being a new conceptual framework, another hermeneutical circle, deconstructs all such structures at their very base by exposing their groundlessness. The adept practitioner of this hermeneutic, far from making any claim to the kind of wisdom sought by those operating within classical culture and its unquestioned universe of meaning, argues that such wisdom is itself really a disguise for something worse than ignorance; for ignorance is only lack of knowledge but prejudice makes its lack of knowledge the dogmatic starting point of a whole system.

However, the person who has fully appreciated the import of the hermeneutic of suspicion will not pretend that it enables one to stand outside all particular cultures or universes of meaning as an unprejudiced observer of them. For one would be capable of such "objective" observation only if one attained the privileged position which the hermeneutic of suspicion argues to be impossible. According to it, there are no privileged positions, no unprejudiced observations, no pure intuitions, no direct grasping of the given, no primary texts.[8] There are only disguised prejudices and undisguised ones. The hermeneutic of suspicion teaches one to glory in one's prejudices, to be naked in one's folly, instead of trying to sublimate it into wisdom. The person who is wise in this postmodern sense is not held fast by the constraining limits of one particular universe, nor does he pretend to have achieved a transcendent vantage point outside all our universes; he lives rather in the very midst of them, aware of their irreducible multiplicity, ready to use them but not believe in them, not depressed by his rootlessness but happy to enjoy the freedom it gives him because it enables him to be at his ease in every world he enters. His pragmatic extemporizing makes him a perfect counterimage to the philosophically wise man of classical culture whose intuition of eternal verities gave him a fixed, immovable vantage point unaffected by any shifts in human affairs. The person who is wise in the postmodern sense is characterized precisely by his openness to such shifts, his willingness to be historicized, his desire to be all too human instead of vainly seeking to be godlike.

THE FLIGHT TO INTUITION

In the hope of leavening the bitter debate between these conflicting paradigms of human wisdom, I would now like to discuss the issue which I have suggested separates them: the possibility of intuition. As John Sallis has explained with remarkable lucidity,[9] there is a profound connection between the privileged status accorded to intuition and what post-modern philosophers have come to call the metaphysics of presence. Understanding this connection may enable us to restate the post-modern suspicion of classical wisdom in a way which sheds more light on the matter than the hermeneutic of suspicion is itself able to do.

Intuition, whether empirical (the arche of positivism) or eidetic (the arche of idealism from Plato to Husserl), is made possible by the full availability of what-is-to-be-known to the knower. To put it in a way that prescinds from the differences between the empirical and the eidetic, intuition can only occur if the to-be-known shows itself, presents itself to the knower without withholding anything or letting anything come between it and him. In other words, intuition depends on there being something that is wholly and immediately given; for it is nothing but our grasp of the given in its givenness. On the side of the knower, intuition requires a wordless receptivity, a willingness to let the given reveal itself, a pure contemplative openness incompatible with any pragmatic concern. Intuition occurs when the pure seeing of the knower recognizes what-is-given as being just what it shows itself to be. In that moment of perfect seeing, seen and seer, known and knower, become one; the knower experiences the pure presence of what is present to him in the present.

What makes such an intuition so desirable to us? Why do we find ourselves so often hoping that the eros of inquiry will be consummated by a perfect seeing? Why are we so devoted to achieving that ocular ideal, that privileged moment of unmediated vision, that ecstasy of presence? Why do we think it would make up for all our false starts and detours, all our wrong turns and misreadings? What sets intuition apart from other cognitive acts and makes us strive toward it as toward the shining light of truth itself? The privileged status of this mode of knowing derives, I think, from its purported unsurpassability, from the fact that the object to be known could never be more perfectly accessible to us than it would be if it were fully present to us in the present without any intermediary between it and ourselves. No grasp of the object could possibly be more re-presentative, no hold on it possibly more secure. It would seem that *whatever is revealed to us in such an ecstasy of presence could not possibly be wrong.* How could we ever discover an intuition to be wrong except by achieving a more accurate, more penetrating view of the object it pretended to reveal? But no view of the object could possibly get us closer to it than we are when, through an intuition, we become one with it in a moment of unmediated vision.

Moreover, if it is true that intuition places us in the unmediated presence of what-is-to-be-known, it would seem to provide us our most direct and dependable access to being itself. For how can we withhold the word being from that which becomes accessible to us in a transparent moment of vision? To what might the word "being" more properly apply? Indeed, the reason why intuition can promise us that it will not be wrong is because it claims to provide us a clean and decisive breakthrough to *being as it is in itself,* a direct contact with being that will enable us to finally transcend our merely subjective images and conceptions of it. Since no more intimate familiarity can be conceived than that which purportedly occurs in intuition, it is only natural to equate being with what is known through it. If intuition is the supreme mode of knowing, being must be identical to what it makes accessible—the given in its givenness, the presence of what is present in the present.

However, we would not give intuition so privileged a status or be so drawn by its promise of an insight immune to error, unless we were already aware of the possibility of being wrong and deeply disturbed by that possibility. We would not be in need of the breakthrough to being which it purports to make possible if we did not already feel cut off from being and in danger of not ever knowing it. Our awareness of this possibility and our dread of it begin to emerge as soon as we begin to realize that there are many possible answers to each of the questions wonder drives us to raise. The very multiplicity of these possible answers requires our prefacing each of them with the word "maybe." To think means precisely to let this array of possible answers emerge, and to grope through the confusion it engenders. Each answer opens up to us a possible universe different from its alternatives. To consider any one of them means precisely to entertain it as a possibility, to conceive of it as something that might be the right answer to one's question. We are tempted to think that such a multiplicity of interpretations, such a plurality of possible worlds, is symptomatic of a particular historical condition, that it is uniquely characteristic of post-modern culture. But, in fact, this wealth of interpretations, far from being an aberration, is engendered by the process of thinking itself, whenever it responds to the compelling exigencies of its questions. The only way to prevent the emergence of this plurality, and the confusion it inevitably creates, would be to inhibit the momentum natural to the dynamism of thought.

Now precisely because it leads us to consider a multiplicity of possible answers to every one of our questions, the act of thinking itself makes it possible for us to be wrong. By enabling us to conceive of a plurality of interpretations, any one of which might answer our question, thinking creates in our minds not just a distinction but a gulf between all our possible answers and the real one. The same eros that drives us to ask a question in the first place, and explore possible answers to it, makes us want to find the answer that traverses the distance, spans the gulf, crosses the abyss which separates us from that toward which the whole process is directed: that which is to become known to us through inquiry, that which alone deserves to be called "being." As soon as one asks a question, one directs oneself toward the answer as toward a destination to be reached by crossing the distance that separates one's question from the insight that would provide a resolution to it. But it is precisely the existence of that destination and the distance separating one from it that makes falling into error possible. *Simply to ask a question is to put oneself in a radically precarious position.* For it situates one on the very edge of a chasm, where the possibility of being wrong yawns before one. The more radical the question raised by the inquirer, the more deeply affected she will be by that vertiginous situation; indeed, if her question concerns the very meaning of her own being, the possibility of being wrong can affect her with the same dreadful foreboding we associate with the anticipation of death itself.[10] For in that case it is the meaning of her world as a whole that is at stake.

When we find ourselves in that mortally exposed position, we are eager not just to avert error but to repress the mortifying possibility of it. When we see the abyss that separates us as questioners from the answer that lies over there on the other side of inquiry, we dream of finding a way to close the chasm instead of bridging it, a way to abolish the distance, instead of merely traversing it. But how can this be done if the act of thinking has already exposed one to the possibility of being in error by confronting one with an array of possible answers, any one of which may be true or false? Only by means of an intuition that would not be a passageway, a medium, a bridge, at all, but a oneness between knower and known so intimate, so complete, that it would allow not the slightest cleft, breach, fissure, fault, to come between them. Is it any wonder that we come to associate the achievement of philosophical wisdom with just such an intuition of presence from which every trace of error and absence has been effaced? Only such a revelation could provide our universe of meaning with the arche it needs if it is to be irrefragable.

But this suggests that the ideal of intuition, like the metaphysics of presence to which it is inextricably bound, originates not so much in the desire to answer one's questions as in the desire to escape the precarious situation we are put in by our very status as questioners. Intuition purports to offer a foolproof way of selecting the right answer from the multiplicity of interpretations which the process of inquiry generates. But its way of doing this is to claim a direct acquaintance with what is to be known through the right interpretation, for only such direct acquaintance could provide one the knowledge one would need to make one's choice of an interpretation foolproof. If such knowledge existed, it would indeed enable us to answer our questions without running the risk of being wrong; but it would also make the entire process of asking questions superfluous since the knowledge to be reached through that process would already be accessible to us without our having to engage in it. The desire to have the object-to-be-known intuitively present comes from our wanting to know it with an immediacy and directness which the process of inquiry, of its very nature, makes impossible. Indeed, it is precisely the experience of being caught in the throe of inquiry which gives rise to our desire to escape from the danger to which it exposes us. Intuition promises the impossibility of being wrong. But the only way it could make error impossible would be by providing us immediate access to what is to be known through inquiry; and if such access were attainable, if intuition could really deliver on the promises it makes, it would make the entire process of inquiry unnecessary. The very fact that we do ask questions suggests that the kind of direct access to reality which intuition promises is lacking. Questioning itself signifies the irreparable loss of presence. That is why, as the hermeneutic of suspicion has helped us realize, the intuition that promises to retrieve presence for us is really only a blind leap of faith by means of which we hope to traverse the abyss of fallibility to which inquiry exposes us; its "eureka" is only the joy of landing safely.[11]

One way to stake out a hermeneutical counterposition to the ideal of intuition, once we begin to recognize the hollowness of its promises, might be to say that real wisdom lies in realizing that the distance between our questions and the right answers to them is not traversable. This would lead us to say that we can always move closer and closer to the truth that lies just outside the edge of our hermeneutical circle, but we can never breach the circle itself. For the horizon toward which we advance recedes with the same speed that we approach it. We never catch up with it so as to stand in the immediate presence of what is present in the present; we are always on the way toward it, always caught in the throe of a question, always, like Socrates, in the position of knowing we do not know. But does not this way of explaining the thinker's situation put Socrates in the position of wanting to be the early Plato and never making it? The hermeneutical critique of the metaphysics of presence remains under the sway of what it criticizes as long as it continues to look forward to the parousia of final arrival, even if it indefinitely postpones it. For in adopting such a hermeneutical perspective, we would still be directing ourselves toward the very destination that intuition would enable us to reach if we possessed it.[12] Reconciled as one may be to the fact that the parousia of presence is unattainable, one is still using it as one's absolute reference point if one understands one's position in terms of its deferral. Even when we admit that thought is moving toward an always receding destination, we continue to plot its course in exclusively horizontal terms, i.e., exclusively in terms of destinations to be reached, distances to be traversed, horizons to be thematized, absences to be presenced, concealments to be revealed. To append a warning that none of these projected closures can ever be achieved does not alter the fact that closure remains the governing objective.

But the act of raising a question and taking it seriously brings us to a place that cannot be found on any two-dimensional map: it situates us at the edge of a precipice, and exposes us to the possibility of a mortal fall. As long as we think that we can avoid that possibility by finding a way to cross over to being itself, we are governed by a horizontal ideal of wisdom. But our reflections suggest that there is an alternative to that ideal. For instead of seeking an intuition of presence, we can entrust ourselves to the eros of questioning itself and plunge into the abyss which it opens up to us, instead of trying to leap across it. Indeed, are not the most radical questions precisely those that pull the ground out from under our feet? Perhaps, then, the distinguishing mark of the philosophically wise person is not that she occupies a privileged position which others envy but that she allows radical questions to deprive her of the arche on which she would like to be able to securely ground her world.

If we turn our thought *down* into the abyss opened up by such questions, instead of trying to throw our thought across it, will we be led to the same conclusions as the post-modern practitioners of the hermeneutic of suspicion? Once we recognize the fallacy we commit in searching for an intuition of presence to answer our questions, what is to prevent us from thinking, like Rorty, that it is a fallacy to search for a "right" answer in the first place?[13] Is the very idea of there being a "right" answer itself derivative from the metaphysics of presence and the horizontal ideal of wisdom? Because we are under the sway of that ideal, we are accustomed to thinking that, when confronted with a multiplicity of theories, interpretations, conceptual frameworks, hermeneutical circles, we are supposed to pick the one most in accord with what we would know reality to be like if we had an intuition of it. But if such intuitions are nonexistent, it is impossible and foolish to evaluate our theories in terms of how closely they approximate it. Does this mean that our original mistake lies in bringing to our theories the inappropriate demand that one of them show itself to be the "right" one? It would seem that the only alternative to that mistake is to evaluate theories in terms of their usefulness instead of their rightness, to select the one that helps us do what we want, without trying to determine if it gives us the kind of privileged access to being which we would get from an intuition, if we could have one.

But what is most striking about this contemporary pragmatic alternative[14] to the classical ideal of wisdom is that it too offers us a way to avoid the very possibility of being wrong. For if there are no right answers but only alternative ways of "coping" and "dealing with" the world, if every universe of meaning is only an elaborately devised therapy,[15] then the decision about which therapy to adopt would not place one in a precarious position; for one would only have to decide what one wanted. This therapeutic pragmatism, schooled in the hermeneutic of suspicion, does not pretend to offer, like any of the wisdoms it critiques, a way to leap over the abyss that separates the questioner from the answer she seeks; it simply tells us to walk away from the precipice, to return to what we were doing before we made the mistake of taking our questions seriously enough to seek true answers to them.

But there is only one place to go when one retraces one's steps back from the precipice to which we are exposed by our questions. For one can stop thinking of alternative theories as possible answers only by ceasing to take seriously the questions which generate them; and one can only stop asking questions by refusing to wonder. And that is not something we need philosophy to help us do. Philosophy originates, in fact, precisely in that act of wonder which, from a strictly practical, common-sense point of view, is spendthrift and superfluous. The practical person who does not allow wonder to disrupt him is completely unaware of any universe of meaning other than his own. Far from helping him become tolerant of and open to alternative ways of understanding the world, his pragmatism leads him to construe every theory as a possible strategy for achieving the results he seeks. It does not offer, any more than intuition does, a kind of wisdom which takes seriously the multiplicity of our worlds and the possibility of being wrong.

THE THROE AS ARCHE

It may seem at first like mere question-begging to say that the kind of wisdom needed in our pluralistic situation cannot come from intuition or practicality but only from the very wisdom generated in and by the pluralistic situation itself. But what I mean to suggest by this is that the pluralistic situation, which is not an historical aberration but a condition that always emerges from the ordeal of inquiry itself, both calls for and makes possible a kind of knowledge which becomes accessible to us only when we let ourselves be caught in the throe of that situation instead of trying to escape it.

I have suggested that the act of thinking generated by a question engenders in its turn a multiplicity of possible answers. In an effort to talk about what happens when that multiplicity emerges, I have employed the image of a gulf separating the questioner from the answer which the dynamism of questioning itself drives her to seek. Now if one is to continue to be governed by this eros, if one is to keep exploring the possibilities it opens up, the next step cannot be a leap over that gulf, as urged by the metaphysics of presence, nor can it be a retreat backward, in the direction of that practicality which the wonder at the root of all questions disrupts. The only way to move forward is to step over the edge of that precipice which both the flight to intuition and the retreat to practicality attempt to avoid. One cannot continue the process of inquiry except by openly accepting the dangerous possibility to which inquiry makes us liable: the possibility of being wrong. One could avoid that possibility if there were no truth to be reached through questioning as contemporary pragmatism suggests, or if what is to be known through questioning were directly accessible through an immediate intuition. But if, as I have argued, what is to be known

through questioning can only be known by taking the steps which
the process of questioning opens up to us, such knowledge is accessible to us only through a mortifying acknowledgment of the
possibility of our inescapable fallibility. For only in and through
such an acceptance of her fallibility does a questioner recognize
that there is a right answer which is not and can never be immediately accessible to her.

Now just as the ideal of intuition is inseparably bound up with
the metaphysics of presence, an acknowledgment of the possibility
of being wrong opens up a metaphysics that is not grounded in that
enduring ocular myth. For if we are to take the possibility of being
wrong seriously, we must cease to think of being as that which
becomes accessible to us through an intuition that occurs outside
the entire process of inquiry itself. But this does not require that we
eliminate *being* from our vocabulary and cease seeking to know it.
That fact that being is not to be equated with presence does not
mean that it must be erased. It means, rather, that it must be
identified with that which can never be either presenced or erased,
since it can never be either immediately known or wholly avoided
(unless we wholly repress our capacity to be questioners). Being is
that which becomes accessible to us only in and through the throe
of inquiry. Insofar as we are in that throe, we are held fast by the
throe of being itself. Therefore, we can know being only by surrendering to the throe of inquiry and embracing the fallibility to which
it exposes us. When we try to escape the mortifying danger of
fallibility, we sever our relationship with being and wrongly identify it with presence. And this means that we can never be right
about being except by realizing that our fallibility, far from being a
barrier to our knowledge of it, constitutes our only possible bond
with it.

To deny that this is the case, we would have to deny that the
throe of inquiry, which requires acknowledging our fallibility,
places us in the throe of being. We would have to claim that the
very process of asking questions about being and exploring where
they lead moves us away from being instead of allowing us to be
governed by it. We would have to argue that being can only be
known by repressing our inquiry into it. But, in the very act of
arguing this, we would be affirming our argument as true and

taking the process of argumentation seriously as a way to know being. We would be caught up in the very throe whose hold on us we would be trying to break. The act of trying to answer a question opens us up to being itself *as* that which is to be known by questioning.

Thus, as soon as we ask a question—*any* question—we find ourselves at a critical metaphysical juncture, even if we do not ordinarily realize it. For we have to decide whether the whole process of inquiry on which we are about to embark is or is not to be taken seriously as our one and only access to being. How we respond when we reach this critical juncture, this jumping-off point, determines how completely we entrust ourselves to the throe of inquiry, and whether we are going to try to protect ourselves from the danger of being wrong to which it exposes us. Indeed, it is the life of the mind in its entirety that is at stake here. For the issue is whether to take the whole process of inquiry so seriously as to allow it to determine everything one thinks about everything. This requires us to make a judgment about the role that the act of thinking is to have in our lives, where "the act of thinking" refers not to a particular mental operation but to the whole process of wondering, questioning, and inquiring that unfolds when we are caught up in the eros of the desire to know.

Just such a critical judgment must be made here, at the beginning of this book. For I cannot take seriously the exploration occurring in it if I do not affirm now that being must be neither equated with presence nor erased but, rather, must be identified with that which we come to know by entering the throe of inquiry and the abyss of fallibility.[16] Given its pivotal character, given the fact that it serves in a sense as the hinge on which everything to be said in this book turns, I would like to be able to refrain from making this affirmation until I am sure of standing on absolutely solid ground. I would like to be able to postpone the beginning of the book until the end of it, so that I could use it to back myself up. But this very desire to secure an unshakable basis for my judgment derives from my not wanting to depend on the process of inquiry, and the judgment to which it leads as my only way of knowing if my judgment is right. I would like to have the truth I am trying to reach directly accessible to me prior to making a judgment so that I could check my judgment against reality before affirming it to be true. But everything I have been saying suggests that the very reason why I ask questions in the first place and get caught up in the throe of inquiry they set in motion, is because such direct acquaintance with being is not available to me. For this reason, I have no choice but to depend on my judgment and on it alone. I cannot check to see if the conclusions I reach through inquiry conform to being because being is to be known, if it is to be known at all, only in and through inquiry. This realization, that we have no access to being outside the throe of inquiry, is the pivotal moment, the fundamental principle, the starting point of wisdom: but far from providing an arche, an unshakable ground, it requires giving up the hope of ever standing on an irrefragable foundation. To the person who experiences it, relinquishing this hope may seem like exposing oneself to nothingness itself. But only by suffering such exposure does one give oneself over wholly to the throe of questioning; and it is only by surrendering completely to the throe of questioning that one is caught up in the throe of being itself. To find being one must remain inside the process of questioning and follow where it leads instead of seeking some magical exit from it; for any such exit, precisely because it promises us a way to escape our fallibility, closes us off to being, instead of opening up a way to it.

But in saying that the judgment I have made—that being is accessible to us only in and through inquiry—does not rest on a secure foundation, I do not mean to imply that it is based on prejudice or arbitrary choice. In making a judgment we have no resources at our disposal except those provided by the process of inquiry itself: we have nothing but the question about the given in which inquiry originates, the multiplicity of possible answers generated by thinking about it, the eros that makes us want to find the truth, and ourselves as questioners, helplessly caught in the throe of questioning. But if we would stop looking for a magical exit out of this throe, we would discover that it has a momentum of its own. We do not judge an answer to be right because it conforms to a reality which is accessible to us before our inquiry begins; we judge it right only because it fulfills that intelligent desire for insight set in motion by inquiry itself.[17] It is the demand set up by the question, as intelligently raised by the questioner, which constitutes the criterion against which all possible answers must be checked, if we are to judge which of them gives us access to being. The word "judgment" does not refer only to the proposition which is affirmed after we have completed the process of weighing as judiciously as possible a number of different theories against the requirements of the question they purport to answer. It refers primarily to the judicial process itself during which we try to appreciate the particular merits of a theory, the scope of its explanatory power, the reasons which give it its plausibility, in addition to critiquing it for possible shortcomings, perhaps for its failure to take into account all the aspects of what is to be explained or for its failure to do so in a way commensurate with the profundity of the issue at stake. Throughout this process, there is no authority to which one can defer, and no prior knowledge against which one can check one's assessment. The act of making a judgment is a firsthand exploration of wholly unknown territory to which we cannot gain access in any other way. We can enter it only if we give up the hope of checking each step we take against a map we already have.

Understood in this light, becoming wise in the philosophical sense does not require mastering a certain set of fundamental truths, or a certain set of primary texts. It requires becoming a good judge of texts, and a good judge of whether the true judgments they purport to contain really do satisfy the exigencies set in motion by intelligence itself once it is caught in the throe of questioning. That a person has acquired such good judgment is not proven by adherence to a particular set of propositions; it is evident only in the quiet tactfulness with which conflicting theories are considered, the attentive hearing that is given to every argument, the calm, deliberate manner in which theories are both appreciated and critiqued. But good judgment is evident, first and foremost, in the humility—we might even say, in the acceptance of one's liability to nothingness—which comes with a profound realization of the fact that one's judgments may be wrong. For only the person whose thinking is conducted in the spirit of such humility realizes that the truths to which her thinking brings her are accessible to her only because she has entered fully into the dreadfully fallible throe of inquiry, and not because she has found some magical exit from it.

That there is a truth to be known through the fallible process of inquiry is itself a truth that the very fact of our fallibility requires us to affirm. For it would not be possible to be wrong unless there exists a truth to which thinking is required to be subordinate. There could be no abyss of fallibility if truth were not *above* us. Indeed, it would seem that the more conscious one is of fallibility, the more prepared one will be to acknowledge that there exists a truth which is not subject to our control or in our possession. An acceptance of one's fallibility and an unconditional affirmation of the superior status of truth itself are inseparable from each other.

But if truth is an indispensable condition for the very possibility of being in error, it would seem that we cannot possibly be wrong in affirming its existence. And if we cannot be wrong in affirming it, it would appear that we are in possession of at least one absolute truth that cannot possibly be false. But if we can possess even one such truth, it would seem to prove that we can transcend our fallible condition after all. Thus, there seems to be a kind of performative inconsistency at the very heart of wisdom as I have tried to define it. For the unconditional affirmation of truth which the principle of fallibility itself requires us to make seems to entitle us to claim that we have exactly the kind of hold on truth that fallibility precludes. And if an absolute truth is accessible to us, in the form of an unconditional affirmation of truth itself, it must be possible for us to attain, in our search for wisdom, precisely the kind of secure hold on first principles which an acknowledgment of fallibility would deny us.

That this dilemma is not an artificial one but lies close to the very heart of the question regarding the nature of wisdom is confirmed by the fact that it is exactly comparable to the dilemma faced by Socrates when he tried, in a single speech, to confess his radical ignorance and to affirm certain unequivocal truths which he thought no one was entitled to deny. There have always been readers who have claimed to detect in this apparent inconsistency the final twist of Socratic irony; they hear, hidden under the humility of his professed ignorance, the arrogance of someone who thinks he possesses a truth which no hermeneutic of suspicion can take away from him. This diagnosis of the *Apology* suggests that the kind of intellectual humility which I have equated with wisdom is an impossible "via media" between skepticism, with its thoroughgoing admission of ignorance, and a dogmatism that claims to be in indisputable possession of absolute truth. Are we forced, after all, to choose between these extremes because the path between them, if followed far enough, always leads back to one of them?

Before jumping to that conclusion, I think we should pause to examine more carefully whether the unconditional affirmation of truth which an acknowledgment of fallibility paradoxically requires of us entitles us to claim that this truth is in our possession. It is true that our acknowledgment of our fallibility remains incomplete as long as it does not include our unconditional affirmation that truth transcends us. But we acknowledge this not to raise ourselves to its level but to clarify our inescapably subordinate relationship to it. Fallibility is precisely the condition of being always in relationship to truth but never in possession of it. We can affirm truth unconditionally and irrefutably not because we are in secure possession of it but because it has an unbreakable hold on us. Our affirmation of it is simply our acknowledgment that we cannot escape our relationship with truth except by terminating the activity of thought itself; it is not our claim to be in possession of truth but our confession that we have been caught irretrievably in its throe. We are fallible because we can neither possess the truth nor escape our relationship to it.

We *would* be able to claim indisputable possession of truth if we could have the kind of direct, immediate grasp of it which an intuition would provide. But far from pretending to rest on intuition, the principle of fallibility requires us to admit that no such direct grasp of the truth is available to us. It is of crucial importance in this regard to notice the kind of argument that leads from the principle of fallibility to the unconditional affirmation of truth. This argument asks us to reflect on what it means to be liable to error and to acknowledge that such liability would not be possible if truth did not exist. It does *not* claim that truth is directly and immediately accessible to us; it claims, rather, that we must affirm truth because of the inconsistencies into which we would fall by denying it. This might seem to be an insignificant distinction. But it means that the argument is not claiming that any truth is intuitively self-evident, not even the existence of truth itself. Rather, it makes an appeal to the good judgment of the reader, as Aristotle did when he argued that we commit a self-referential inconsistency when we try to deny certain propositions.[18] Such truths are not irrefutable because they are self-evident but because, try as we might, we are powerless to escape their sway, except by abandoning the entire process of rational inquiry.[19] Given the fact that we can come to know it only in this way, knowing that truth exists does not give us possession of it, if by possession one means the kind of secure hold on truth we would have through an intuition that made it directly accessible to us. The knowledge of truth gained from a self-referential argument, far from putting us on the same plane with it, makes us realize that truth is never available to us as a foundation because we are always in a subordinate position to it. We never stand on the same firm ground as the transcendent itself, as the intuitionist would like, because it is always possible that we are wrong; but neither can we rest securely in our ignorance, as the skeptic (and contemporary pragmatist) would like, because the very possibility of being wrong makes our relationship with truth inescapable. There is no firm position at all, no unshakable arche, except to be in the throe itself, held fast by a fallibility one can never transcend and a truth one can never possess. We become wise only by letting go of our secure foundations and abandoning ourselves to the abyss opened up by our questions.

On the other hand, both the dream of intuition and the metaphysics of presence are bound up with a possessive attitude toward truth, an attitude which is the exact opposite of the humility one begins to acquire by acknowledging that one is always liable to be wrong. To be in possession of the truth—would that not mean to be in such sure control of it as to be incapable of being mistaken? Were not those who claimed such control the favorite targets of Socratic irony? The alternative to such *sophos* is not a skeptical or pragmatic retreat from truth-seeking but the realization that we can never escape truth and never be in possession of it. Our fallibility prevents our ever having the kind of control over truth we would be entitled to claim if the dream of intuition could be realized. But far from cutting us off from truth, fallibility presupposes that we have an inescapable, and inescapably subordinate, relationship to it. Both intuition and pragmatism promise an exit from the tenuous rapport of that subordination. Wisdom lies in accepting it not just as a temporary stopping point on the way of inquiry but as our permanent condition.

The pursuit of such wisdom, philos/sophos, does not begin with the securing of indisputable first principles, on the basis of which one could go on to build an impregnable universe of meaning. The only way to engage in *philos/sophos* is by giving up one's secure foothold and plunging into the dreadful throe of inquiry which is governed by truth itself. One has not fully surrendered to that throe as long as one retains even the slightest doubt about whether there is a truth to be known; but neither has one surrendered to it as long as one retains the hope of terminating one's subordinate relationship to truth by possessing it. To be fallible means precisely to always be under the sway of truth and never in control of it, to always be in the position of having to look up at it from the vantage point of that abyss into which we plunge when we realize our liability to error. But it is never an error to be in that helpless, ridiculously privileged position. For only someone secure in her fallibility knows how insecure she will always be in her relationship to truth. She alone is wise enough to know that by not claiming to have a hold on it, she allows truth to exercise its gentle but inexorable influence over her. What does one have to do to begin developing such wisdom? Only ask a question. Only be struck by wonder.[20]

CHAPTER 2

Wonder as Hinge

It is the experience of wonder which Heidegger, like Aristotle, places not just at the origin of philosophical wisdom but at the origin of all human inquiry. Because wonder makes "the 'Why?' spring to our lips,"[1] it is the hinge between ignorance and knowledge, between oblivion and insight, and perhaps for that reason the hinge between every past and future. What door is opened by that hinge? What place are we about to leave as we approach that doorway, and where do we find ourselves after we have passed through it? As the originating point of thought, wonder is the point of departure par excellence, the beginning that is prior to and in that sense has priority over every other starting point. Can we say what gets it started? Or whether we will ever arrive at the place to which it leads us? Perhaps we are always in the doorway, never completely on either side of it, always in between genesis and parousia, always in the between which, if Heidegger is right, is time itself.

I find this image of hinge and door, borrowed from Derrida,[2] especially suggestive when it is associated with those childhood experiences which most of us can remember vividly: the wondrous (and yet also dreadful) experience of venturing into a secret room, or exploring an uninhabited house, or even opening the lid of a chest hidden in the attic and found unexpectedly. If, as children, we seemed to live closer to the source of ourselves than we do now, perhaps it was because we were more eager to be venturers, and less able to resist the lure of dark woods and untried paths down which we were drawn by the very fact that we did not know where they led. I think here of the remark Derrida is reputed to have made some years ago when asked where his thought was headed: "'. . . I am trying, precisely, to put myself at a point so that I do not know any longer where I am going.'"[3] If this suggests that Derrida seeks to return to the originary situation of childhood, he does not do so out of nostalgia for its naivete. What children do better than us is precisely to leave their childhood behind, to risk opening even that door whose hinge makes a terrifying sound, as if to warn them, in the only language they understand, of death itself.

As I reflect on such childhood experiences of wondrous (and dreadful) venturing, I am tempted to say that they gave all of us our first intimations of being. However adept we become at handling our philosophical language, that word is always ready to break free of the associations it has acquired and become again an evocation of all the things which, even as we held them in our small hands, turned into mysteries. If there is in our childhood wonder some Socratic wisdom that is worth retrieving, it lies in the fact that, as children, we did not yet have the illusion of understanding what being means. In these reflections I have no desire to go back to the past of childhood in the hope of restoring a present when the future did not exist yet; rather, I would recollect that time when the present moment was full of hints and promises, so that it seemed like a door that was ready to open on the mystery of being. For it is no exaggeration to say that everything hinges on that turning and re-turning door.

WONDER AS RUPTURE

As children, we do not know what is hidden behind the doors we are on the verge of opening. We stand there on the verge, on the threshold of a forbidding place we are sure it is dangerous to enter. If another child is with us, we vacillate between terror and giggling, each of us depending on the other's courage, and yet at the same time afraid of following the other's lead. It is hard for us to imagine, now that even the most remote peaks and distant poles have been reached, what it must have been like to be an original explorer. Some child in us still starts at the sight of a pathless wood, or at the thought of venturing alone into the unknown waters beyond the lifeguard's reach. Explorers had to be foolhardy, or believe, like Socrates, that dying itself is the ultimate venture.

What is the phenomenological structure of wonder as exemplified by such venturing? Let us concentrate, for the moment, on the example of the child on the verge of opening the door to a secret room. What fascinates the child, and terrifies her at the same time, is the unknown in its very character as unknown. To the degree that she is held in the grip of that fascination and terror, she is incapable of picturing or imagining what lies behind the door. This inability to picture is not a consequence of her being seized with terror; rather, it would be more accurate to say that the sense of terror is awakened by her inability to picture, by the fact that she finds it impossible to homologize what lies behind the door with the contents of her small but familiar universe. It is precisely this otherness, this heterogeneity, which gives what she wonders about its element of dreadfulness.[4] She has not yet opened the door; indeed, we might imagine her paralyzed, unwilling and perhaps unable to either withdraw or venture further. But if she is paralyzed, it is because she has already been seized by the unknown that lies behind the door. She is not frozen in the present so much as she is held spellbound by a future she cannot reduce to any present she has ever known. In that sense, even though the door itself is still closed, her small world is already ruptured. There is already an outside that is external to what had seemed to be its all-inclusiveness.[5] Wonder prevents us from living inside our little worlds. Even if we do not venture out, it prevents us from any longer believing there is only an inside. Wonder is already the rupture of the same by the other, where the other is simply the unknown itself in its difference from the known.

This rupture could not occur unless the unknown were known in its very character *as* unknown. This paradox makes wonder itself a mystery that confounds our ordinary understanding, operating as it does according to the logic of identity. No analysis will make that mystery evaporate. If the unknown behind the door were known, it would lose its otherness and consequently its power to hold the child fast in dreadful fascination. If the unknown were simply and utterly unknown, its otherness would be too remote to be disruptive. To account for the event of wonder we have to affirm that the child experiences the unknown *as* unknown, that she has an awareness of the other in its very otherness.[6] She knows nothing of the unknown except the one thing she must know if she is to be fascinated by it: that it is unknown. In this regard, the child is exactly like the explorer who differs from all other kinds of traveller because she really and truly does not know where she is going. But the fact that the explorer does not know where she is going does not mean she is lost in the ordinary sense of the term. For we consider ourselves lost when we cannot find the way to where we are headed, and the explorer has no destination except the unknown as such; she is not hoping to get anywhere except into it. She is not aiming toward a goal that has been fixed upon ahead of time, over there on the other side of the untravelled country. What beckons to her in the here and now is the beyond as such.

This begins to suggest how profoundly the experience of wonder and temporality are related to each other. In exploring, we are neither on the side of the known nor on the side of the unknown but exactly between them, already uprooted from the present, and on the verge of the future that beckons us. We have imagined a child standing transfixed by wonder before the door to a secret room. But this image is misleading if it is taken to suggest that the experience of wonder freezes us or makes time stop still in a frozen moment. Perhaps the child gets the courage to raise her hand toward the latch—and then, just as she is about to lift it, she stops her hand under the influence of a final, unnerving premonition. She pulls back from the door, surprised that she could have come so close to opening it; she is ready to turn and run back into the past where this future cannot get to her. And yet she does not flee but advances again. For wonder puts into motion precisely this dreadful play between withdrawal and venturing, retreat and longing, reluctance and urgency, delay and hastening. When caught in its sway we do not stand motionless; we are held fast in the throe of an ambivalence between the known and the unknown, the same and the other, the past and the future. That ambivalence gives us an evocative image of temporality itself which never allows us to stand still in a univocal present but rather always points us beyond it. In fact, since wonder engages us in the throe of temporality, it suggests that time itself is a kind of exploration and longing in which we are permitted to actively participate. (Into what, one wonders, does time venture? Is time itself caught up in the throe of an other?)

Is the unknown, the other, the future, really as irreducible to the known, the same, the present, as our characterization has implied?

The child stands before the door to the secret room as if she knows, or at least suspects, that behind it lies something unalterably strange and foreign, another whole order of being, another dimension heterogeneous with the one she is familiar with. That toward which wonder points lies in the future which precisely insofar as it is the future, is now absent. But when one actually opens the door of wonder and finally gains access to what is on the other side of it, it would seem that the strange and unknown are transformed into the known and familiar. For this reason, the absent seems to be always, at least in principle, collapsible into the present, to be no more than another present that has not arrived yet. Insofar as the "whence" and "whither" of wonder are correlative with presence and absence, the "whither" of wonder would appear to be reducible to the "whence." However, if this were true, no explorer would ever step into a truly strange, truly foreign land; for the very moment she set foot in it, she would annex it to the familiar world she calls home. From this point of view, wonder would always result in our making the other over into the same; exploration would always be colonization.

But if that toward which wonder points us were only another present that had not yet arrived, we would only be able to wonder about the absent future, and not about what is right here now in front of us. For when what is right here now before us saturates us with the perfect plenitude of its presence, it does not give rise to any experience of absence and so, in the above analysis, would give us no reason to wonder. But in fact we know that, as children, we marvelled over the very things that were closest to hand and most familiar to us. We have never been closer to things, never had them more immediately present to our direct, unclouded vision, than they were in the instantaneous sureness of originary perception. But it was precisely then, when they were fully present in the present, that things struck us as unfathomable.

What is immediately present before us can awaken our wonder, and this means that we can know we do not know it. It is only because we know it is unknown that we ask, What is it? But to what does the word "it" refer in this question? "It" is both that-which-is-immediately-present-before-us and that-which-is-as-yet-unknown. The from-which and toward-which of wonder are concentrated here in a single term whose sameness is the hinge of their difference.[7] The it which is immediately present to me awakens wonder but the it toward which wonder points me can only be known by trying to answer the questions wonder asks. The presence of what is present to me in the present, this plenitude without lack, this fullness—far from answering any of my questions, only enables me to raise them.[8] Wonder is the hinge that turns my attention away from the immediately present toward what can only be known through questioning. In making that turn, one opens the door to another world—indeed, to all those worlds, all those universes of meaning which can become accessible to us only through inquiry. They are not accessible to us in any other way. That the ball which the child holds in her hands has a certain atomic structure, obeys the chemistry of rubber, can be pitched and caught in an exciting game, can be used as a symbol for a planet or as an example in a philosophy essay—all of this the child can come to know if she follows wonder where it leads, into one universe of discourse after another. None of it can be known by looking at what is right there in front of her in its immediate presence. We might think that children enjoy staring at things in their brute givenness. But if they turn things over and over in their hands, or gaze at the most ordinary objects in dreamlike reverie, it is because they are always already caught in the throe of wonder which turns even the most obvious, familiar objects into mysteries. Like all of us, they would like to be able to see their way right into that mystery with their very eyes.[9] But the it which wonder makes us hungry to know cannot be found by going back to the it from which wonder arises. Wonder is the hinge that opens up the absolute future, by which I mean a future that is not another now, a future so different from the now that opening the door to it is really the beginning of a new world. To put it in other words, the real explorer dies with every step she takes because for her the familiar is constantly turning into the strange, the obvious into the questionable, the it of immediacy into the it to be known only through inquiry. Real exploration is always an experience of being dispossessed, a disruption of the same by the other.[10]

Thus, the future toward which wonder projects us is not merely an absent version of the already present. For the "object" which is to be known through questioning can be reached only by leaving the immediate behind and moving not toward a new immediacy but toward a universe mediated by the act of questioning. Merely moving from one area of immediacy to another is not exploring at all, no matter how much ground one covers. The only thing that makes movement exploratory is my not knowing where I am going. But in order for me not to know where I am going, I have to be aware of the unknown I am entering as unknown. Were it nothing more to me than an addition to the immediate in its immediacy, it would not ever hold me fast in its spellbinding strangeness. Wonder "go[es] before [us] into emptiness, raise[s] strange suns for [our] new mornings."[11] It makes the universe itself come into existence for us.

It is difficult to articulate more precisely the distinction between the whence and whither of wonder because of the fact that the words we might employ to do so themselves belong to the world opened up by wonder. We cannot find any meaningful words to describe that pure presence of original immediacy since every such word already belongs to one of the many universes of discourse whose doors are opened by the hinge of wonder. We can ask, What is this "it" whose presence is so present to us, this "it" which precedes wonder not in the sense that it comes before wonder temporally but in the sense that wonder presupposes it? And then, as soon as we ask that question, we realize that it is the one posed by wonder itself, and that any answer we might give to it would describe the "it" as it is known through inquiry, not the "it" which precedes inquiry. Were we to continue trying to figure out what the "it" is, in its immediate presence, we would have failed to realize that the very process of inquiry in which we are engaged points us forward toward the universe of meaning, not back to the level of immediacy from which wonder beckons us.

Should we then leave the from-which behind us, even perhaps to the point of denying this "it" completely?[12] If we cannot say what the given is in its immediate givenness, should we say it isn't at all? The path of wonder and inquiry can never carry us back to where we were before taking our first exploratory step. But how could there be any dreadful steps, any opening of doors or crossing of thresholds, any exploration at all, without a from-which, even if the from-which is never accessible to us, except as that from which we are being drawn away? What starts us on the path toward the universe of meaning is the fact that the given always turns out to be simply there in its mute immediacy; but that very dead end is always our starting point. Were there no given, wonder could never spring on us its unpredictable surprise, would never be able to sneak up and startle us into realizing that we do not know what lies right here in front of us. The given is indispensable not because it gives us something without which we cannot know but rather for just the opposite reason: we must be given the given so that we can realize that, even in the plenitude of its complete givenness, it does not make accessible to us the knowledge of what it is.

THE RE-PRESENTATIVE PICTURE AND THE VOCATIVE IMAGE

As even this brief excursion has made clear, the phenomenology of wonder is rich with implications, which I will be trying to explore throughout this book. Here I would like to make a first attempt at probing the ontological import of the distinction between the from-which and the toward-which of wonder. The pivotal question which arises in this regard is this: which "it" more appropriately deserves to be called "being"?

Being, it would seem, comes first, before our understanding of it. Knowing, it seems, comes after being; for being is here already before we set out to understand it. Isn't this prior-ity, origin-ality, of being over knowing inscribed in the very nature of knowing itself? When we seek to know something, does not the "it" to be known already lie out there, like a target to be hit? Is not inquiry the arrow of intentionality shooting toward that target? Or, to switch to the image Derrida uses in *Of Grammatology*,[13] is not the relationship we try to achieve between being and knowing like the relationship which exists between an original and the copy made to duplicate it? The ideal copy is so like the original that we cannot distinguish them: the difference between them evaporates. Just so, it would seem, we treat being as the original which our knowing seeks to re-present. The more perfectly re-presentative our thinking is, the closer it comes to being; we strive, it seems, asymptotically perhaps, for a parousia of coincidence where knowing would so perfectly copy being as to be self-effacing and thus present to us no mere re-presentation but the original presence itself. The end of knowing (in the sense of both its purpose and its terminal point) would be its returning to the beginning. In putting an end to inquiry, the eschaton would bring us back at last to the original plenitude of genesis.

This way of construing the purpose of inquiry (which Derrida imputs to the whole history of Western metaphysics[14]) comes from likening thought to vision. We see well insofar as we see just what is there before us with flawless accuracy; we know insofar as we are faultless mirrors of nature as it is without us. For the eye to become what it sees is the consummation devoutly wished; if the mind could, indeed, know things so well as to become them, it would be comparable to God, who is said to create things by seeing them. The correspondence theory of truth, as traditionally understood, comes out of this copy theory of knowing. Our ideas are true insofar as they conform to being; and how is this conformity to be achieved if not by our making our ideas the self-effacing servants of the things they are meant to re-present? Thus, thought is conceived of as a replication of what is, and judgment as a checking of the replica against the original.

However we put it, we find again and again at the basis of this view the same prior-ity of presence over re-presentation, original over copy, nature over imitative replica. Knowing is always a kind of image whose veracity lies in its referring back to what is literally given. I do not mean to recapitulate here the devastating critique of this theory worked out in *Of Grammatology*, but to explore the possibility of an alternative to it by following the intimations of the phenomenology of wonder.

For while we are tempted to think of images as always pointing back to some literal given, and to be mere appurtenances, excrescences, when compared with the present itself which they mimic,[15] our analysis has suggested that the same cannot be said of wonder. Even when the object that provokes our wonder is right in our hands, our wonder does not refer us to that object in its givenness; rather, it surprises us into realizing that, as perfectly as the object is given to us, we do not know what it is. When consciousness is filled with wonder, it is precisely its image of the given that is effaced, under the advent of an amazement which leaves the literal imagination nonplussed. In our becoming conscious of the unknown, in its very character as unknown, our literal pictures of the given waver and fade, giving way to the influence of the unknown as such in its very unpicturability. Sometimes we say quite frankly, as we turn a thing over and over, looking at it from every possible angle, "I cannot imagine what it is." Wonder is not a picture of what is present in the present. It is our falling under the spell of the unknown in its utter strangeness, its radical heterogeneity from the given. Indeed, it is just this heterogeneity, this impossibility of picturing it at all, which gives the toward-which of wonder its power to fascinate and terrify at the same time. How could we not feel compelled to explore this whole other universe, once we have been seized by the fact of our ignorance of it? And how could we not be terrified of taking even a single step in its direction, once we realize it is impossible to picture where we are going? The other which becomes accessible through wonder, and only through wonder, swallows all our images in one terrifying gulp of its darkness. That is why, when we were children, we were afraid to open even an inch the door leading into the secret room. For an imagination used to re-presenting the given, the other opened up to us by wonder is entirely other, and so can be as dreadful as nothingness itself.[16] If the deepest truths are found only by following those intimations, in all their dreadfulness, death is, as Socrates suggested, the mother of wisdom.

However, we would be doing imagination a grave injustice if we identified it with the ability to picture literally, and so denied it any role in our wondrous (and dreadful) venturing. Are there not, in fact, images which provoke the very fascination and fear which are constitutive of wonder?[17] Are there not images which fill us with both longing and foreboding, which heighten our sense of strangeness instead of alleviating it, which, far from filling the dark with familiar presences, give us intimations of realities which are radically other than everything present to us? I am not thinking here only of those images (discussed by Edmund Burke) whose effectiveness comes from their very vagueness, their sonorous, rather than their ocular, import. I mean poetic language in general, as Gaston Bachelard understands it,[18] the language which does not just make our daydreams come alive but convinces us, at least while under its influence, that there is more truth to them than to memory's literal accuracies. Whether it accents the tone of dread, or gives us inklings of some unexpected joy we cannot picture, the poetic image has a vocative, not an imitative, import. When the poet remembers being

> . . . young and easy under the apple boughs
> About the lilting house and happy as the grass was green,

and recalls how

> Time let me hail and climb
> Golden in the heydays of his eyes[19]

what is being praised is not the morning that can be seen with the naked eye, but the morning which wonder once made us eager to embrace. If the poetic image would take us all the way back to the first day of genesis, it does not try to do so by purporting to present us with a literal image of it.[20] It would retrieve for us, rather, the origin-ary amazement which made every literal object into something seen and yet marvellous, present and yet unfathomable, given and yet transcendent. In paradise itself, we would not have known where we were. What we have lost is our origin-ary openness to the unimaginable future.

The "lilting house," insofar as it does not refer to any literal given, is considered a "figure of speech," just as what it images is considered fanciful. But such a way of construing both the phrase and its meaning presupposes the priority of the speechless given as the criterion of the real against which images are to be compared, with the consequence that poetry comes to be viewed as a distortion of language's natural and origin-ary usage, which is to record the literal. The factual given is that houses are not lilting. But the house that is not lilting is the house we walk through thoughtlessly every day on our round of appointed chores, the house which we take so much for granted as the context of our lives that it would take a Sabbath to startle us into realizing we do not even know it exists. The poetic image is a pro- and e-vocation of the house as it is destabilized for us on the Sabbath by wondering. Its "truth" lies precisely in its vocative effectiveness, its power to make real to us what we become conscious of in amazement. Poetry is not to be checked against the literal given in its givenness but against that to which wonder beckons us.

But this suggests that the poetic image does not come after some original truth which it fancifully deconstructs. Rather, the poetic image as it is engendered by our marvelling, gives us the first inkling of that which we cannot know except through wonder and the inquiry it provokes. Poetry does not refer back to literal presence but leaps ahead toward something which becomes accessible to us for the first time in the poetic evocation of it. We might say that poetry makes the world begin for us for the first time.[21] It is, as the romantics suggested, the origin of all our worlds.[22]

If we find it surprising that a philosopher of science like Bachelard ends up writing an encomium to reverie, it is because we are used to thinking of enchantment as a departure from rationality, instead of as the origin of it.[23] Bachelard points out[24] that our reveries about our childhood do not carry us back to the literal house we lived in; rather, they return us to the houses we inhabited in our original daydreams. For the child, the tree-fort is more real than her literal bedroom, even if it exists nowhere except in what we call the fantasies she entertains of it as she lies in her room on Sunday morning, with the sun streaming in from outside, as if it had been sent to beckon her. Such daydreams are truer than we ever suspect; everything we know comes from following their intimations.

BEING AS THE TOWARD-WHICH OF WONDER

I mean this last claim to be more than a poetic exaggeration on behalf of the vocative image. Whether it is more than that can be determined only by asking what the phenomenology of wonder requires us to say about the relationship between language and being.

For it seems, again, that being comes first, and thought comes after it, like a hunter chasing its quarry after giving it a head start. In *Of Grammatology* Derrida explains that this is just how we ordinarily conceive of the relationship between thing and language or, to be more specific, the relationship between the signified and the signifier.[25] We think that the signifier does its work when it calls no attention to itself so that, presented with it, we think only of what it re-presents; we seem to succeed in catching up with being when the signifier disappears completely into the signified. Language purports to be perfectly transparent at such moments so that we see right through it to the thing itself, to the presence of what is present in the present—to being.

But it is just this ordinary way of conceiving of the relationship between the signified and the signifier which the phenomenology of wonder requires us to revise. For in thinking that the signifier refers back to the signified, we are thinking of it as a copy that is trying to duplicate an original that is already given. In thinking of language this way, we make it the servant of the immediate, something not just derivative from but wholly reducible to what precedes it. But we would not need language to refer us back to the immediate if we had not already gone beyond it. And what sense would it make to institute a signifier whose sole purpose is to get us back to the given in its immediacy? If that were where we wanted to go, a quicker route would be to do away with language entirely. Why institute a signifier for the purpose of making it disappear?

The theory of language that has it pointing back to the given leaves one critical fact unaccounted for. It explains language as a retrieval of the prior but it says nothing about what has drawn us away from the given in the first place so as to be in need of returning to it. What breaks us out of immediacy, what introduces the origin-ary separation which it is the purported role of language to heal? The answer is wonder itself. On its hinge we turn from the "it" of immediacy toward an "it" to be known only by following where wonder leads. Wonder, far from turning us back, opens a door onto a world that is accessible to us in no other way except through the questions it awakens in us. Language could not exist prior to wonder because only wonder opens that distance between our selves and the world of immediacy which language, in any theory, presupposes. But if language only emerges once we have turned away from the given toward the world opened up by wonder, what justifies us in continuing to think that language refers back to the given that is accessible without it? Might it not beckon us instead toward a world accessible in no other way except in and through its mediation?

If the clues wonder gives us are to be trusted, language is vocative; it calls us into the world of meaning and makes it real to us for the first time. Words do not refer back to things, as copies refer to an original. Rather, words beckon us ahead to things which become accessible to us only in words and through them. The signifier is not an excrescence. For it is not to be understood by reference to a signified that can be known without the signifier. If the signifier disappeared, were utterly effaced, we would be back where we started before we became wonderers. But, in fact, we were never there, even in our childhood; we have always been on our way toward the world of significations which signifiers make accessible to us. No signifier refers us back out of the world of signification; there is nothing outside language which we can use to check our language to see if it holds true; for that against which we must check what we say is accessible to us only in and through language itself.

But none of this need be construed in such a way as to imply that the signified is reducible to the signifier. The signifier does not refer back to the (lost) present in a vain attempt to re-present it. But this does not mean that the signifier refers to nothing beyond itself. One would jump to this conclusion only if one thought there could be nothing beyond the signifier except the given in its givenness. But instead of referring back to the given, the signifier can refer ahead to an "it" which is accessible to us only because the signifier signifies it to us. One is tempted to think that language, once released from its purported obligation to copy the given, can only float freely and aimlessly, without relationship to anything beyond itself. But this temptation comes from our attachment to the given, from our presumption that the given is being itself, and from our presuming that beyond the given there is precisely nothing. But, in fact, language needs its freedom from the given precisely so that it can open up to us a world which we cannot reach in any other way.

In doing so it opens the door to a revolution in our whole sense of reality. For it suggests that the given is that *from* which wonder turns us, but being is that *toward* which it beckons us.[26] Being is not to be known by going back as far as we can to the given; it is to be known by going ahead as far as we can into the unknown of which wonder itself first makes us aware. In calling that unknown being itself language is only saying what wonder already taught us: that there is a plenitude to the mystery of the unknown that is lacking in the given.

When wonder frees language from the given, it does not give it free rein, uninhibited by any bonds or relationships. It frees it, rather, for a higher calling. Far from being a copy of the given, the whole vocation of language is precisely to uproot us from it, to enchant us with its web of significations to the point where the latter becomes the world in which we live and move and have our being. Under its influence, one is led to understand and assent to the claim that being itself is not the given to be known by looking at what is right here in front of us; being is what is to be known through enchantment and exploration, wonder and inquiry, reverie and the questions it prompts. The given is the whence of wonder but being is its unknown whither, that toward which we are called, by which we are beckoned; it is that which is known when we operate inside the world language opens up for us—the world of language itself. But this does not mean that being is reducible to language. It means that when we speak of there being something "beyond" language, we must explain whether we are referring back to the given, which is prior to language and in relationship to which language seems like a mere excrescence, or ahead to a world of being that becomes real to us through language, and in no other way. Being is beyond language, not in the way an original is prior to a copy, but in the way that what we come to know through inquiry is distinguishable from and transcends it.

As I understand *Of Grammatology*, it does not explore these different meanings of what is "beyond" language. It would free language from its re-presentative bonds without ascribing to it a vocative import. It suggests, as I read it, that there is nothing "beyond" any signifier, nothing to which any signifier points, except other signifiers.[27] It suggests that nothing could be "beyond"

language except the given to which language is referred when it is
construed as a copy. The "beyond" is here identified with the "outside," with that which is external to language, that which lies right
here in front of me. But the "beyond" can have an entirely different
meaning: it can refer not to the given which lies outside of language
but to the world to be found only by operating *inside* language.
Because wonder leads us to move beyond the given into the unknown, as into an unknown plenitude, it requires our affirming
that the real world is not the given at all but the world to which our
questions bring us—the world as spoken, the world as it is found
in language. What transcends language is precisely the world contained within its meanings, the world that can only be said.

Whenever we try to put this peculiar kind of transcendence
into words, we are tempted to fall back on the picture model of
language, to say that words refer to objects as a replica to an
original. But words give us our origin-ary access to the reality they
refer to. That is why the poet, who lives that origin-ary experience
so intimately, treats every word as a sacrament: not as a symbol
that can be dispensed with as soon as it is understood, but as an
indispensable annunciation which makes reality accessible for the
first time. The thing to which the word refers transcends the word
and yet one cannot reach it if one leaves the word behind; one
reaches the thing only by getting inside the world contained in the
word.

In short, there is a transcendental signified; but it is accessible
only by our remaining immanent within the web of signifiers. Only
when we affirm such a transcendental signified do we have a way to
talk about being that does not equate it with the presence of what
is right-here-now, prior to wonder. It seems to me that *Of Grammatology* stops halfway between the rejection of being as presence
and the affirmation of being as it becomes accessible to us through
the sacramentality of words. It is as if, after liberating language
from its obligation to copy the given, *Of Grammatology* is afraid
of saddling it with any vocation that might inhibit its autonomous,
self-satisfying play. It would have being give way to a writing in
which being is not mentioned at all, not even to be crossed out.
Being, it seems in the end, cannot be anything but presence, and
the idea of transcendence cannot be anything but a hankering after

the given in its (never given) immediacy. And this would be true if it were not for the event of wonder which, even as it uproots us from the given, points us toward the other in its otherness. The word for that other, in its otherness, is being.

In saying that it is the vocation of language to speak it, one might be accused of weighing it down with a responsibility the gravity of which is incompatible with its untrammeled play. But perhaps here again we should think of ourselves as children, standing before a door behind which, we suspect, lies something fascinating and dreadful. For us, as children, such experiences were unspeakably serious; we felt, when held fast in the grip of such longing and anxiety, that we were on the brink of something wholly other, and that, once we opened that door, our lives would not be the same again. And yet if such moments retain their immemorial appeal for us, it is because in them we were consummately explorers; we did not know where we were headed and, precisely for that reason, we felt quickened, all the way down to our bowels, by our mortal venturing. And yet we know too that, for us as children, opening that door was the supreme experience of play. Only the diversions of adults are frivolous. For children, the act of venturing where one has never been before serves no purpose external to itself. What makes exploration dreadful is the very same thing that makes it playful: the fact that one does not know where one is heading. And it is precisely because one does not know that one is drawn on, as by the irresistable power of the unknown as such.

INTIMATIONS OF THE SACRED

Thus far I have been able to give no more than intimations of the world opened up by wonder. In the chapters to follow I will be trying to explore in greater depth some of their radical implications—especially the ontological implications which follow from identifying being not with the given but with that toward which wonder beckons us. I will not, in these final paragraphs, try to anticipate where this exploration might lead, except with regard to one theme which deserves more than the oblique reference I have given it thus far.

I have suggested that, when one follows the inklings of wonder, one finds oneself opened up to the world discoverable through questions and inquiry, the world of being mediated by meaning. But, however far one goes in that direction, one keeps on venturing only insofar as one is stricken again and again by wonder and surrenders again and again to its throe. Implicit in our experience of that throe is an ambivalence of fascination and dread, longing and horror. But each of these just-mentioned terms is heavy with connotations which I have refrained from explicating. If we return to the situation which we have been treating as paradigmatic of wonder in general, we may make it easier for the implications implicit in these words to emerge. The door before which we stood as children with such fascination and dread, precisely because it was a door, presented itself to us simultaneously as a barrier and an entrance. It kept us out at the same time that it invited us in; it warned even as it beckoned, it barred our way even as it made a promissory appeal. We shrank back from it—but only because its appeal had already touched some deep and mysterious chord in us. The very fact that the door is there enables us to know that on the other side of it is something forbidding in its otherness. Somehow we know we cannot open that door, cannot cross that threshold, without leaving everything behind. If dread is implicit in wonder, it is because wonder can so easily turn into a matter of life and death: it is childhood itself we lose when we wholeheartedly follow its intimations. What could make us raise our hand to the latch, put our fingers on the cold handle, push the door open with the full weight of our small bodies, at that very moment when we are melting with horror? The fact that we are drawn to the other seems to be paradoxically linked to the fact that it awakens such dread in us. Perhaps the explanation for that link is to be found in the fact that the horror we feel when on the verge of gaining access to that other comes from our realizing how transcendent its import is. Precisely because it is more worth knowing than anything we are familiar with, it is capable of devastating us.

That is what has always been meant by the sacred: that which, beyond us, other than us, it would be utterly dreadful to know; a mystery that beckons even as it horrifies, an other which bids us approach at the very moment we find it to be most forbidding. The place reserved for the holy because of its holiness is a place we are forbidden, on pain of death, to enter; but which of us would not feel, if she found this place, that she stood on the threshold of what had been sought all along with such indefinable longing? It is, I think, no accident that the toward-which of wonder evokes the same richly ambivalent response which aestheticians, phenomenologists, and historians,[28] with remarkable unanimity, have found to be characteristic of religious experience. For it is wonder and wonder alone that makes accessible to us the other as other and this other, precisely because of its otherness, evokes the realization that we are standing on the verge of a reality that is awe-full and terrifying—but a reality toward which we are implacably drawn because it makes everything we already know pale into insignificance. Wonder, of its very nature, is an eruption of the numinous in human life. Religion, origin-ally, is our dreadful marvelling.

And if, as the argument has led us to think, being is not the from-which of wonder but that which wonder alone makes accessible to us for the first time, then it will not do to dismiss the holy as an illusion. We would have to say it is being, precisely because it is the toward-which of dreadful marvelling. The real world is full of the gods. We cease to take them seriously as we learn how to repress our origin-al dread of them. We flee from them because we know all too well how devastating it would be to stand on the threshold of their sanctuary, as children stand before a door which leads to a wholly other world. Perhaps we should not cross it without genuflecting into our own nothingness.

This, too, is an issue whose radical ramifications I will be trying to explore here. For after the first door there are many others,[29] each of which opens up to us a universe we hadn't expected to exist. These universes are not, I have suggested, the playthings of language. Rather, if we are to trust the testimony of wonder, we are to say they are, each one, a universe of being, holy and wholly real, though we have no access to them except through childlike astonishment. If Socrates was right, the purpose of all thinking is not to get us through that door once and for all but to get us, over and over again, into the throe of opening it. His word for wonder was wisdom.

CHAPTER 3

On The Way between Heidegger and Lonergan

One way for me to deepen the exploration of the themes I have started to address is to situate them in the context of those texts where they were first awakened for me. I have for many years now been under the sway of two great thinkers and their two great works: Martin Heidegger's *Being and Time* and Bernard Lonergan's *Insight*.[1] To be under the sway of a great work does not only mean that one assents to a particular set of key propositions contained in it; it means that one is so deeply engaged by the way of thinking which animates it that one's own way of thinking is profoundly and permanently transformed.[2] This can only occur when we allow ourselves to enter inside the body of a work, instead of trying to seize on a list of theses that can be extracted from it. A great text is a world which we can understand only if we inhabit and learn to feel at home in it. As this process progresses, we find that we cannot enter and leave the world of the text as casually as we pick up and put down the book; for our thinking gradually comes to be governed by the same throe of questioning which generated the text. This does not at all mean that we have mastered the text; it means, in fact, something nearly the opposite of this— that we are surrendering ourselves to the eros of inquiry which moves the text, and spending ourselves in service to it. To claim to have mastered a text would itself be proof that one had not understood it.

I have lingered over this preamble because the two texts which I am to discuss are acts of world making in a special way. Every great text, or work of art, is like the creation of a universe. But in these two philosophical works, the act of creation is fully self-conscious and reflective since the author of each is fully aware of the fact that he is generating a new world. Indeed, both of these works are explicitly self-referential: each of them is about itself as a universe of meaning.[3] In this regard one might view them as examples of the same kind of self-conscious world making which occurs so widely in twentieth century literature, from Faulkner to Barth, from Joyce to Garcia Marquez. But since the *Euthyphro* philosophy has never been satisfied with simply providing examples or studying them: it always strives to become conscious of that which the example is an example of. The thinking of both Heidegger and Lonergan is an exercise in self-appropriation,[4] an attempt on the part of thought not just to create a world of meaning but to understand itself as the act of creating such a world. Each of their texts is a world about the meaning of worlds.

I assume that a comparison of these texts, these worlds, with each other will be of interest at least to those who have been fascinated and affected by both of them. But whether such a comparison is possible is a more difficult question and not one which can be answered without plunging headfirst into the very issues raised in the texts.[5] What is the meaning of these worlds of meaning which great texts create for us? If each text is a world, it seems at first glance that one cannot enter one without leaving the other. Inside which of them, if either, should one reside when one does the work of comparing them? Where is the comparer of these worlds to stand if, as an outsider, she can understand neither and, as an insider, she cannot get far enough outside one world to understand the other? We assume that each of these thinkers was at home in his own world. On the other hand, those of us who would like to compare them represent, as it were, their strangeness to each other. Is there room, in either of their worlds, for the stranger in his strangeness? It is unlikely that any of us is as much at home in either text as its author was. Instead, we are somewhere between these worlds, neither residents nor aliens, neither lost nor found, wishing that each would send some signal that would show us the way to the other. But it seems we have to think our way between them for ourselves.

But all this is how it seems at first glance, and both Heidegger and Lonergan tell us to distrust first glances, especially when they seem like certain intuitions. In what follows I will try to go as far as

I can beyond my initial experience of the strangeness of these worlds to each other. If it is impossible for me to pinpoint at the start of these reflections the position I am standing in or the perspective I am using when I make them, it is because locating myself in this way would require beginning with a well-defined map of the terrain to be explored. But then the thing that makes exploring exploratory is that when it is done no maps exist yet. The cardinal rule of exploring is to let oneself be surprised by new worlds. I am writing these reflections precisely because I do not know where I stand, only that I am caught between these universes.

THE EMERGENCE OF THE WORLD AS WORLD

Only the reader who enters into a text in the way I have described is able to discover it as a world. It is easier to do this when one does not know what to expect and has no guidebook at one's disposal for locating the principal sights. The citizens of a country do not especially appreciate the kind of tourist who has no heart for learning how to be at home with them. For such "sightseeing" tourists are not much different from trespassers; they travel mainly in order to have pictures of where they have been. When we sightsee in this way, we fail to appreciate even what is right in front of us since we look at it for only as long as it takes the eye of the instamatic to see it. The instamatic tourist has too many pictures to take to stop for long before anything.

I have been using the image of discovering a new world as a metaphor for the experience of entering a text. But the converse metaphor is also illuminating and pregnant with richer implications. Exploring a world is like reading a text. In *Being and Time* and *Insight*, Heidegger and Lonergan talk about entering into a written work as one particularly important example of the activity in which we engage all the time, though we are for the most part unconscious of doing so—the act of entering into the world.[6] We explore texts only because at a more primordial level we are always readers of the world. Dis-covering the universe is not one among many human acts; it is, for both Heidegger and Lonergan, constitutive of being human, though both would be quick to admit that ordinarily we travel as tourists, not as pilgrims. For none of us, even the most hardened travellers, can the world ever completely cease to be something unexpected.

The unexpectedness of the world, the suddenness with which it comes upon us, its ability to sneak up on us and take us by surprise—this is not something over which we have control. We have no choice about whether to be subject to this riveting suddenness, this experience of being caught unaware by something in the world that makes the world as such abruptly real as if for the first time. A story told about the sculptor Donatello perfectly illustrates this.[7] Walking home one day from market with an apronful of eggs, he happened to pass by the door of the chapel in which the newly finished crucifix of Brunelleschi had just been hung. Donatello was so stricken by the beauty of what he saw that he dropped all his eggs and stood there transfixed. The crucifix, in this example, is not something ready-to-hand within the orbit of Donatello's circumspective concern, nor is it simply a new object he finds alongside others already present-at-hand. It is something like the suddenly revealed center of a new universe, the existence of which he could not have foreseen.

Such an experience of beauty, like the experience of falling in love, gives us a kind of priveleged access to the world; to use Heidegger's phrase, it allows the worldhood of the world, the very fact that there is a world, to reveal itself. Such experiences have the power to be radically transformative; they can alter in the most profound way our whole circumspective, practical way of approaching things. But both Heidegger and Lonergan think that while such experiences seem to come from out of nowhere to suddenly interrupt our habitualized lives, they actually effect a return to and redis-covery of our most primordial condition: they make us wonderers again. They enable us to go back to the original human situation which was not an experience of presence but an experience of being thrown headlong into an unknown future. From whence spring all the whys we ask if not from some primal desire to know? And how could there be any desire to know if we were not from the beginning thrown forward in astonishment into the unexpected world? No matter how many techniques we acquire for handling the ready-to-hand, no matter how exhaustive our catalogue of objects present in the world, the world itself can never completely lose the astonishing character it had when all we knew was that we did not understand it.

Because he is intent on tracing our intellectual life back to its unremembered source, and uncovering its transcendental conditions, Lonergan identifies our primordial astonishment before the world with the simple experience of wonder itself.[8] Heidegger, on the other hand, emphasizes the fact that, in our everyday, circumspective concern, this original amazement is repressed; only the horrifying possibility of losing one's world as a whole can reawaken it.[9] And yet these two experiences, wonder and horror, have more in common with each other than appears on the surface. It is true that we are inclined to follow where wonder beckons but want to pull back from what horror threatens to reveal to us. But just as there is a dreadful dimension to wonder, so there is operative in horror a wonderlike sense of being held fast in the spellbinding sway of the unknown. According to both Lonergan and Heidegger, to be human means to be always caught in this sway which at the same time carries us outside of ourselves and, for that very reason, enables us to be ourselves. Indeed, in Heidegger this sway turns out in the end to be the work of that ecstatic temporality which is constitutive of our very being: in astonishment we are caught up (thrownness) in the spellbinding grip (fallenness) of an unknown which both beckons and horrifies (projection).

For both Heidegger and Lonergan transcendental reflection on this primordial experience enables us to appreciate the constitutive role it plays in all intentional acts. The event of astonishment, whether it takes the form of dread or wonder, is not one happening among others in our biographies. It gets its primordial status from the fact that it constitutes the condition for the possibility of human existence as such with its polymorphic and historically differentiated character. Astonishment founds all our worlds. But while it underlies all our practical and theoretical acts, we are too used to operating inside the worlds that have been founded on it to be aware of its transcendental function. Hence the importance of philosophical reflection which enables us to re-trieve the event of astonishment not by a reimmersion in the primitive experience itself but by understanding for the first time its role as the condition for the possibility of every mode of consciousness.

What gives astonishment, whether in the form of dread or wonder, its transcendental import? Why do Heidegger and Lonergan claim it to be the ground on which our worlds are constituted? It might be helpful here to return again to the childhood experience discussed in the previous chapter. Exactly what is it that fascinates the child as she looks at a block and turns it over and over in her hands? She does not yet recognize the block *as* a block, as an item of equipment needed for the accomplishment of a building project. In fact, she does not recognize it *as* anything. Shall we say then that the "as" of interpretation is simply inoperative for her? If that were the case, it would mean that what she is looking at would be for her nothing but what is "already out there now"[10] in front of her. She would then be aware of what is there before her only in its sensory immediacy to her, as the cat is aware of its saucer of milk.[11] Her consciousness would then be operating solely on the basis of what Lonergan calls biological extroversion, with the consequence that the object before her would be simply a meaningless datum of experience: it would certainly not be an "object" because for it to be a thing of any sort it would have to be loosened from its pure uninterpreted immediacy.

But in this description of the child's experience, it is precisely wonder that has been left out. If the child experiences nothing but the sensory immediacy of what is "already out there now" in front of her, wonder has not yet arisen; if the child sees what is out there as a building block, wonder about it has already been supplanted by the circumspective use of it. But there is a third possibility—the possibility that she is experiencing what is right there in front of her as unknown. In this experience, what is before her could not be any more immediately present to her than it is and yet in its very accessibility to her she recognizes it as beyond her. The "as" is operative in wonder—without it wonder would sink back into sensory immediacy. But it is operative as an unfulfilled intention, as a future that breaks in upon the present and uproots it, as the unknown known in its very character as unknown.[12] To be seized by wonder is to be carried outside of and ahead of oneself into mystery.[13] When we say, as we are tempted to, that the block awakens wonder in the child, we are importing into the child's experience the very interpretation of what is in front of her that can only be reached as a consequence of wondering. It is not the block that awakens her wonder. It is wonder that leads her to recognize what is in front of her as a block.

If we move from this example to the general point it illustrates, we have to say that wonder is not an event that happens *in* the world like other events. It is not the world that makes wonder possible; it is wonder that makes it possible for the world as such to happen to us.[14] One might say that the central purpose of both *Being and Time* and *Insight* is to persuade us to take the ontological and epistemological ramifications of this reversal seriously. Both Heidegger and Lonergan think traditional metaphysics needs to be radically rethought on the basis of a transcendental turn that makes wonder and dread constitutive of the world. The world that takes us by surprise and seizes us so unexpectedly is not already out there now in front of us; it only becomes accessible to us in and through the very surprise by which it seizes us. The correspondence theory of knowledge as traditionally understood breaks down, according to both Heidegger and Lonergan, right here at the forgotten beginning of all our truths. Wonder itself does not prove its epistemic worth by being in conformity with what lies right there in front of us. Rather, the importance of wonder lies precisely in its capacity to beckon us beyond what lies right in front of us toward the unknown as such. What the universe is is not to be known by looking at it as it lies there; it is to be known only by going where wonder beckons when it makes us fall in love with questioning.

In short, wonder is not a copy since it projects us into a world to which we can have no access except through the questions which it provokes. But the world wonder discloses must not be thought of as lying out there just over the horizon—as if it were something not-yet present which will be lying right there in front of us as soon as we catch up with it. The future toward which wonder projects us is not going to be just another instance of immediate experience. All the answers given to the child's whys do not give her information about what is in front of her; they transport her out of the immediacy of what is in front of her and situate her in the real world for the first time. Would it be intelligent to ask her, after she has become comfortable in this world and can readily distinguish between "toys" and "furniture," etc., if this world is an accurate copy of the one she was acquainted with before she entered it? Perhaps she is too at home in this world that is so different from her earlier one to even remember the transformation of one into the other. We forget that the world we move about in so naturally and take for granted as obvious does not lie "out there" waiting for us to find it but reveals itself only when wonder makes room in us for its appearance. To use a Heideggerian image,[15] we do not have to construct a bridge to connect our thoughts with the world because the world we seek to connect up with is not to be found anywhere outside of our wonder. It is futile for us to try to conform our thinking to the world because the world only becomes accessible to us for the first time in and through our thinking it.

That is why the world is not reducible to the sum total of entities; it is the condition for the possibility of there being any entities at all. For the entities which we come to know and name are accessible only as they emerge from the unknown; the unknown precedes them as the condition for the possibility of their emergence. The world is the unknown itself as a whole from which everything we know emerges, and we become ourselves only by entering it. In wonder, the unknowing subject and the unknown object have not yet become separated; the event of astonishment holds them together in a single ecstasy. The unknown, which carries the subject outside herself, and the unknower, who makes it possible for the unknown to be recognized as such, are one.[16]

THE TRANSCENDENTAL TURN TO WORLD-MAKING

I have been trying to suggest, in this Heideggerian/Lonerganian return to the theme of wonder, that their thought takes a transcendental turn which is similar to but in the end more radical than Kant's. For both of them the turn does not just transform the meaning of "object" but the meaning of being itself. However, they are Kant's successors insofar as they think that the understanding of understanding is the hinge on which the turn is made. Both

Being and Time and *Insight* aim at revolutionizing the way we think about being by first revolutionizing how we think about thinking itself.

Just as we are never mere experiencers, so we are never pure wonderers. In fact, Lonergan helps us realize that pure wonder as a kind of self-contained condition is a contradiction in terms. Wonder is precisely our being projected from the immediacy of expeience toward the world mediated by meaning. To be human means to operate within a world of meaning and to be concerned about things of which we would not even be aware if the insights that enable us to understand meaning were not accessible to us. Acts which, on the surface, seem to involve nothing more than an immediate recognition of what is present-at-hand—my recognizing what is in front of me as a set of blocks, my remembering that they were a birthday present given to my child, my surprise that they have been left lying on the floor and not cleaned up—actually presuppose and help to constitute a whole framework of meaning which defines the boundaries of my world. I see the blocks *as* toys or clutter only because I interpret them in terms of the underlying project of meaning by which I orient myself in my day-to-day life. Particular events that happen and particular things I encounter acquire their meaning from their location within the horizon of an order in terms of which I interpret my life as a whole. The parameters of this horizon are the limits of my world. When operating inside them, I feel at home.

In a very radical sense, we ourselves constitute the world we live in by adopting the horizon of meaning in terms of which events are to be interpreted. We are all world makers. Such world making would never be possible were it not for the fact that wonder frees us from the given in its givenness. But this liberty to create meaning is far more dreadful to exercise than we would like it to be; for we have no secure framework inside which to operate when making judgments about the meaning of our world as a whole. Perhaps for this very reason, we do not ordinarily operate on this primordial level.[17] In fact, we are ordinarily so accustomed to operating within the limits of a particular horizon of meaning that we treat the things which are meaningful to us because of that horizon as things that should be immediately self-evident to anyone. The more ex-

clusively we live within the limits of a horizon, the less aware are we
of there being any limits to it. We tend to become so comfortable in
our world that we cease to be aware of the possibility of any others.

This power we have to constitute our own world is most clearly
evident in the way we construct a practical framework for our lives.
But according to Heidegger and Lonergan it is wrong to think that
the shift from the practical to the theoretical, from praxis to theory,
entails a shift from *making* our world to *looking* at one that exists
"out there," independently of all our meanings. Heidegger and
Lonergan agree that the world of the physicist differs dramatically
from the world of the factory worker but both reject the traditional
explanation that explains this difference as a difference between
looking and making. For this would make theory, as contrasted
with practice, a matter of staring at what is right here now in front
of us, a matter of merely eyeing what is present-at-hand, instead of
working to change it. Were thinking an act of seeing, the thinker
would be required to seek a perfectly pure and direct vision of the
object since it would take such vision to make the object immediately and wholly accessible to the viewer. Both Heidegger and
Lonergan argue, each in his own way, that this is precisely the kind
of intuition which Kant was right to say we do not possess.[18] We
are never more immediately, more intuitively, related to what is
present-at-hand than when we are standing right in front of it
looking at it in wonder—but it is precisely then that we are aware
of it as *unknown* and *inaccessible* to us in the here-and-now of a
direct seeing. Wonder itself is the only kind of "intuition" we have.
But it is of course intuitive only in a manner of speaking because it
does not instantly deliver knowledge to us as we expect intuitions
to do; instead, it delivers us over to the unknown and makes us
aware of the fact that it transcends us. When it comes to knowing,
there are no instamatics, no Polaroids, no cameras of any kind.

This means that theory, for all its difference from techne, is just
as dependent as the latter on our capacity to be world makers and
to constitute the world through acts of insight. The theorist's world
too is defined by a horizon of meaning which fixes the basic framework in terms of which everything is interpreted. It makes no sense
to ask if this theoretical framework enables the theorist to have an
accurate picture of what the world is like in itself if by "the world

in itself" one means what is directly accessible to us in our immediate experience. For the whole purpose of a theory, of interpretation of any sort, is to make sense of something whose meaning I do not grasp in my immediate experience of it. And this can be done only by generating, through my own intellectual creativity, insights which direct experience never delivers to me. Thought is an act of making, not of looking—but, unlike techne, it seeks to create meaning for its own sake. It is the act of thought, and thought alone, that enables the world to become an intelligible whole for us. The leisure of the theorist, her freedom from exigencies of circumspective concern, permit her to engage in world making as an end in itself. The theorist is the world maker par excellence insofar as her leisure permits her to lose herself completely in the activity of creating meaning.

But if she is absorbed in a world of meaning that is of her own making in the sense that it is accessible only through the insights which her thinking generates, how does her theory differ from a fiction? With this question we broach for the first time the issue on which hinges the transcendental turn as Heidegger and Lonergan make it. It is the same issue which Kant had to address because, like his successors, he rejected the copy theory of knowing from the ground up. But this is no longer an issue of relevance to technical philosophers alone. Indeed, I do not think it is an exaggeration to say that our assessment of post-modern culture as a whole hinges on how we respond to it. For the distinguishing trait of this culture is precisely its plurality of apparently incommensurable worlds, its willingness to accept different, even incompatible universes of discourse, its sympathy for the kind of relativism and historicism which emphasizes that we are the makers of culture.[19] Not only are our best literary fictions those which create, as it were out of whole cloth, their own mythical universe; there is now a tendency to think of scientific and philosophical theories themselves, which until recently were read as competing pictures of the one and only real world, as projections of alternative worlds no one of which we have any reason to call truly real. Once the picture theory of knowledge is rejected, theoretical thinking is no longer bound to the "external world," as it exists "out there now" prior to our inquiries. In the post-modern age, even the plastic arts, the most

pictorial achievements of insight, are not considered to be re-presentative. Heidegger and Lonergan explain this post-modern experience of world making in a way which makes clear that, far from
being an aberration, our power to generate a universe of meaning
is grounded in the primordial exigencies of wonder itself and the
drive toward meaning which is animated by it. That neither of
these thinkers is himself a relativist or historicist, though both
recognize that different epochs live in different worlds of meaning,
suggests that there is a critical dimension to their thought which we
have not yet explored.

As I turn to that dimension, I should mention that on it depends the status of my own reflections, which are written from a
point I have not yet located somewhere between the worlds of these
two theorists. Would it even be possible to raise the question of
comparing them if each of their worlds was closed in upon itself? Is
there something about the very concept of a world of meaning
which leads us to think it is shut in upon itself so that those who
are at home in it never have the sense of being explorers? Were
Lonergan and Heidegger comfortably at home in the world of their
texts? Or does the fact that both of them made turns after writing
their great texts suggest that we cannot fully enter the world of
those texts except by moving beyond them? Perhaps the "world" of
meaning is such that only the explorer is truly at home in it. But if
that is true, in what sense can we speak of meaning as a world?
Might it be better to speak of it as beyond every world that attempts to enclose it?

DECONSTRUCTION AND ONTOLOGICAL CONVERSION

It will be easier to address these questions if we examine briefly the
experience of dread which, for all its similarity to wonder, differs
from it in certain crucial regards.[20]

None of us is indifferent to the end of the world we customarily
inhabit. We hold onto whatever horizon of meaning has enabled us
to make sense of our lives and avoid as best we can any questions
that might pull out from under us the foundation on which we
have grounded the world in which we feel at home. That structure

is more fragile than we realize when we are habituated to living within it. Accustomed to operating inside the limits of its presuppositions, we treat the latter as given and the horizon of our world as the horizon of being itself. Irrespective of what our presuppositions are, irrespective of the particular horizon in terms of which we think and live, we tend to repress as effectively as we can those horrifying intimations of its collapse which sometimes assail us. Such intimations afflict the intellectual when something calls into question the theory in terms of which she thought she could explain everything.[21] They assail all of us when some event radically disrupts the fundamental project in terms of which we ordinarily operate. In either case, one's world as a whole is in jeopardy. Every such disruption gives me an intimation of my own death for it exposes me to the possible shattering of my whole existence. It is not just that we avoid thinking about death because it is a threat to what we conceive of as the meaning of our lives; the deeper truth is that we try to avoid thinking about radical questions because being assailed by them is a form of dying.[22] The last thing in the world we want to experience is the deconstruction of our world as a whole.[23]

Wonder, we have said, is an awakening which provides us our way of entry into the world of meaning. Horror too is a kind of awakening—but what it awakens us to is the possible disintegration of our world. Caught in the sway of such horror, we find ourselves on the verge of our complete undoing.[24] Whereas wonder beckons us on toward knowing what we know to be unknown, dread makes us recoil from knowing what we want at all costs to keep unknown. We would not recoil so if we did not already know enough of this unknown to realize that knowing it would be shattering. Avoidance has the same fundamental structure as wonder but it moves, as it were, in the opposite direction. Just as wonder holds us in the sway between not knowing and knowing, and would not be possible if we were simply knowers or unknowers, so too avoidance presupposes an awareness of the unknown to be avoided and would not be possible if we were not already caught in the grip of a horror whose meaning we would like to repress.

Is it possible for us to form at least a heuristic notion of what awakens such intimations of horror and prompts the recoil of avoidance? What is so shattering to us that it threatens to bring our whole world down on us in this way? Certainly something lying right here now in front of us, while it might serve as the occasion for our experience of horror, cannot itself be that by which we shattered. For what is right here now is as accessible to us as it will ever be. Intimations of horror, on the other hand, prompt us to recoil in avoidance from that of which we know nothing except that it is able to shatter us—something which is not right here in front of us but unknown, except for the dreadful intimations we have of it. Indeed, someone aware of nothing but what is right here now in front of her could not possibly be the recipient of an intimation of horror. For what one pulls back from in such an intimation is the radical disruption of one's world as a whole, and only someone who has a world can have a horrifying anticipation of its undoing. Thus, horror presupposes that one is at home in the universe of meaning one has developed to make sense of one's life, and it is precisely this being-at-home that it radically disrupts.

In recoiling from such a disruption, we seek to avoid undergoing an experience that threatens to change our world entirely. What is jeopardized by such a threat is not the meaning of this part of our life or that but the meaning of everything—indeed, the meaning of being itself.[25] What we retreat *to,* and try to protect, is the meaning of being which our entire way of living and thinking presupposes; what we recoil *from* and try to prevent is a revolutionary challenge to our basic ontological presuppositions, and the experience of nothingness that such a challenge necessarily entails. To call into question the meaning of being on which one's life rests is to raise the ultimate issue than which none more upsetting can be conceived. For such a question leaves literally nothing in one's life untouched or intact. It sets in motion an experience of nothingness because it undermines everything one thinks about everything. In fact, an event can precipitate a crisis in our lives only to the degree that it imperils the underlying ontological principles which give them structure and stability. It is just this imperilling of our whole sense of being that we are desperate to prevent when we repress our horrifying intimations.

It is true, of course, that a profound upheaval can occur in a person's intellectual or personal life without the person explicitly realizing that her customary understanding of being is in jeopardy. In Heidegger's terms, a person undergoing an existentiell crisis does not necessarily appreciate its existential ramifications. But an existentiell crisis would not be radical if it did not upset one's most basic presuppositions about everything, even if one cannot articulate those presuppositions or appreciate how the crisis is undermining them. Ordinarily we are too deeply governed by our presuppositions to be explicitly conscious of them. Even in an intellectual crisis we might not realize, with any depth of insight, that it is our ontological presuppositions that are being jeopardized. But for a crisis to be fundamental, it must disrupt in a primordial way everything we think about everything, and so it must disrupt our understanding of being, whether we are philosophically conscious of its doing so or not. For whatever being turns out to mean, there is nothing that is not included in some way within its meaning. "Being" is said of everything that can be said to be in any sense. That is why a rupture in one's understanding of it is not just one among many intellectual or personal transformations that can occur; rather, any transformation of self is fundamental only to the degree that it disturbs one's customary understanding of being.

I am suggesting, then, that a crisis which shatters one's world cannot occur unless one is already operating comfortably within a universe of meaning; that when it does occur it uproots the presuppositions that form the parameters of one's universe; and that at its deepest level this uprooting of presuppositions disturbs the meaning of being itself since this is, for all of us, the ultimate horizon in terms of which everything about everything is understood. Now up to this point I have spoken of *Being and Time* and *Insight* as if each of them is a kind of insulated, self-contained world which its author wants us to enter. But this would imply that both Heidegger and Lonergan would like nothing better than for us to make ourselves comfortable inside the universe of meaning constituted by their texts. And in fact that is exactly what is not the case. For both *Being and Time* and *Insight* invite the reader to undergo an intellectual conversion—and not a conversion about this issue or that but one regarding the meaning of being itself. Indeed, according to the transcendental argument which these texts share, the truth of

being is not accessible to us in any other way except through the
kind of intellectual crisis and conversion which they try to make
compelling for us. *Being and Time* and *Insight* are not texts that
have to be violently broken open in order to make them comparable to each other because each of them is already caught up in the
throe of the same crisis in the meaning of being to which radical
thinking must always be drawn.

We can now begin to realize why the transcendental turn leads
both Heidegger and Lonergan further than it led Kant himself.
Seriously as he took our power to constitute the world through our
understanding of it, Kant continued to identify being not with that
which becomes accessible to us through insight but with the thing
in itself of which we can know nothing except how it appears to us
right here now in front of us. From Heidegger's and Lonergan's
point of view, Kant did not realize the revolutionary possibilities
implicit in his own thinking insofar as he was not led by it to the
most radical, and for that reason the most upsetting, question—
the question about the meaning of being itself. But, while he did
not do so himself, Kant put us in a position to realize that being is
not that which lies behind what we immediately experience, nor is
it what can be known by taking a look at or directly intuiting what
is present-at-hand. Rather, being is what we come to know by
following the throe of inquiry even when it leads us to ask those
radical questions which articulate our most upsetting intimations.

To put this point into Lonerganian terms, we might say that, in
addition to direct insights and inverse insights, there are certain
radically upsetting insights which we try to avoid having because
they require us to alter everything we think about everything.[26] For
they undermine the presuppositions about being on which our
world as a whole is grounded. The possibility that being does not
lie behind what is right here in front of me but is accessible only
through a radically upsetting insight is itself a revolutionary
thought which calls everything into question in a primordial way.
The intellectual conversion which is set in motion by this question
is not so much achieved as it is suffered; it involves undergoing
what Heidegger calls an experience of nothingness. For both
Heidegger and Lonergan, philosophical thinking is once again
what it was in the beginning for Socrates himself: an undermining

of our ordinary presuppositions which is so radical that it is likened to dying. Or, rather, it would be more accurate to say that this turn is so radical that, in the end, dying is likened to it.

Death, Socrates says,[27] is something the philosopher has to practice over and over again. This, I take it, is what Heidegger means by repetition:[28] the turn from the ordinary view of being is not something that happens once for all. To think always means to be caught up in the throe of this turn, to undergo a revolutionary change in one's sense of being itself. To be subject to this undertow is so dreadful that we realize, when we experience it, that we are caught in the throes of nothingness itself. But it is only by surrendering to that nothingness, and the loss of our ordinary way of understanding everything, that being itself becomes accessible to us.

JUDGMENT AND THE CALL OF BEING

We can now look back over the path we have taken from the perspective of this radical turn to which the path has brought us. Wonder, while ignited by something directly experienced right here in front of us, beckons us away from the immediate toward the unknown in its very character as unknown. When caught up in the sway of such wonder the child knows the unknown only as unknown; she does not know yet that it is being itself that beckons her. The questions wonder compels her to ask lead her into the universe constituted by meaning—first the world of circumspective concern which interprets everything in the light of practical imperatives, then the world of theory which tries to make sense of what is experienced not for an ulterior motive but simply for the sake of understanding itself. Once settled into the world constituted by meaning we seem to have arrived at the place to which wonder intended to lead us. For the meanings grasped by insight answer the questions raised by wonder. But just as wonder beckons us into the world constituted by meaning, dread leads us, if we do not repress it, beyond our horizon of meaning to an experience of nothingness that makes possible a revolutionary change in our sense of being itself.

From the perspective of this transformed sense of being it might be possible to begin unravelling the nexus of problems that need to be thought through once one realizes that the correspondence theory of truth as traditionally understood cannot survive for long after the copy theory of knowledge has been rejected. The correspondence theory, in requiring the conformity of thought with the reality of the thing itself, implies that the thing itself can serve as our criterion of truth because it is right here in front of us. It is tempting to argue in defense of it that by requiring us to check our thoughts against the cold, hard givenness of the directly experienced, this theory insures that we will not become narcissists absorbed in worlds of our own making. That there is a danger of such narcissism should be apparent to anyone familiar with contemporary literature and art in general, where it often seems that everyone tries their best to be a world maker, and to live inside the fiction they have created for themselves. Once we reject the correspondence theory, we seem to sever the only bond that held our myth-making in check and kept it rooted to reality. It seems that what is right here now in front of us is our one sure anchor, the only secure and certain hold we can ever have on being. Were we to lose it, would we not end up floating aimlessly, in the airy clouds of our imaginary universes?

The unnoticed presupposition at the bottom of this fear is that the further we get away from what is right here in front of us, the greater the danger of our losing our grip on being. But this cannot possibly be true if it is being itself that is beckoning us. If being is the destination, not the starting point of all inquiry, we should never think of it as lying right here in front of us but as always situated beyond the radical turn our thought is required to take. The whole point, it would seem, is not to think we can catch up with it but to surrender to its ineluctable sway. Being is what would be known if our thinking about it could ever make a final turn. But, even then, we would only be able to retain our knowledge of it if we remained in the throe of that turn—and did not pretend to have completed it.

Now if being is not what is right here now in front of us but that which beckons and horrifies, truth cannot be reached by trying to get as close as possible to what is present-at-hand to us before we start to think. Rather, truth can be reached only if we yield to the beckoning of the unknown, as it draws us beyond the immediate to the world of meaning and beyond the world of meaning to being itself. Truth does not get its binding power from the fact that it keeps us tied down to the given, but rather precisely by virtue of the fact that its call uproots us from the given. It does not hold us as chains hold the slave but as the beloved holds the lover in spellbound eros. The relationship of accord with it is not conformity or possession but surrender and spendthrift devotion.

The call of the unknown breaks through every world of meaning which we develop to make sense of what is given us, just as it initially broke through the given so as to beckon us into the realm of meaning. Can we say that this call, which is finally the call of being itself, exists independently of us? Does one have to affirm this independence in order to keep from falling into the narcissism implicit in the claim that we are world makers? Everything depends here on what one means by "independence." The differences between Heidegger and Lonergan hinge, I believe, on the ambiguities of this term and how one tries to unravel them. These ambiguities are intimately related, of course, to what is meant by "being" itself. I have used this term as a heuristic notion to refer to that which holds us in its sway when we are called to question everything about everything. I have suggested that it is, all along, the noema of our cognitional acts, although we know it all along as unknown. While Heidegger and Lonergan agree that being is accessible only through an intellectual conversion that upsets one's world as a whole, it still needs to be asked if they agree about what is known when one undergoes that conversion. It may be that, while being is knowable only through a radical turn, the same radical turn can lead different thinkers in different directions.

To say that the call of being exists independently of us must inevitably suggest to us, given our customary way of thinking, that the call of being is something like a sound that goes off even if we are not around to hear it, something that is there, in its givenness, whether we happen to notice it or not. But the very nature of the call is that it is issued by the unknown, not by what is given. And only a being who has the capacity for wonder and horror is able to be held spellbound by the unknown, and to know it *as* unknown. Lonergan would affirm just as emphatically as Heidegger that the call of being, indeed, that being itself, does not exist independently of us—if by "independently" one means that being lies right here now in front of us, waiting for us to copy it. But if by "independently" one means to emphasize that being is not a merely subjective projection of consciousness which man produces and has control over, Heidegger would affirm just as emphatically as Lonergan that being is so independent of us that we can never control it but are always held in its sway.[29] We have no access to being except through our inquiring consciousness of it—which seems to make it dependent on us. But our consciousness is what it is only because it is governed at every step by the beckoning call of being—and, for that reason, we are contingent on it.

Nevertheless, in spite of this profound agreement, I think the ways of Heidegger and Lonergan part on this issue. For thought to answer the call of being, it must break radically free of its ordinary re-presentational mode of operating. It must cease interpreting its thoughts in a re-presentational manner. But Heidegger and Lonergan disagree about how and in what direction our ordinary re-presentational way of thinking needs to be transformed, though both insist that the transformation must be primordial and responsive to the unrelenting rigor of being. I think their differences on this crucial issue emerge most decisively in their differing assessments of the role of judgment in knowing.

In the tradition of the correspondence theory, truth is achieved when thought is in conformity with its object. To meet this requirement it is not enough for me to think; I have to check my thought against reality. When I make that check and reality confirms what I have been thinking about it, I make the judgment that I am justified in asserting that reality is as I think it is. Now it is clear that this traditional understanding of the function of judgment presupposes that knowing consists in taking a look at what is present-at-hand. For in this interpretation, what convinces me that my judgment is correct is the act of checking my thought out with things as they are. And only my looking at them would enable me to carry out this kind of check. As Heidegger and Lonergan explain, looking in this way will never enable us to do anything but see what lies right there in front of us. Trying to reach "accurate objective judgments," if judgment and objectivity are understood in terms of the correspondence theory, would cause one to subordinate knowing to looking, and thus betray the call of being. Understood in this way, "objective judgments," far from signifying a responsiveness to being, signify a fall into the fatal confusion of being with what is present-at-hand.

I think Heidegger implies in *Being and Time* that this confusion is brought about by the very nature of rational judgment itself. He wants us to reflect on what makes an assertion assertive.[30] Assertion appears to differ from inquiry and surmise, musing and imagining, insofar as it makes a claim to rightness. By virtue of its mode as an assertion, every assertion claims correctness for itself. Implicit in the idea of correctness is the idea of being perfectly in accord with some standard—and what would the standard be in this case if not reality as it is right here in front of us? An assertion's claim to rightness seduces us into thinking it offers a picture-perfect view of the real. And that thought is made all the more seductive by the fact that an assertion corners us into giving it an unconditional yes or no. For in the unequivocal yes of assent, I seem to grant the assertion's claim to be the absolutely correct, the definitive, unsurpassable picture of what is.

But if truth becomes accessible to us only by virtue of our responding to the call of being, it is profoundly inappropriate to treat it as something to be achieved by making assertions which correspond to what is present-at-hand. The assertoric mode itself encourages us to construe the assertion as an accurate presentation of what is. But real thinking, according to Heidegger, begins with our awakening to the difference between what is present-at-hand and being itself. Fidelity to the path of thinking would therefore lead us to eschew the assertoric mode itself and to develop in its place a discourse full of hints and intimations whose purpose is to evoke being, not to produce a set of propositions about it.

Lonergan's thought takes a different path because he thinks the very features of rational judgment which, in the Heideggerian view, tempt us to go back to the correspondence theory of truth, enable us to move in the opposite direction—toward being understood as other than what is present-at-hand. Lonergan invites us to reflect on how the process of making a judgment differs from both the proposition which is generated and the insight that is judged.[31] It might seem at first that a judgment is nothing but an insight that has become sedimented into something present-at-hand. But this characterization fails to bring out how radically original judgment is—how it introduces something completely new into the process of thinking. For the very moment I begin to wonder whether an insight which seems to make sense of my experience *really does* make sense of it, my attitude toward my own insight undergoes a fundamental change. Or rather, we should say that my authenticity in asking this question is tested precisely by my willingness to change my fundamental attitude toward my insight—from an attitude of unquestioning excitement over its explanatory power to an attitude of critical scrutiny. Why is there something deflating about this transition from insight to judgment? Why would we prefer to dispense with judgment and embrace our insight with headlong enthusiasm? For the simple reason that we do not want to think that our insight could possibly be untrue. After all, why is there any need to check one's insight when, at the moment one hits upon it, it possesses such perfect clarity and self-evidence?

Judgment seems then an irritating and unnecessary precaution, one that interferes with our absorption in the insight that has taken hold of us. We would like to be carried away by the self-evidence of the thought that has seized us. But judgment whispers, "Not yet." It whispers, "Wait a moment. Don't rush into this. Be careful." Is it an accident that we find ourselves using here terms whose temporal connotations Heidegger would be the first to notice? Judgment, we said earlier, acts like a brake, a check—and so it seems to hold us up, to make us tarry when we would like to rush ahead. But toward what do we rush when the truth of an idea seems self-evident to us? It is precisely the present that has captivated us in such moments. We would like the whole truth to be present right here in the perfect self-evidence of this thought that is present to us. When judgment whispers, "Not yet, think this over," it is trying to break our headlong plunge into the present. The sound of the future is no more than a whisper because the appeal of the present is so urgent and insistent. Only the prudence of judgment can make it heard. It appeals to us on behalf of being.

What does it urge us to do? The process of making a judgment is set in motion, as thinking is, by wonder and the question that gives expression to it; it begins with my wondering if my insight is really true. What is it that enables me to raise this question? I would not have any inkling that my insight might be false unless I were aware of a criterion in terms of which it must be evaluated. But when I wonder whether my insight is true, I am not asking if it accurately copies what is right here in front of me; rather, I am asking if it enables me to understand the unknown which provoked my initial wonder and set my inquiry into motion. Thus, the criterion against which insight must be evaluated is not the given but the unknown as such. And the difficulty is that I have no access to this unknown except *through* insight; apart from my insight, I know it only as the unknown which beckons me. How, then, is it possible for such a check to be carried out? How am I to check my insight when that which is to serve as the standard for the check is accessible to me only through my insight—and only if my insight is true?

Lonergan solves this dilemma by arguing that, in forming a judgment, we check our insight against the unknown as it has manifested itself in and through the exigencies of the question it has prompted us to raise about it. Being, the unknown, is not directly available to us. Our only access to it is through wonder and horror, and the insights to which their intimations lead. But we can test our insights against the compelling exigence of the questions themselves which those experiences arouse and which our insights purport to answer.[32] It is possible for me to check my theories against being not because I can take a look at being but because I can "measure" my insights against the questions being has compelled me to raise. My questions make being itself, in its very character as unknown, accessible to me—the very unknown which is to be known through my insight if my insight is true. And I can know that an insight is true, Lonergan says, if it completely answers the particular question which being, as the unknown, has beckoned me to ask.

The function of judgment, then, is not at all to hold theory down to the hard, cold givenness of what is right here in front of me. Rather, just the opposite: in calling into question the very insight I have reached in trying to make sense of my experience, it calls my thinking itself into question and re-minds it that it has not yet finished satisfying the call of being. In thinking about whether our insight really answers the question we have been asking, we come to realize that it is by no means the answer to all questions but at best only the answer to one particular line of inquiry. If we assent to it, we give our assent precisely to this insight whose limits we have come to recognize. The infallible sign of a person with good judgment is her not taking even her profound insights too seriously; judgment humbles us just when we thought we had found the insight that explained everything. Because of what Heidegger calls our fallenness, we are tempted to think that, if our judgments are true, it must be because we have reached the destination toward which thinking tries to move. Having arrived, we are tempted to think we have no further need for staying on the path. A true thought, it seems to us then, is the end of thinking. But this would be the case only if we could reach a thought that put an end to wonder and horror themselves. I might suggest here at the end of this chapter an insight which I will later[33] try to thematize: namely, that if, as Lonergan says, the unrestricted desire to know can never be satisfied in this life, that has to do with the fact that, as Heidegger explains, we are irremediably caught in the sway of a temporality that keeps uprooting us. Judgment, we might think, is an ending. We fail to realize that whenever we judge an insight to be true, the world we live in changes. Reality is not what is right in front of us. It is what is known through insight and judgment. And that means that after every judgment we find ourselves in a strange new world we have never been in before—one which, gifted as we are with the power to marvel, we cannot help but find wondrous or horrifying.

As thrown, we are brought up against the given, as what is right here now in front of us; as fallen, we are easily seduced into believing that we can know being by taking a look at it; but as projected into the unknown, we can know enough to judge ourselves destined to be pilgrims on the way toward being which keeps surprising us with its primordial strangeness. One of the reasons that I find Lonergan's theory of knowing, as it moves from the given to insight and from insight to judgment, more convincing than Heidegger's is because it accords so deeply with Heidegger's theory of ecstatic temporality according to which we are carried beyond whatever experience or insight or judgment we have reached by the throe of a mystery which we can try to repress but whose grip we never escape.

It is perhaps no accident that Socrates formulated at the end of his philosophical life, not at its beginning, the dictum which identifies wisdom with wonder and both wonder and wisdom with philosophy itself. The child who is only on the verge of inquiry already knows that she does not know; but only the philosopher who has died over and over realizes that the end of all exploration—not just in the sense of goal but in the sense of purpose—is to arrive where one started from and know the place for the first time: to fully know the mystery—*as* mystery. Old men, in their dying, ought to be as childlike as explorers, as exploratory as children. Their end then would be a kind of beginning.

CHAPTER 4

Worlds

A world is not a collection of things. When we become engaged in the world of a piece of music, the world of a text, the world of a story as told by a master storyteller, we enter a universe of meaning which differs from any we have inhabited before, even if all the things included within it are already familiar to us.[1] Even those works of art which have traditionally been described as representational, indeed even the genre paintings of the Dutch realists, surprise us by creating a world we have never seen out of the most ordinary things. Although we have used pitchers and sat at tables similar to those pictured in them, the light that comes through the window in Vermeer's pictures transforms the familiar world of domesticity into a wondrous universe that is as unexplored as a new-found continent. In entering into the world created by such a work, one experiences something like the birth of being itself.

As post-modern intellectuals, we live in a situation that exposes us to a constantly expanding multiplicity of such universes, each of which makes its own unique appeal to us. As members of a pluralistic culture, we need to be able to operate within a variety of different conceptual frameworks or hermeneutical circles, different structures of meaning, different models and paradigms, different language games—different worlds. And yet precisely insofar as we are post-moderns, we seem to have lost our capacity for genuinely belonging to, or fully participating in, any of these worlds. At home in none of them, we try to negotiate our way among them; but while each separate world provides maps and compasses for its own terrain, none of these guides is usable in the no man's land that lies between them. In the past, philosophy has often tried to provide a total map of all possible universes without abridging any of their horizons. But instead of helping us sublimate the multiplicity of perspectives within one all-encompassing universe of meaning, philosophy today seems to have become irremediably pluralized itself, and its history looks to us like a scene of incommensurable worlds, each apparently entire unto itself, governed by its own irreducible terms, held together by its own self-imposed presuppositions. Most of us no longer take seriously philosophy's claim to have reached, or ambition to achieve, a priveleged position from which we might be able to have a God's eye view of all worlds at once. For we know that every prejudice is treated like a priveleged intuition by the philosopher who is governed by it.

But while a systematic integration of all our worlds may not be feasible, it may be possible for us to come to a richer understanding of the concept of "world" itself. I have spoken of the world as a text and of the text as a world. More generally, I have been speaking of the world which becomes accessible to us through wonder and the process of inquiry it initiates. But while the word "world" has been used repeatedly, its meaning—which is intimately related to the meaning of meaning itself—has not yet been thematized. How appropriate is it for us to use the word "world" to describe the inside of a theory or an artwork? What consonances make it sound fitting to say that there are entire universes awaiting us within these discourses? I do not mean simply to ask whether there is an analogy that justifies our thinking of a painting or philosophical theory as a cosmos in its own right. I mean, rather, to address the prior question of what we mean by cosmos itself, whether we are referring to the microcosm of a Vermeer interior or to the macrocosm of the physical universe. What gives any of these worlds its very character *as* a world and encourages us to speak of it in cosmic terms? The radical character of such questions derives from the fact that, in asking them, we are broaching not one of our worlds but all of them, for the purpose of understanding what entitles each of them to be accorded the status of being a world. In this chapter, I do not hope to provide any final insights on this matter, but rather to explore certain possible ways of access to the intricate web of issues implicated in it.[2]

WORLDS AS HIEROPHANIES

Let us begin by reflecting on the beginning of a world, by which I mean that event of revelatory surprise by virtue of which a world begins to be a world for us.

We might think, for example, of the revolutionary break-through which occurs when a child discovers the world of the book. In and through its language the child immerses herself in a universe not accessible to her in any other way. The book which seems at first to be like any other object situated in and understood in terms of everyday practicality, is actually a door opening upon another realm, of an entirely different order. (To which world does the door belong? If it were included within either or excluded from both, could it function as a door?) What draws the child into that realm and makes it fascinating to her is precisely the surprising fact that it promises to be different from the given one. How does this other world come into being?

Just as the book itself seems at first to be merely another object within the everyday world, so too it seems to be about something that belongs to that world. When the child chooses to read a book about horses, she expects it to talk about something she has al-ready encountered in a variety of everyday situations: she has glimpsed horses grazing in fields, as the car she was riding in sped by them; she has a cousin who takes riding lessons, and rode a pony once herself at a firemen's carnival. These casual, accidental encounters have piqued an interest, ignited at least a brief flare of wonder; if she elects to read *this* book, and not one on cars or firemen, it is because even so fleeting an acquaintance with horses was sufficient to make her think of them as somehow special, set apart, extraordinary, different from everything else in a wondrous, inexplicable way. The suspicion that there are worlds other than the one we ordinarily live in is always awakened by just such fascinat-ing differences, by the surprise of heterogeneity, by the sudden, unpredictable strangeness of something that is found in our world and yet stands out from it in a way that breaches its boundaries.[3]

In this other dimension—or perhaps it would be better to say in this dimension of Otherness—opened up to the child by the book, the horse ceases to be one object among the many which occupy the ordinary world as it is ordinarily conceived; indeed, precisely what constitutes the other dimension *as* another dimen-sion is the fact that the same horse which was just one object among many in the ordinary world is there the center of attention around which everything revolves. In entering it through the book the child enters the world of the horse, a world radically heterogeneous from our own because in it the surprising difference which distinguishes the horse from everything else becomes the absolute principle of reference in relationship to which everything else acquires meaning and import. What entitles the horse to this status is the extraordinary heterogeneity which set the horse apart in the first place and made it impossible to enclose it within the parameters of the homogeneous. Difference is a constitutive principle of every world.

If there are millions of libraries filled with millions of books about everything, it is because everything that exists contains within its very difference from other things the possibility of becoming a world for us. Of everything about which a book has been written we can say that at least one person, the author of it, was seized by its fascinating otherness to the point of letting that otherness mean the world to her. The insect crawling across the sidewalk, the glass of water which momentarily catches the afternoon light like an unexpected benediction—every one of the things we casually encounter in our everydayness is capable of breaking free from the role given it in our ordinary world and becoming the center of a cosmos that radiates from itself, even if it takes the genius of Chardin's still lifes or Darwin's treatises to illuminate it for us. What is genius except the capacity to be astonished by worlds no one expected to exist?[4] The one we ordinarily live in is ready at every moment to break into a million others. If our own experience of wonder is to be believed, worlds are waiting to be born like novas; all it takes is our being awake to notice them.

Now the only way to enter into any one of these worlds is to become immersed in it to such a degree that it becomes one's own principle of reference. The painting that hangs on the wall in my room only becomes a world for me when, instead of limiting it to its position in space as ordinarily conceived, I let it draw me out of my room and into the virtual space that opens up inside its frame.[5] The space of the painting cannot become real to me unless I cease viewing the painting itself as an object that is observable within the context of the ordinary world. A world cannot be observed; it can only be lived in. For any vantage point that one takes up outside it would situate it within a surrounding context or horizon and thus restrict it to being an object *in* a world rather than a cosmos in its own right. A world becomes accessible to us as a world only by our stepping inside it and leaving the one we previously occupied. The heterogeneity of the other creates, as it were, a gap in the ordinary context of our lives through which we must pass if we are to discover that other on its own terms, in its own right, as a universe not containable as an object within the bounds of the ordinary.

Now what can this mean but that, to enter a world, I must accept it as the center of my own life? This way of putting it may seem at first to exaggerate the import of the shift that occurs when, by reading a book or looking at a painting, I temporarily allow myself to be drawn inside its parameters. And yet, to the degree that we are caught up and held fast by what a book is about, we are given over to its world and no longer aware of our own. To be lost in the world of the work means to forget one's ordinary concerns so completely that one is wholly engaged by what holds sway in that other world. And while it is true that such experiences are often short-lived and do not prevent us from resuming our lives as they were before, it is also true that there are worlds we enter and never want to leave because we find at the heart of them an other on which we would like to lavish all the time and passion we have. One look through the eye of a telescope may be all it takes for a child to become an astronomer in her heart—if the glimpse of the stars it offers her makes her feel like she has been given access to an inexhaustibly fascinating world in comparison with which her ordinary world suddenly seems not just uninteresting but insubstantial.[6]

In short, to enter a world is to fall in love with the other which in its very character as other is at the center of it. We are capable of eros only because we are capable of being invited into and held spellbound by something that is not a thing at all but means the world to us. Among the distinctive traits of eros are the extravagance of its longing, the unreserved character of its enthusiasm, the eagerness with which it spends itself without caution or restraint.[7] Spending oneself so extravagantly is no merely metaphorical death; it signifies a willingness to give up one's entire life as one has lived it until that moment for the purpose of re-centering it around this other which, instead of fitting within one's world, has caused a radical rupture of it. This other could not provoke a desire to leave one's ordinary world as a whole behind if it were simply one object among many, or even if it were one other among many others. In order for it to mean more to me than everything, I must think of this other as a reality that deserves an uninhibited self-expenditure because its worth surpasses every effort I make to estimate it. Indeed, if every other either loses its significance when compared with it or acquires its meaning only from reference to it, this surpassing other must seem, to the one who is centered on it, something like being itself.

Now when we gather together the aspects of the world which have been gradually unfolding in our reflections—the fact that a world begins to be when the heterogeneity of an other breaches the ordinary, the fact that we cannot recognize such a world as a world except by entering into it, the fact that we cannot enter into it except by thinking of the other at its center as a kind of transcendent good which deserves an uninhibited self-expenditure—all this suggests that our discovery of a world is intimately related to our recognizing something as sacred. For in treating something as sacred, we not only acknowledge that it is set apart from everything else by its extraordinary character, but also admit that all the sacrifices we might make in its honor fall short of expressing the gratitude we feel just for being able to make it the object of our reverence. In this sense of the word "sacred," every one of the worlds waiting for us to discover it is a sacred world that has nothing in common with the profane homogeneity of the ordinary.[8] Understood in this light, all things are, indeed, full of the gods because each thing is a world in its own right.

This makes understandable to some degree the otherwise inexplicable fact that, for the primitive religious consciousness, "the multiplicity, or even the infinity, of centers of the world raises no difficulty."[9] There are, indeed, an infinite number of worlds for us to fall in love with, each accessible to us through a distinctive intimation of the sacred, each governed by the unique other at its center, each constituting a distinctive hierophany. Even as it pierces the heart with its heterogeneity, each of these worlds awakens our repressed longing to spend ourselves completely and profligately, in a way analogous to worship. Each of them has the capacity to touch us with its promise of inexhaustible plenitude. Would we not like to enter every one of these worlds whose intimations have beckoned us, instead of having to choose between them? We are apparently forced to make such a choice because of the fact that each one of them seems to issue an unconditional appeal to us and make an absolute claim on us. How are we to reconcile the multiplicity of these worlds with the all-important character which each apparently purports to have? Does not each of these worlds promise to give us access to the entire universe? Should we be suspicious of such promises and wary of entering any world lest we fall victim to its seductive falsehoods? What if all these worlds are only so many blind alleys promising everything but leading nowhere? If we enter wholly inside any one of them, and lose ourselves in it, it will seem to be a complete universe from which nothing has been left out. But does not the very fact that there is an inside and an outside to each of these worlds suggest that none of them can be as all-encompassing as it promises to be? In surrendering to it because it liberates us from the ordinary, are we in danger of being imprisoned anew?

CENTRIPETAL PULL AND CENTRIFUGAL RADIANCE

To appreciate and explore the complexity of the issues these questions raise, we need to shift our attention from the genesis of a world, our intimation of it as a world, to what we might call the structural form which a world, as it is being constituted, tends to assume. I have already been compelled to employ terms like center and breach, whole and part, context and parameter, which are indispensable in our talk about worlds because they help to form the complex web of meanings constitutive of worldhood itself. I would now like to explore some of the nuances of this web.

Let us return to the example of aesthetic experience. What happens to us when we leave the room inside which a picture is hung and enter the world that exists inside its frame? One enters that world and becomes engrossed in it by allowing one's eyes to be guided by whatever drew one to the picture in the first place. The delicate fold of drapery, the ephemeral play of light and shadow, the quiet subtlety or outspoken extravagance of a certain color—

any such surprise can give a work its captivating character and put
one on the path that leads into its deeper intricacies. One's eye
picks up a line that curves and bends, and then twists abruptly at
some right angle of unforeseen seriousness; or one follows lines
that at first seem disconnected until one realizes that they form a
circle which embraces everything with a kind of maternal solic-
itude. Usually the lines themselves give way to the shapes they
form, sometimes calm and dignified, sometimes monumental, even
fearful, sometimes poised together in graceful equilibrium. The
more faithfully one follows the paths of a painting, the more completely one allows oneself to be affected by the grace or grandeur of
its space, the more deeply one is drawn into the interplay of its
colors and shapes, the more likely one is to finally realize its consummate integrity, the way all its elements are gathered together in
an order that does not just integrate but animates them. I do not
mean there are no great paintings (or texts) that lack such order,
either classically or dialectically achieved; I mean that paintings
without such order do not, strictly speaking, attempt to create a
world for us.

Our recognition of this order, in a painting whose elements are
held together by it, makes it possible for us to have an insight into
its embodied meaning. Whatever else we might mean by meaning,
it always signifies just such an ingathering of elements into a
whole, an integration of multiplicity into a single fabric.[10] We
begin to recognize how painfully fragile such an order is when we
realize that no stroke of the brush, and no summation of all its
strokes, suffices to create it. For the order itself cannot be painted
in the same sense that one can paint any of the objects contained
within it; it does not exist in the lines as such but *between* the lines,
in the relationships that simultaneously distinguish and connect
them. Moreover, this order does not exist before its ordered elements; it is not an already constructed framework which the content can be made to fit. It comes into being only in and through the
tact with which the elements are connected, the fragile balance by
which their differing weights are distributed and coordinated.

Is it not an analogous balance, a similarly delicate conjunction
of elements which makes a text or theory meaningful and thereby
enables it to be a world? Drawn into a text by the leading question

or the unexpected intimation of insight contained in its first paragraphs, we follow from then on the often torturous curve of its inquiry. The coherence of the text is not to be found in its individual sentences or chapters but in the insights that join and thereby animate them, the matrixes which generate its terms, the connections which make it possible for its various themes to be included within a single embrace.

Now irrespective of what it is about, irrespective of how "small" or "large" its world appears to be, any text (work of art/theory) held together by such coherence makes an (intellectual/aesthetic) experience of wholeness accessible to us. What is constitutive of that wholeness is not the particular elements that enter into it but the fact that each of them is embraced in a particularly appropriate way by an inclusive order. Even though there are a multiplicity of such worlds, and each of them promises us a universe in its entirety, these promises are not hollow pretensions. For every one of them does make the universe as a whole accessible to us in the sense that it makes an experience of wholeness possible. A world can be whole without including everything within it because its wholeness does not depend on or derive from the number of constituent elements but from the fragile structure, the painstaking form, that unites them into a single coherence. Though it is true that each of our many worlds draws us in its own direction and fascinates us in its own particular way, they all open up to us an analogically similar experience of integrity. Each of them invites us inside its own unique circle, but irrespective of which one we enter, we find ourselves connected to a center of meaning that means the world to us.

We enter and participate in a world of meaning only by coming to some understanding of it, i.e. only by having an insight which enables us to recognize the particular connections and relationships constitutive of its order. Only because we are capable of insight are we able to belong to a world and consciously appreciate it *as* a world.[11] And, conversely, only because a world is constituted by an intelligible order is something like an insight possible. There is no world except the world mediated through meaning, and no meaning except that which becomes accessible when an insight enables us to recognize a world as a world.

Now as soon as we become aware, through an insight, of the order which makes a world the integral whole it is, we naturally begin to think of its structure in centripetal terms. For a whole cannot be integral unless its order pivots on a unifying principle toward which its many paths converge and by reference to which everything is given a rightful place and appropriate role.[12] We might say that a centripetal exigence makes all the elements that belong to a world turn toward its center as toward their source and sustaining power. But if, indeed, the center is the *source* of the world it centers, then it attracts things *toward* it only because of the transformative energy and beneficient light that emanates *from* it in all directions with a centrifugal radiance. Just as all the paths leading into the center of a circle are also radii emerging from it, so too the center of the world not only gathers but also sends forth; it not only unifies, it also disseminates.[13] Or rather, it only unifies by disseminating, by expending itself—by exploding.

That is why the wholeness we experience when we have an insight is not enclosing but ecstatic: it *sheds* light, scatters it profligately, throws it in all directions at once. It can do so only because the order which insight enables us to understand, far from being enclosed and repressive, is open and self-dispersing. The world constructed around such a self-dispersing center has no outer limits, no defined circumference, no fixed boundaries—just as, once we are inside a painting, its frame disappears and we find ourselves lost in a universe that keeps extending its horizons indefinitely. Because the ramifications of an insight have no definable limits, the world of meaning in which it enables us to participate is of its very nature expansive—not like an empire seeking to enlarge the territory it controls but like a radiance which places no restraints on the profusion of its brightness. Every world, I suggest, is a centrifuge toward whose radiating center we are drawn with centripetal urgency because we can find there, at the center, an exploding source of meaning which differs from that found everywhere else. What Eliade says of primitive people holds for everyone affected by the radiating effulgence of any world: we seek "to live as near as possible to the Center of" it.[14] But we seek that sacred ground because it opens out to an infinite universe. In that sense all our worlds are unlimited—not in spite of the fact that each emanates from its own center of radiance but because of that fact.

But while a world has no boundaries because there are, in principle at least, no limits to its centrifugal brilliance,[15] its integrity as a world is entirely dependent on its center remaining in its central place.[16] Any dislodgment of the center from its primal position, indeed, even the slightest decentering of it, would deconstruct the world it centers in the most fundamental way. Things fall apart if the center does not hold; and the center does not hold if, instead of remaining in place as the principle of centripetal and centrifugal order, it leaves, or is removed from, its position.

Our reasons for resisting such a displacement of our center are not difficult to appreciate. We enter a world only by participating in it, and we participate in it only by allowing its center to become our own and letting it become the ordering principle in terms of which we live and move and have our being. In many cases a painting or a text only becomes our world for as long as we are caught up in viewing or reading it. But sometimes through the pages of a book, or the lens of a microscope, a person enters a world that radically and permanently alters her because it persuades her to make it the center of her entire life. And if no world is more fascinating, more filled with promise, more evocative of an inexhaustible plenitude, than the one we begin to enter when we look into the eyes of another person, it is not because they blind us to everything else but because we see reflected in them every one of the worlds that beckon us. To lose such a source of blessing and illumination, after one has made it the focus of all one's ardor, would mean the loss of what means more than anything. That is why all the enthusiasm one was willing to spend on its behalf is likely to be marshalled against any mortal threat to it. We cannot bear the thought of losing what we have decided to live for. The wholeness of our own lives, the coherence which sustains all our acts and longings, the intelligible order in terms of which we govern our very selves, all depend on that center which is not in us but whose loss nevertheless portends our own disintegration.

What happens to our worlds when we realize they are liable to such decentering? How do our efforts to resist it affect the very structure of the world whose deconstruction they are designed to prevent? What must we do to our world to exclude from it the very possibility of it collapsing around us?

THE TRAGIC QUEST FOR AN
UNDECONSTRUCTIBLE WORLD

Because our wholehearted participation in it makes the integrity of our own lives contingent on the integrity of our world, any threat to the latter is bound to awaken intimations of our own nothingness. Only if we stop to reflect on this "nothing" will we be in a position to appreciate the impact which such intimations of it have on the fundamental structures of our worlds.

The possibility of its own deconstruction cannot be included within any world as one of the many things that might conceivably happen in it. The end of any world is not an event that can be integrated into the context of meaning, the web of relationships and connections, that constitute its very worldhood.[17] Indeed, precisely because a world is not a thing or a collection of things but a centifugal order, the end of it necessarily involves the deconstruction of that order itself. The difficulty in conceiving of such deconstruction derives precisely from the fact that within the context of meaning which constitutes a world, the end of that world is, strictly speaking, unthinkable. The kind of thinking which occurs inside a universe of meaning founders when it comes to thinking about its liability to nothingness. For nothingness of its very nature deconstructs the centrifugal principle which, in every universe, is the generative principle of insight.

Now because the possibility of nothingness is not assimilatable within a world but always deconstructive of it, our only option, if we are to insure that the world we live in is kept intact, is to exclude that possibility from it. Such an exclusion cannot be effected except by creating a system of defenses that will keep out trespassers and strangers, a set of barriers whose purpose is to separate the inside of our world from the outside and thus from the possibility of its deconstruction.[18] To do its job properly these barriers must prevent encroachment from any direction, and close off every possible opening that nothingness might try to take advantage of. And how can such foolproof protection be afforded except by constructing a circular system of defenses that completely surrounds our world and encloses it? A world of meaning becomes a closed space when, in the attempt to render it immune to the deconstructive gambits of nothingness, we enclose it within what we hope will be unbreachable ramparts.

Now while they are laid down on the outskirts of our world, as a network of outer defenses, the ultimate purpose of such fortifications is to prevent a mortal attack on the most vulnerable of all places—that center which constitutes its radiant core. Damage to one's world can be endured, breaches repaired, trespassers disarmed, but only if the principle that inspires and animates one's efforts remains intact. The best defense, therefore, is an invulnerable center, one that is absolutely immune to deconstruction, a center that is inviolable, impenetrable, an inside which no outside has even a possibility of breaching. Only such a center can provide the kind of "undecenterable" principle which a world needs to have if it is to be fundamentally secure. Without it, the world is susceptible to deconstruction by virtue of a mortal weakness at its heart; with it, the world becomes an impregnable whole.

A world with an immovable principle at its center and a fixed barrier surrounding it is protected from disruption by anything heterogeneous to it. The center of such a world governs it according to a principle of Sameness on the basis of which every other is to be excluded, or its otherness suppressed. Differences are tolerated, even encouraged, in such a world, but only after the very differences that differentiate them have been brought under the influence of the primary principle of homogeneity. However, even an excluded other would continue to have a destabilizing, decentering impact if, after having been excluded from one's world, it continued to exist outside it; in fact, its excluded position would enable it to evoke in us precisely those intimations of horror which are so upsetting. Consequently, it is not enough to have an impregnable center and inviolable barriers. The inside of one's world can be perfectly safe from the outside only if there is no outside, only if the excluded other is unreal, only if the possibility of nothingness itself does not exist. But this requires that one's world be not just a world but a totality[19]—and, indeed, not *a* totality but *the* totality, the total whole, the all-encompassing one, the absolute itself. There cannot be many such worlds but only one of them, and that one must be a total unbreachable system.

What is it that makes such a system so attractive to us? Why do we often find ourselves drawn toward it, as toward the best of all possible worlds? Its promise of closure and impenetrability, its unequivocally defined boundaries, its imperturbable center—all of this can appeal to us only if the possibility of death, the possible loss of our world as a whole, which it promises to prevent, has already filled us with dread. We recoil from the possibility of such a loss as from a horror than which none greater can be conceived. But our horror at the prospect of this loss, and the desperate urgency of our desire to prevent it, both derive from our uninhibited love for that radiant center which has become the centripetal and centrifugal principle of our lives. When we find something sacred, something which we think deserves to be the focus of all our care and enthusiasm, we want to build a sanctuary to protect it from violation and prevent its deconstruction.[20] But such a haven is not perfectly secure until it is transformed into a fail-safe system whose borders cannot be trespassed and whose inner sanctum has no entranceways.

And now, I think, we can begin to understand the terrible irony and tragic futility of all efforts to create such a system. The only way to make the radiant center of a world secure from the threat of nothingness is to enclose it inside an impregnable network of defenses. But the very barriers set up by such an enclosure to protect the radiant center keep it shut up within itself and thus repress its radiance. For, once closed in upon itself, a center can neither beckon nor pour forth; it can neither unify nor disseminate; it cannot draw things toward it, nor can anything emanate from it; it cannot exercise the pull of centripetal fascination nor can it explode with centrifugal brilliance. It is as still, as inert, as passive and impassable, as death itself. We can make what we love invulnerable only by killing it. We can prevent the loss of what means the world to us only by making its sanctuary a tomb. Any world that is closed off to the possibility of its own deconstruction is by virtue of that very fact the kind of world which it is suffocating to enter.

That is not at all what our worlds are like when we are first enraptured by them. I have spoken in earlier chapters of that revolutionary breakthrough which occurs when children start discovering all the worlds to which their capacity for wonder gives them access. These childhood ecstasies are themselves prefigurements of the most dramatic and deeply felt experience of entering a world—the experience of falling in love with another person. But all such experiences have acquired a terribly poignant character for most of us because of the fact that the worlds to which they once gave us access are now lost to us. And they were lost as soon as our desire to hold onto them led us to prefer the closed totality of a system over the vulnerability of an open world. We do not realize, when we make that choice, that by enclosing what we love in order to protect it, we bring about the very loss we are trying to prevent.

The possessiveness which at the beginning seems so foreign to the experience of romantic love, but which in the end we think of as inseparable from it, is only the most obvious example of how an effort to keep what is loved destroys it. More pertinent for us as philosophers is the temptation to try to make philosophy itself a total system, an irreparable whole constructed around an undeconstructable arche.[21] No mere insight, however much light it might shed, however many connections it might enable us to make, possesses the kind of invulnerability to error which an arche would have to possess in order to function as the center of an all-enclosing structure. For insights, by their very nature, can be wrong, and need to be critically assessed before they are affirmed. In addition, when an insight explodes with ramifications, there is no way to foresee where they will all lead; the further one follows any one of them, the more likely one is to find oneself asking questions which jeopardize at least the centrality, if not the truth, of one's original insight. To prevent oneself from being put in such a precarious position, one would have to find a principle that contained within itself not just indisputable evidence of its own truth, but an exhaustive revelation of its own meaning. To possess such a truth would seem to put one in the most privileged of positions insofar as it would give one a vantage point from which one could judge all possible theories. But a principle can be immune to deconstruction only if it is self-contained and self-sufficient, and thus accessible to us only through an intuition of its self-evidence; and a principle that is closed in upon itself in this way, instead of opening out like an insight that radiates in all possible directions, actually cuts us off from the entire open field of thought itself. Instead of illuminating a world, it requires us to look exclusively and directly at its own blinding light.

This implies that the openness of an insight, its power to generate a world through the centrifugal radiance of its meaning, is lost as soon as we try to repress the possibility of its losing its centripetal power. We like to think that by making an insight invulnerable we gain for it the security that will enable it to function as the immovable arche of our thought. But, in fact, such invulnerability transforms the open world of insight into the closed world of a system inside which the process of thought itself thickens and congeals because it has neither room to expand itself nor reason to expend itself.[22] The only way to prevent the death of thought is to keep thought open to the possibility of its own undoing. For it is our trying to avoid that possibility that causes us to protect our open worlds by closing them. We keep them open only by allowing them to be exposed at every turn to that nothingness which cannot be included within any world because it undermines all of them.

The fact that the centrifugal radiance of a world is inseparable from its vulnerability to nothingness, the fact that we cannot protect what we love without violating it ourselves, the fact that, to be fully receptive to a world we must be open to the possibility of its deconstruction—all this means that if we are to fully enter a world in wonder, we must be ready to lose it in horror. We do not suspect, when we are first drawn into it, that we cannot be caught up in the spellbinding throe of a world without exposing ourselves to the devastating possibility of its annihilation. Indeed, we find a world inviting precisely because it promises a fullness of life, an animating plenitude, we have not experienced before. But the very openness that makes a world radiant makes it vulnerable. Its susceptibility to annihilation is no accidental flaw that just so happens to mar what would otherwise be the best of all possible worlds. Vulnerability and radiance are inseparable aspects of that openness which enables the center of a world to open out upon the world it centers. We would prefer to keep life and death separate by erecting barriers around the center of radiance which means the world to us. But it is precisely the life-giving power of that center which would thereby be suffocated.

None of the worlds that fascinate us are closed systems, all-consuming totalities. The effort to create such a system transforms the heterogeneity of the other into a principle of sameness, to whose rule of homogeneity everything must conform. A real world of meaning, a real text, a real painting, a real culture, is not turned in upon itself in this way. Precisely what makes it radiant is the fact that, at its very center, it opens out into a multiplicity of different directions, each of which has the possibility of leading us to another world. The distinguishing characteristic of a real world, as contrasted with a system, is precisely the fact that it does not try to protect itself from a collision with other worlds or from nothingness itself, but rather gives us a way of access to the very possibilities of its own deconstruction.[23]

This, I think, is what Plato was suggesting when he argued that if the lover were to "abate his violent love of the one"[24] person on whom he has concentrated his passion, he might be led to all the other worlds he first became aware of through her radiance. But if, instead of letting go of the one, he holds onto her, he will lose not only those other worlds she beckoned him to enter, but her own surpassing strangeness, the universe he originally saw open to him in her eyes.

WORLDS AS GAMES AND THE DEMISE OF THE SACRED

I suggested at the beginning of this chapter that, as post-moderns, we are familiar with a multiplicity of different worlds, different hermeneutical frameworks, different universes of discourse, and that we are suspicious of any attempt to systematize this multiplicity into an all-encompassing totality. This seems to imply that we are in a privileged position to appreciate the distinction I have been trying to draw between the open nature of a world and the closed nature of a totality. Acclimated as we are to shifting from one text, paradigm, culture, to another, we seem to be particularly adept at juggling worlds, and to have no interest in tightly holding on to any of them. Indeed, is it not liberating to be exposed to so many worlds and yet be held fast by—imprisoned in—none? A tradition-bound mind would describe such a person as profoundly decentered, but such a willingness to live without a center would seem to indicate a readiness to participate in "the joyous affirmation of the play of the universe."[25]

And yet to participate in the play of any universe requires, we have said, precisely a willingness to surrender wholeheartedly to its gravitational field. The passionate character of such a surrender enables a world to mean the world to us. But it is the absence of just this kind of eros that characterizes our post-modern kind of openness. In its place, post-modern culture cultivates the knack of playing in a world without letting what is at stake in it become a matter of mortal gravity. Someone adept at such play is able to treat the worlds which eros enters so passionately as so many games. This capacity for turning worlds into games is intimately connected with what Philip Rieff describes as our success in turning beliefs into therapies.[26] This is a much more radical change than that which occurs when we shift from one world to another or one belief to another. For when a world is transformed into a game, its very character as a world is fundamentally altered.

It is true, of course, that in playing a game we enter a world. A game has its own special field of play set apart from the mundane space of our everyday activities. To play it one must enter into the fascinating order composed by its dramatic rhythms, by the harmony of its special movements, by the counterpoint of its rival strategies. What unifies a game and makes all its plays coherent— what constitutes it as a world—is the goal one has to score to win it. All the action moves toward and around that goal as the center of the world of the game. But if it is the goal that makes the game a world by giving it a central, organizing focus, what makes this world a game, and no more than that, is precisely the fact that the goal does not really matter, has no intrinsic meaning, is not something which we can ultimately take seriously. Children, in their naivete, play games with an uninhibited passion as if everything were really at stake in them. But that is precisely because they have not yet realized that what distinguishes the game from all of our real worlds is the fact that its do-or-die situations, its sudden deaths, are not as mortal, or as mortifying, as they seem to be. For the child in all of us, a game can be a prefigurement (and ritual enactment) of life and its radical vulnerabilities. But once one has recognized a game *as* a game, once one realizes that the central point around which it revolves and which constitutes it as a world, has no intrinsic importance, one can take it seriously only by taking it metaphorically.

Now just as a game is a kind of world, a world becomes a kind of game when those who enter it, and play within its order, do not recognize its center as sacred. And if one thinks that nothing has any intrinsic worth, that nothing deserves to be the object of uninhibited enthusiasm, in short, if one considers nothing to be sacred, then however many worlds one enters, one empties all of them of that mortal seriousness they must have if they are to be different from games. From the point of view of such disbelief, all worlds are make-believe, are fictions centered on an illusion of self-importance, are wish fulfillments which disguise themselves as religions. And once worlds have been interpreted as fictions, the thinking which might have tried to explore their centrifugal insights will take the form of hermeneutical suspicion, which is itself understood as a game whose purpose is to expose the slips of pen or tongue that have led others to mistake mere games for matters of life and death. Underlying and governing every such diagnosis is what might be called the master suspicion that there simply are no matters of life and death because life and death themselves are not matters of ultimate gravity. There is nothing, this view suggests, that should mean the world to us.

Articulated in philosophical terms, such an attitude describes itself as cheerfully pragmatic, and celebrates its recovery from the age-old philosophical quest for a non-deconstructible system of doctrine.[27] The adept practitioner of such an attitude, precisely because he has not been caught up in the throe of any world, can move among all of them with the cosmopolitan ease of a connoisseur. The imperturbability with which he shifts from one to another, his way of "caring and not caring" about whatever world he chooses to be in, are the characteristics of a distinctively postmodern version of the peace that surpasses all understanding. Instead of taking any world seriously on its own terms as an order of meaning, the pragmatist approaches every world either as a strategic option whose network of techniques and tactical maneuvers it may be beneficial to use, or as a playful diversion it may be therapeutic to enjoy. In either case, what ultimately matters, from a thoroughly pragmatic viewpoint, is not life itself but our being able to get out of life what we decide we want from it.[28]

This helps us understand where the post-modern pragmatist belongs in the geography I have been charting in this chapter. For if one's principle concern, as one approaches anything—the peach ripening on the windowsill, the blossoming forsythia across the road—is "what can I get out of it?," one is viewing it precisely from the vantage point of that practical everydayness which the world of the other is capable of disrupting. Instead of allowing the heterogeneity of the other to have its captivating effect, everyday practicality concentrates on using the other, dealing with it, managing it, coping with it, precisely in order to subordinate its otherness to the requirements of everydayness—the requirement of control itself. The fact that, in our everyday lives, such control is of central importance to us, the fact that ordinarily we evaluate everything we encounter in terms of its being beneficial or detrimental to our practical purposes, the fact that these purposes give our lives a stabilizing order, all this may be interpreted to mean that everydayness too is a world, a pattern of meaning, an experience of wholeness. And yet in this "world" what matters most is to be in control; and the only way to be in control is to let nothing mean the world to you. The distinguishing trait of the everyday "world," what makes it everyday, is precisely the fact that there is nothing in it that matters ultimately.

It is not hard to understand why we are all "drawn" to live in such a "world." For if we love nothing with uninhibited enthusiasm, there can be no danger of suffering a terrible loss and no need to try to avert it. Someone completely in control is completely invulnerable. But the "world" of practicality is not a world at all in the sense we have used the term, for at its center is not something sacred but rather a determination to never recognize anything as ultimately important. The real purpose of everydayness is precisely to keep the center of one's life empty because only if we love nothing are we perfectly insulated from the devastating possibility of losing what means everything to us. The "world" of everydayness does have a certain unifying coherence and sustaining integrity, but it does not emanate from a central life-giving principle. Rather, everydayness is in its very essence a carefully constructed order of avoidances, a structure of interlocking denials, a near-perfect system of mutually dependent repressions whose unifying purpose is to prevent anything from rupturing them. The threat of such rupture does not come from death itself but from the other in its very difference from us. That is why, to protect the integrity of the ordinary, we have to exclude from it everything that might begin to matter to us, everything which might evoke that trembling delight, that presentiment of the sacred, which is the first stirring of an ecstatic and mortal passion. Of all our worlds, the everyday is the closest to being a completely dead one.

THE RETURN OF THE REPRESSED

But not even the empty "world" of practicality can be completely moribund. For even in a "world" from which life is totally excluded, even in a world which gets its character as a world from its network of avoidances and denials—even there the upsetting heterogeneity of the other holds us in its mortal sway. For we have to constantly renew our efforts to repress it. If we find it necessary to construct a whole network of repressions, if we need to keep moving from one diversion to another, it is because at every moment every one of them is in danger of breaking free and becoming a world for us. To prevent any world from coming into being is an exhausting business, in spite of the fact that it only requires us to play at everything as if it were a game.

If the work of repression is never finished, it can only be because we keep encountering the other and hearing an invitation to enter its world. However, entering any world, after one has worked so long to close oneself off from all of them, is not a quick or easy passage. For when we cease participating in any world other than the ordinary one, we do so because we do not want to suffer the anguish, be touched by the horror, be torn apart by the pain that must, in one way or another, come to us from loving them. And when we transform all our worlds into diversions to prevent this pain from happening to us, we do so by draining from each of them that seriousness, that terrible weight, that unbearable preciousness which would make it mean the world to us. To re-discover a world as a world, to experience once again its overwhelming gravity and centrifugal radiance, would involve opening oneself up to all that repressed suffering, all that denied anguish, all that avoided horror. It would be something like the ordeal of dying and being born, experienced simultaneously and understood as inseparable.

The world to which one gains access through such an ordeal is no system immune to deconstruction, no distraction drained of sacral import, no game plan for getting what we want. Entering it costs not less than everything, and its ecstasies are no more beneficial to us, in the ordinary sense, than are its horrors. But it is as radiant (and vulnerable) as all the things that beckon us to love them. Choosing whether to accept that invitation or refuse it is a matter of life and death. But it is not a choice between life and death, anymore than it is a choice between love and suffering. Only by being open to both in their inseparability are we in the world at all.

CHAPTER 5

Amphibolies of Love and Death

The great project of the hermeneutic of suspicion, as practiced by such masters as Nietzsche, Freud and Heidegger, has been to diagnose the amphibolies of the heart, to explore the interplay of their double meanings, and to trace them back to their forgotten origin. The heart has its reasons but, unlike Pascal, these masters suggest that we can come to understand them if we learn how to see through the disguises, and ignore the misdirections, which the heart uses to keep them secret. It may be true that we do not want to know ourselves, and that our deepest selves do not want to be known. But the hermeneutic of suspicion works to overcome this double resistance, and to wrench from the heart an acknowledgment of its buried truths and untruths, its original recognitions and self-deceptions.

In the previous chapter I was led to suggest that the deepest ambiguities of our hearts have to do with love and death, and with the terrible ironies that result from their inseparability. These very ironies came to preoccupy the great practitioners of the hermeneutic of suspicion. For their archeology of the heart led them to realize that we bury in its secret chambers both what is most precious to us and what is most horrifying to us; sometimes we hide things in order to safeguard them, and sometimes in order to repress them. The hermeneutic of suspicion tries to convince us that all our feelings spring from these buried loves and repressed horrors, and that our ordinary lives as a whole, though they may seem on the surface to be rationally designed and freely chosen, are unconsciously governed by them. This argument has been made so persuasively that we have come to think that our very authenticity as persons depends on the degree to which we acknowledge the buried truths which we ordinarily try to keep most deeply hidden.

My intention in this chapter is to plumb this hermeneutic by exploring some of the questions that arise in my mind when I juxtapose the Freudian and Heideggerian versions of it. Freud's hermeneutical efforts were primarily focused on understanding the vicissitudes of our primal desire, Heidegger's on understanding the import of our primal dread. Because of that radical difference, I find it most perplexing and thought provoking that each of them found death at the bottom of the heart, and argued that our feelings about it profoundly influence our whole way of being in spite of, and because of, the fact that they are so profoundly repressed. According to both Freud and Heidegger, death is our primal reality. But while *Beyond the Pleasure Principle* suggests that the best kept of all our secrets is our primordial desire for it, *Being and Time* argues that we repress death in order to bury our primal dread of it. In the one case, death is interpreted as what we secretly seek, in the other as what we secretly avoid; in the one it is the object of unconscious longing, in the other the object of unconscious horror. Although he was venturing beyond the pleasure principle in hypothesizing a death-instinct, Freud remained faithful even then to the basic explanatory insight which had governed his hermeneutic all along—that we repress what we want. Heidegger, on the other hand, argued a more straightforward position which is not so obviously dependent on the hermeneutic of suspicion: that we cover up death not because of any secret desire for it but because we want to protect ourselves and our world from its shattering impact.

One is tempted to ask how two thinkers so practiced in unravelling the tangled logic of the heart could have disagreed so profoundly about the nature of its deepest needs and primordial impulses. But since both Heidegger and Freud had a genius for unmasking our disguises and uncovering our dissemblances, perhaps it would be wiser to try to put their hermeneutics together instead of trying to choose between them. On the surface, their theories require us to decide whether the deepest thing in us is our love of death or dread of it, whether we spend our lives secretly longing for death or secretly fleeing it. Reading them together, one is driven to ask which of two directly opposed passions underlies all we seek and suffer. However, if we have learned one thing from both of them, it is that the heart can harbor just such contraries, just such opposed passions, as their opposed theories of death ascribe to it. The part of us in love with easeful death may, as the poet suggested, be only half of us; the other half may be recoiling from a death it always finds horrifying. My purpose in this chapter is not to do an exegesis of the Heideggerian and Freudian texts but to explore the ambivalent images of death and ambivalent attitudes toward it which the conflicts between their texts help to crystallize. Freud and Heidegger make the importance of such an exploration obvious. For if they were right in claiming that death is what is closest to our hearts, an insight into the logic of these ambivalences will shed light on the nature of all our anxieties and longings, all our desires and terrors.

If I do not set forth here at the beginning of this exploration a theoretical framework that might help the reader anticipate its direction, it is because I would like to try to understand our feelings on their own terms, instead of bringing a precast theoretical perspective to bear on them. The attempt to develop a theoretical explanation for our feelings should be preceded, I think, by an effort to articulate, in a phenomenologically rigorous way, the meaning of the feelings themselves. To achieve such phenomenological rigor requires that we keep our reflections as true to our feelings as possible, without surrendering in any way to our ordinary way of interpreting (and dissembling) them. To know what our feelings are, especially those feelings which we have done our best to keep silent, to be able to describe them with such expressive accuracy that our feelings recognize in our words the exactly appropriate articulation of their meaning, is an underlying purpose of both phenomenological reflection and psychoanalysis itself. What makes the achievement of this purpose so difficult is precisely the fact that, as both Freud and Heidegger have helped us realize, we do not ordinarily want to know what we feel, especially about death; and in order to prevent ourselves from knowing what we feel, we keep the feelings themselves unconscious and uncommunicative. For that reason, phenomenology, when it operates in this context, cannot limit itself to describing our feelings, as they are consciously experienced; rather, it must try to uncover, through the elusive hints and intimations which our feelings sometimes succeed in sending us, their unspoken meaning and repressed import.

INSTINCT AND THE DESIRE TO CONTROL

On the chance that it will show us a way into the deeper passageways of the heart, let us begin with one of our more accessible feelings about life and death—the self-preservative instinct which we have all experienced in dangerous situations. It would seem that here, if nowhere else, we will be able to find a straightforward drive, a compulsory biological urge whose meaning is univocal because it operates in us at so basic a level that it has no opportunity to become compromised (and complicated) by the kinds of ambivalence which emerge when we enter the universe of meaning. But does anything "primitive" retain its primitive, uncomplicated character when it is incorporated into a being capable of meaning? At first, nothing seems so directly life affirming, so single-mindedly vital as the biologically conditioned urge to live. And yet there are those who would say that someone who operates primarily at such a level "might as well be dead." This frequently heard expression implies that even the most basic of all urges has an ambivalent character; we need to examine the nature of the self-preservative instinct more carefully before deciding whether there is any wisdom in this criticism of a life focused on it.

First of all, we have to admit that even our ordinary way of using the word "survival" complicates its meaning. Thoreau, for instance, knew that those whom he accused of being slaves to their possessions would reply that they only worked so hard and long out of practical necessity—i.e., because their "survival" depended on it. One can read Thoreau's experiment at Walden as his attempt to prove that survival required far less than his neighbors supposed. Construed in this way, his imperative to simplify urges us to revert to a primitive way of life centered primarily on biological necessities. One could argue that, by showing us how much we could do without, Thoreau hoped to restore the idea of survival to its original pristine meaning. But such an argument overlooks the fact that, for Thoreau, the emphasis on survival is itself a disease of the modern spirit, and the underlying cause of its obsession with mechanical innovations. His complaint was not that his contemporaries had moved too far away from the basic necessities, but that they insisted on always thinking about the world and seeing it in terms of its ability to satisfy them. To look at the earth as a piece of property is, he argued, only a sublimated version of a sensory hermeneutic which interprets everything as potential food. Our desire for luxuries is not a betrayal of our survival-instinct but a continuation of it in a disguised form.

Though we may be sympathetic to such a critique of the acquisitive life, we know how easy it is to fall under the sway of its compulsions, just as it is easy to fall under the sway of those instinctual desires after which the acquisitive life is modelled and from which it seems to borrow its compelling power. We may think ourselves too human to regress to the point where we are completely absorbed in the pure, uncomplicated present of sensory consciousness. But we do regress to a condition which approximates pure sensory immediacy when the urgency and intensity of an instinctual desire efface everything from our intention except the fulfillment of it. When a sense-desire (e.g. for a particular food or for sexual pleasure) is aroused to the point of becoming a craving, it insists that we suspend our involvement with everything else and concentrate exclusively on finding an immediate satisfaction for it. And in the moment when that satisfaction is attained, the pleasure it brings is such that intentional consciousness itself is temporarily suspended. Pleasure pure and simple does not include an awareness *of* anything; all noema disappear into the direct immediacy of pleasure itself.

Our desire to live, our instinct to survive, is at least in some ways analogous to (and has sometimes been interpreted as the original cause of) such pleasure-focused sense-desires. In situations where mortal danger is felt to be imminent, a drive even more urgent and intense than a sensual craving is spontaneously aroused in us. Like sense-desires, this survival drive is only awakened on specific occasions and is always experienced as a need which demands to be immediately met. Just as the craving for food or sexual pleasure makes itself felt as an emptiness that must be instantly filled or as an exigence that must be instantly satisfied, so the instinct to survive makes us desire immediate relief from a threatening situation. And just as a sense-desire ceases as soon as its demands are met, so too we cease to experience the survival instinct as soon as the threat which awakened it is removed. But because the survival instinct is primarily defensive in character, the satisfaction of its demands brings only relief and not the kind of culminating pleasure which characterizes the fulfillment of sense-desire. One satisfies it simply by terminating the experience of danger, so that one is able to return to the relatively undisturbed state of being one enjoyed before danger disrupted it.

Nevertheless, the fact that the sense-desires which culminate in pleasure, and the survival instinct which is satisfied by the removal of danger, are both experienced as needs which cease to directly affect us as soon as their demands are met explains at least in part the conservative character of our instinctual life in general. Because the instinct to survive becomes quiescent as soon as the danger which called it forth is removed, it makes sense to interpret homeostasis as its real objective. But as Freud realized and tried to explain,[2] a similar return to quiesence occurs as a consequence of the fulfillment of *any* sense-desire. The fact that instinctual desire of whatever type disappears as soon as its demands are met encourages us to think of it as a negative condition which the instinct urges us to remedy so that we can return to the undisturbed condition which preceded its arousal. It can easily be argued, in response to this suggestion, that, in the case of sense-desire, we do not seek the restoration of equilibrium but the intense pleasure which fulfills desire and terminates it. But even if this is the case, it is still possible that there exists an underlying similarity between equilibrium and pleasure, due to the instinctual nature of our desire for them. Is there some primal, instinctual objective which is common to both of them in spite of their differences?

Let us first consider an often unnoticed irony in the concept of equilibrium itself. Ordinarily we define psychic equilibrium in terms of the absence of disruption from our lives, and this naturally leads us to think of it as an essentially passive condition which does not presuppose or require the active exercise of our powers. But, in fact, we can be in a state of uneventful equilibrium only if we have found a way to prevent upsetting events from happening, or a way to deprive such events of their upsetting impact on us. Psychic equilibrium is therefore not a condition of passive acquiescence but a consequence of successful control. We achieve it only by finding a way to make ourselves imperturbable and immune to disruption. Far from suggesting that we are willing to be passive, our desire for homeostasis reveals that we would like to be impassive, incapable of being upset. The perfect form of such impassivity would be to live in the world of an impregnable womb which nothing could penetrate and inside of which one could enjoy perfect invulnerability.

But the quest for homeostasis which leads us to seek control and avoid disruption would not be necessary if we had not already been upset by something or at least exposed to the possibility of being upset. And, indeed, that possibility becomes real to us as soon as we become aware of anything other than us in its very otherness from us—for our very exposure to otherness puts us in a vulnerable position. Every other, precisely because of its otherness, is a threat to homeostasis. The pursuit of homeostasis and the flight from otherness are therefore dependent on and inseparable from each other; they are two aspects of a single movement—the self's instinctual recoil away from the other and back into itself. Now it is just such a recoil which seems to be at work in both the desire for sensory pleasure and in the desire for self-preservation. For at the moment when the desire for pleasure or self-preservation is satisfied, the other (which was either the object of desire or the cause of danger) ceases to be of any concern to us; indeed, our very awareness of the other is either greatly diminished or completely effaced. In the experience of pleasure, my very consciousness of the other evaporates into the pure immediacy of the pleasurable sensation itself; and while there is only a sense of relief after successfully avoiding a threat to my survival, that relief comes from the fact that I can relax and stop worrying about the other because the danger it posed has been evaded. In both cases there is operative the same regressive recoil from otherness, the same instinctual recoil toward the self, and, underlying them, the same original dream of there being nothing at all that is other than oneself.

In the light of this analysis, it is not surprising that, hard as he worked to develop a dualistic theory to explain the frightful, internecine conflicts which occur in the psyche, Freud kept uncovering disguised, even contradictory, versions of the same primal drive. For underneath the distinctions he drew (and redrew) between the ego and the id, consciousness and the unconscious, underneath even the distinctions he tried to draw between the different instincts, the same drive to be in control, the same desire to eliminate otherness, kept reappearing, although, as far as I know, Freud did not describe it in these exact terms or explicitly thematize it. The ego's efforts to acquire technical mastery over nature, and even more importantly its constant attempt to deal with, handle, manage, cope with, its own life, are only the conscious, rationally organized manifestations of that desire to control otherness which operates in us unconsciously in both our desire for pleasure and our instinct for self-preservation. Freud even understood psychoanalysis itself as a method for helping the patient cope with the opposing forces within him.[3] Just as he saw all those forces as contending for mastery of the person, so he hoped that therapy would provide the ego a way to keep them all in equilibrium and thereby be the master controller. The ideal of control is, in this sense, the unexamined but governing principle of psychoanalytic theory itself.

But no matter how effective the ego becomes in controlling its life, its successes always fall short of the kind of control we experience in those pleasures in which the other is completely effaced. If our desire for that experience has to be repressed, it is not because the kind of control it gives us is undesirable but because, in the world as it is and always will be, it cannot be our normal condition. The reality principle requires our acknowledging the ultimately irrepressible fact of the other, in its ultimately irrepressible otherness. But, as Freud understood it, even a life lived according to the reality principle is not based on accepting reality; it is based on accepting the fact that we have to work on reality if we want to control it.[4] Thus, even in the most mature, most pragmatic individual, the pleasure principle retains its ascendency insofar as all his work is devoted to approximating that mastery of the world which he still occasionally experiences in his pleasures, and in the magic world of dreams.

Heidegger and Derrida have helped us understand the meta-physics of those dreams by diagnosing the dream of metaphysics: the dream of abolishing not just this or that danger to our equilibrium but the underlying source of all danger which is death itself; the dream of being utterly immersed in the fullness of a present that not only has no beginning and no end but no duration either, an experience of presence which is immune to both interruption and succession, a presence not contaminated by any hint of absence, a presence purified of temporality itself. The only way for us to realize this dream of presence would be for us to find a way out of the world and its otherness, and back to the original condition of being for which we are nostalgic, even though we have never experienced it. What inspires this nostalgic quest for presence, according to Heidegger, is our flight from death as the ultimate other whose otherness cannot be domesticated; from it we flee toward the plenitude of an eternal presence, toward a timeless heaven.

But Freud gave that heaven the exactly opposite name: he interpreted our desire for an untainted experience of presence not as a flight *from* death but as a desire *for* it. Although Freud tried to distinguish between life-instincts and the death-instinct, he thought that even the life-instincts seek to restore us to a state of homeostasis, indeed, to the "state of things that was disturbed by the emergence of life."[5] If, as Freud has led us to suggest, it is the very nature of instinct to seek homeostasis and ultimately a homeostasis that is imperturbable and immune to disruption, it is difficult to avoid the conclusion that death is the ultimate objective of desire. For, in fact, it is only in death that we find an inviolable haven, an impenetrable womb. Only the dead are so perfectly immured within themselves as to be completely invulnerable. The equanimity we instinctively seek can be perfected only if the very possibility of experiencing otherness is eliminated. But to eliminate that possibility entirely would require not just temporarily suspending intentionality, i.e. our very capacity to be aware of the other, but permanently eliminating it. Insofar as we seek an imperturbable homeostasis we recoil from the life of intentionality as a whole because of the vulnerability to otherness to which it always and necessarily exposes us. And we can preserve ourselves from the threat of such exposure only by acquiring the perfect impassability, the flawless protection which death alone provides. In this sense, only death can provide our instinct for self-preservation the kind of guarantee from danger which it seeks.

EROS AS CELEBRATION

Even if it were more fully elaborated, the hermeneutic of desire which I have just sketched cannot be the whole story of the human psyche. For while it might be able to explain the various ways in which we recoil from the other, it does not help us understand the experience of otherness from which we flee. In the Freudian corpus, for instance, dominated as it is by the effort to unravel the logic of regression, much is said about the tactics we (unconsciously) use to outwit the reality principle, but little is said about the experiences in which we respond to the other positively, instead of merely giving its existence our grudging acknowledgment. Indeed, one of the tasks of the hermeneutic of suspicion, as Freud taught us to practice it, is precisely to help us recognize, in the purportedly positive responses we sometimes make to the other, disguised versions of our primal desire to recoil from it and retrieve the homeostatic primacy of the self. But if the other never awakens in us anything except our primal desire to efface its otherness, our hearts would harbor none of that ambivalence, none of the excruciating tension between conflicting feelings, which Freud himself found so fascinating. All the ambivalence would be in our situations, none of it in our selves. We would be, in our heart of hearts, just as simple, as single-minded, as we imagine animals to be when we think of them as wholly absorbed in the pure presence of sensory immediacy. But no matter how close we come to approximating that immediacy, we cannot completely eliminate the possibility that the other will break through to us and awaken us to its mystery. Such an awakening can simultaneously provoke both our instinct to protect ourselves from the other and the opposite of this desire—a longing to respond to its beckoning.

This sensitivity to the other is not a one-time or some-time thing. It is, rather, the primal human experience which differentiates us from beings who have never left the world of immediacy and so have no reason to nostalgically dream of returning to it. We are always already human, always looking back to an original plenitude, an unbroken presence, which we have always already left because the very existence of the other deconstructs it.[6] Pleasure gives us the only taste we ever have of what we never were. But there is always already in us a sensitivity that pulls us in the other direction—the direction of the other itself.

The fact that this sensitivity makes us susceptible to a kind of longing which is radically different from desire will be easier to appreciate if we relate it to the event of wonder which is so intimately connected with it. That what is immediately given to the child's senses, and thus directly accessible to her, nevertheless strikes her as wondrous, means that even she does not live in a primitive world where the otherness of the other is completely effaced by the givenness of the given. Thoreau would say that being caught up in the throe of wonder enables the child to "progress" further than those of us caught up in a goal-oriented culture because it carries her outside of herself and thus awakens her to mystery. Thoreau's call to be awake meant more than opening one's eyes, just as by living simply he meant something more than satisfying one's basic instincts. This "more," this excess by virtue of which we exceed the given, can never be given to the senses and, in that sense, is never self-evident; but it cannot be denied except by denying the revelatory import of wonder itself.

Longing is awakened along with wonder because the latter affects us in our entirety when it opens us up to the unknown other in its very character as unknown and other. The breach caused by wonder in the otherwise perfect plenitude of the present creates the condition which makes possible the instinct's conservative, regressive recoil *from* the other; but, at the same time, it makes possible the emergence of an entirely different kind of feeling—a fascination *with* the other, a sense of being captivated and held spellbound by it, above all a sense of being beckoned toward it, of being drawn not just through the breach but further and further out into the wholly unfamiliar territory of its otherness. What gives the other this drawing power? What makes me even consider responding to the intimations it evokes in me, when doing so runs so contrary to the conservative imperatives of instinct and desire?

Even if we do not follow where they lead, our intimations of the other awaken in us an unexpected gladness, a tender and tentative delight which we feel toward it simply because it *is* wonderful. We might think here, for instance, of the happiness we expect to see spread over a small child's face when she opens the gift we have bought her, only to find her so fascinated by the wrapping that the toy inside never captures her attention. If the child could put her fascination into words, she would include, I am suggesting, some expression of surprised joy,[7] some exclamation of assent and celebration. As contrasted with sensual pleasure which is so centered on itself that consciousness of the other is effaced, such joy delights in the other and forgets itself. The best way to express this delight would be to exclaim, "It is good that the other exists!"[8] But it is important to note that this existential endorsement, because it is a response to the other as encountered in wonder, is addressed to the other not as something present-at-hand but precisely as a reality which breaches the present and transcends it. From the very beginning, the relationship between the self and the other which exists in wonder is exactly the opposite of the relationship which exists between them in the experience of sensual pleasure when the latter is pursued for its own sake. For the gladness implicit in wonder delights in the very otherness of the other which the pursuit of pleasure seeks to efface. Pleasure promises to close the breach in the present through which the future itself in its unknown otherness becomes accessible to us. It is pointed back toward a past where nothing was real beyond what-is-given-in-the-present. Delight, on the other hand, celebrates what occurs when the other breaches the present with intimations of its otherness. Gladness is glad to be carried out of itself, in the throe of the future. Its ecstatic character, far from making it analogous to pleasure, confirms the fact that the two move in exactly opposite directions. For ec-stasis shatters precisely the homeostatic present in which pleasure loves to be wholly absorbed.

I have called the joy within wonder tentative in order to emphasize the fact that this joy is no more than a beginning, since the good which it affirms is the unknown other in its very character as an unknown whose being only the future can unfold. Since it originates in that primal gladness and tries to explore its promise, the longing generated in us by wonder must be radically different from desire and its search for pleasure. But that difference is difficult to conceive because we tend to construe the future in terms of a future present, and so are inclined to interpret any movement toward the other or into the future as an effort to reduce the other to what-lies-right-here-now-in-front-of-us. Does not longing, like desire, seek first to reach the good and then to possess it? What would longing seek if not the attainment of what it longs for? We might be persuaded to agree, for instance, that romantic passion differs fundamentally from sense-desire, but how can someone be filled with such passion and not be filled with the desire to become one with its object? Indeed, are not these precisely the terms Plato used to describe not the common, vulgar love of the appetites but the ennobling eros of the soul?[9]

But if eros does desire to possess its object, it is difficult to understand why we should not interpret it, like Freud suggested, as a disguised form of sense-desire, sublime in character but only in the sense of being a sublimated form of appetite itself. And to move in that direction would require effacing all the distinctions I have been trying to draw between wonder and immediacy, between response to the other and recoil from it, between surrender to the throe of the other and flight from it. If we are to take these distinctions seriously, as a phenomenology of the experiences from which they arise requires, we have to consider the possibility that the vocabulary of desire, convenient as it may be to use, does not do justice to the kind of longing by which we are animated when the goodness of the other beckons us.

This possibility becomes more plausible when we consider the fact that Plato himself, even though he describes eros as desiring the possession of its object, often speaks critically of an acquisitive attitude. While possession and consumption of the object are the natural goals of appetite, we know that, if we approach the beloved with such goals in mind, we will be in danger of repressing the very otherness of the other in whose existence we delight. The very attitude which, from the viewpoint of desire, would be most natural, seems to be a violation of a norm which ought to govern treatment of the beloved—a norm which derives from the very nature of wonder itself. For implicit within wonder is an imperative to leave untouched the other whose goodness we become aware of through it. The longing generated by wonder's initial encounter with that goodness, far from being analogous to desire, moves in the exactly opposite direction—not toward possession of the other but toward a deeper and deeper "letting-be" of it.

However, this Heideggerian expression, helpful as it is for emphasizing the lack of possessiveness in genuine eros, fails to convey the powerful yearning to move *toward* the other which eros makes us feel. Heideggerian letting-be must be operative in eros if eros is not to violate the norms implicit in its own genesis as a longing fundamentally different from sense-desire. But someone falling deeply in love can never be satisfied with so passive a response to the other. The lover is filled with a spendthrift enthusiasm for the beloved which he does not want to suppress or inhibit. And the more we reflect on the nature of this enthusiasm, the more careful we are to describe the kinds of gesture and action which express it, the easier I think it will be to distinguish it from appetite. For whereas appetite operates speechlessly and moves toward consuming the other, eros inspires us to invent the poetry of praise, to practice an etiquette of reverence, to pour out of ourselves a love for the other which we cannot bear to keep contained. Eros, like desire, does not want to hold itself back; but whereas desire cannot restrain the urge for pleasure which effaces the other, eros cannot restrain its enthusiasm for the other in its otherness. Desire wants to possess the other; eros longs to spend itself wholeheartedly and unreservedly on the other's behalf. Desire makes us aware of a void to be filled, whereas enthusiasm springs from an overflowing heart that is eager to empty itself. Desire is a regressive impulse which leads to an effacement of the other, and the pleasure in which it culminates is as safe a haven as we can find. Enthusiasm, on the other hand, is a celebration of the other and urges us to throw caution to the wind—to risk everything on the other in a single act of self-abandonment.[10]

Far from being motivated by an expectation of getting a return on its investment, eros wants us to spend ourselves completely and receive nothing back, because only by retaining nothing can we let the beloved be everything to us. Such self-expenditure is as contrary to the conservative common sense of the ego as it is contrary to the conservative logic of consumption which governs sense-desire. Its extravagance flies in the face of rational calculation, just as it upsets the homeostasis which our instinctual desires always urge us to safeguard. More fundamental than any of the conflicts which might exist between the ego, understood as a rational agency concerned with "dealing with" its life, and the id, understood as an unconscious fund of instinctual desire, is the complementary roles they both play in the economy of control. The fundamental conflict in us is the one which exists between the extravagant self-expenditure of eros and the economy of control itself. The possibility of that conflict arises out of the primal event of wonder, which is grounded in the immediacy of the present and yet breaches it by exposing us to the unknown. To be situated in that juncture means to be torn between desire and longing, between consumption and enthusiasm, between self-absorption and self-abandonment, between control and eros, between the desire to retrieve a lost presence and the willingness to risk everything on an unpresenceable future. But, as Heidegger has explained, to be thus torn means to be already irretrievably caught in a throe which carries one outside of oneself, and thus to have irretrievably lost that which desire, and the instinct of self-preservation, would have us recover. We could achieve our deepest wish fulfillment only by escaping from temporality itself, whose ec-stasis necessarily upsets the homeostasis we instinctively seek. For us, time means precisely not to be in the present, but to always be already on our way toward what is always beyond it—on our way into the beyond as such. That beyond, even as it breaches the present, and so renders the entire project of control impossible, awakens in us a fascination and longing—an eros—which no present, and therefore no fulfillment of desire, can possibly satisfy. We live in human time precisely to

the degree to which we give ourselves over to the spendthrift enthusiasm of this eros.

And, indeed, what do we mean, when we describe someone
as "full of life," if not that she is animated by an apparently
inexhaustible enthusiasm which transforms even the mundane
chores of everydayness into expressions of love? If we have not
found a way of access to the reservoir of eagerness and intensity
which makes such self-expenditure possible, it is because our way
to it is blocked by the fears and appetites, the insecurities and
possessions, which keep us attached to our lives. We are unwilling
to give up all we would have to lose to be spendthrift in our
enthusiasms. But this means that it is our very holding onto life
which prevents us from being able to fully enter into it. We are not
full of life because we are unwilling to stop trying to control it. We
flee from the fullness of life because embracing it would cost
us everything, and for that reason would be as exacting as death itself.

The mortal import of eros, the fact that it costs the lover not
less than everything, and actually requires a willingness to die, has
always been symbolized by a wound. But from the viewpoint of
eros, it is a privilege to be vulnerable to this wound and a joy to
suffer it because only in and through one's suffering of it does the
other become accessible. The mortal consequences of self-expenditure may not be evident to those who are in the first blush of the
enthusiasm which inspires it. The more wholly given over the lover
is to what he loves, the more his love approximates dying, but it
may very well not seem like dying at all but rather like being truly
alive for the first time. But sooner or later, in one way or another,
the terrible paradox of eros will open that wound, originally
effaced, and make it pour out its anguish. For precisely because
eros prompts one to spend oneself *on* the other and not possess her,
one cannot remain faithful to its life-affirming impulse except by
giving *up* the very other to which one is giving oneself. To give
oneself to the other always means precisely to lose the other. For to
prevent the loss of the other, one would have to strive to retain one's
relationship with her, and such an attitude would involve just the
kind of possessive grasp or conservative recoil which we have seen
to be characteristic not of eros but of its opposite. We are ac-

customed to thinking that the loss of the beloved only occurs in
tragic circumstances, that only an unfortunate few are required to
undergo the kind of suffering, the kind of death, which such a loss
would entail.[11] But the experience of mortal loss, far from being a
tragic accident, is required by the very nature of eros itself, and can
be prevented only by deforming eros into a sublimated form of
desire. One either makes the kind of complete self-expenditure for
which eros asks, in which case one is willing to lose the beloved on
whose behalf it is made, or one works to retain the beloved, in
which case one's very relationship with the other regresses to possession. Here too, as before, one must choose between control and
vulnerability, between the unknown otherness of the other and the
primacy of the self, between the unimaginable future and the
homeostasis of unbreached presence. But if the other has come to
mean the whole world, being receptive to the future, as eros itself
requires, means being open to the loss of this other and thus to the
shattering of one's world as a whole. Suffering that loss, undergoing that deconstruction, requires surrendering to the throe of nothingness itself. The ec-stasis into the future which was originally
experienced as wonderful thus leads us directly toward an experience which is devastating.

The inseparability of wonder and horror, of eros and mortal
anguish, seems to me to be one of the great truths one can retrieve
from *Being and Time*, after long reflection on it. In our initial
experience of eros, as in our childhood experience of wonder, we
are too carried away by our enthusiasm, too delighted by the goodness of life as a whole, too eager to be profligate in our celebration
of being, to be more than subliminally aware of the fact that we
have to give up our hold on life if we are to be faithful to our love of
it. But once that realization becomes explicit, its devastating impact
transforms the character of eros itself. What wells up within one is
an anguish coeval with eros's enthusiasm, and requiring the same
spendthrift self-expenditure. In his effort to emphasize the equi-
primordiality of ec-stasis and anguish, Heidegger does not so much
reinterpret eros as replace it with care, in the hope that we will hear
in this world, often used as a synonym of love, the reverberations of
an inexhaustible hurt. Once we are smitten we are never healed. To
be human means to be an open wound.

One's experience of that wound, like the experience of eros, would not be complete if any part of one's self were held back from it. That is why we speak of both love and anguish as matters of the heart, where this term does not refer to a particular organ but to the very core of our being.[12] It is as impossible to say which part of us weeps as it is to say which part of us overflows with enthusiasm; it is the self as a whole which sorrows and celebrates. That care can run so deep and be so uninhibited as to leave no part of us unaffected, suggests that the tension which exists at the heart of us, the tension between desire and ec-stasis which exists in our very core, is ultimately resolvable. But it is resolvable in either of two ways: we can recoil back to that motionless homeostasis in which all otherness is effaced, or we can give ourselves over wholeheartedly to that throe of the other which is simultaneously the throe of love and anguish. In the former case, the tension is dissolved by repressing the throe of temporality, in the latter by completely surrendering to it. When nothing is held back from it, such a surrender creates a kind of serenity which a superficial observer might be unable to distinguish from the inert impassivity of homeostatic equilibrium. But the serenity of the person who has wholly given herself over to the throe of temporality comes from her defenseless openness to suffering, while the imperturbability of the person recoiling from the throe comes from knowing that no suffering can affect her. The distance between these stillnesses, similar as they may seem to be on the surface, is all of time itself.

IRONIES OF DEATH AND DYING

Having followed the instinct for self-preservation and the eros of self-expenditure to their opposite extremes, we may now be in a position to appreciate the paradoxes of the heart which led Freud and Heidegger in different directions toward the same final ironies. As practitioners of the hermeneutic of suspicion, they were convinced that our everyday lives, and everyday way of understanding ourselves, are governed by the very realities we spend our lives trying to avoid and repress. To explain the workings of avoidance requires uncovering both that from which avoidance turns and that toward which it flees. Insofar as we are unaware of our avoidances, we are equally unaware of both the from-which and the toward-which of our flight. The unchanging objective of Freud's evolving hermeneutic was to wrench from himself and us an acknowledgment of that which we all secretly desire; in *Being and Time,* on the other hand, Heidegger tries to wrest from our everyday self an acknowledgment of that which we all secretly flee. The two hermeneutics move in different directions from the same starting point of avoidance, the one to uncover our deepest wish, the other our deepest dread. Each names what he finds death, but as we have found by retracing their paths, these deaths are precisely the opposite of each other.

There would be no possibility of avoidance in the first place if it were not for the event of wonder and the tension it creates between the given and the emergence of the other. Only because we know the unknown as unknown are we exposed to it in all its unimaginable otherness. It is in the experience of that tension that the unknown becomes dreadful and the given desirable as an escape from it. No matter how wonderful the other which beckons us, it could not become accessible to us in its otherness except through a rupture of the present. In that rupture, which is first experienced as wonder, the possibility of nothingness is already implicitly present, as an irreparable breach of presence itself.

To close that breach, to repair that rupture, requires finding a way to back out of the experience of wonder and into an experience of unbroken immediacy, where one would not be exposed to the other in its otherness. From the very beginning there is implicit in our appetite for such immediacy, however pleasurable we might imagine it to be, a desire to be invulnerable, to be immune to rupture, to be in a homeostatic condition which nothing can upset—not even nothingness itself. Such invulnerability is indistinguishable from being dead, and, in fact, it is only the dead who have reached it. For only someone who is dead has an unconditional guarantee against the possibility of being upset. To be invulnerable would mean to be incapable of losing life, to be immune to dispossession, to have one's instinct for self-preservation perfectly fulfilled. But the only way one can have so secure a hold on life as to render its loss impossible is to drain life of everything which might make it vulnerable to rupture. And what remains of life when it is drained of that possibility is precisely a motionless impassivity indistinguishable from death.

What follows, then, when we integrate these Heideggerian and Freudian paradoxes? What makes life different from the condition of being dead is precisely its vulnerability to nothingness, its liability to rupture, its dreadful openness to an unpresenceable future. The reason we seek death, as Freud understood it, is because our deepest wish is to avoid an encounter with it of the type Heidegger described. Death offers us our only fail-safe way of escaping an experience of nothingness. But the experience of nothingness is not a one-time or some-time thing, a tragic accident that befalls us once in a lifetime. It is the (ordinarily repressed or implicit) meaning of that ec-stasis which is human living itself. When we flee it in order to preserve our lives we smother the animating eros, the spendthrift enthusiasm, which arises within us when we are so in love with life that we do not think of holding onto it.

These ironies are not a philosopher's invention. We can find them operating in those all-too-human addictions which, as they drive us to seek an always purer, always more intense experience of presence, drain us of our capacity to experience the kind of eros that is inseparable from suffering. Such addictions stop only one step short of being literally suicidal, of seeking in the undisturbable repose of death itself a permanent release from that tension which keeps bringing the experience of nothingness alive for us. But we see these ironies at work at the other extreme as well. I am thinking of the kind of unreserved self-expenditure which we associate with the highest reaches of sanctity. We are sometimes led to think (not only by our own misconceptions but also by a faulty theology) that what distinguishes people like Mother Teresa from the rest of us is their willingness to renounce life and root out of themselves that eros which is awakened by the goodness of things. But in fact what distinguishes such a person is precisely the extravagance with which she gives herself to life, instead of trying to control it, the lack of reserve in her expression of eros, the depth of care in her appreciation of being. Someone who lives in this way stops only one step short of literal martyrdom, of giving herself so completely to life as to die of it. What, we might ask, does it take to awaken such a passion? Some small child in us, standing at the nexus of all desire and all longing, knows and has forgotten. There is a way, apparently, for a mortal wound to be a blossoming flower, a way for the most upsetting of all experiences to become serenity, a way for the experience of death to be the most life affirming of all our celebrations. In these matters, perhaps the saints are our best teachers.

CHAPTER 6

The Experience of Horror and the Deconstruction of the Self

All our thinking may begin in wonder, as Aristotle suggests, but our deepest, most radical questions originate in horror.[1] From its inception philosophy has been perceived as an upsetting ordeal somehow comparable to dying because it raises the questions that horrify us instead of helping us protect ourselves from them. Understood in this way, philosophy is an activity from which we are always tempted to recoil because it seems to be self-destructive and even suicidal.[2] Examining the presuppositions on which one's life as a whole is based is like cutting off the limb on which one is sitting. When it encourages us to engage in such self-examination, philosophy is not just reminding us of death but inviting us to participate in our own undoing.

One of the distinctive characteristics of post-modern thought, from Nietzsche to Derrida, has been its insistence on the deconstructive import of philosophy. But since many great philosophers from Plato to Hegel have also tried to provide access to eternal verities or to develop the architecture for an undeconstructible system of truths, this emphasis on deconstruction has precipitated a crisis among philosophers themselves about the very nature of their enterprise. This crisis comes to a head in *Being and Time* where the effort to philosophize about death leads, if not to the death of philosophy, then at least to a deconstruction of the philosophical tradition. It is plausible to argue that such a radical dismantling of the tradition is a uniquely post-modern phenomenon. But it can also be argued that the possibility of such a crisis is always implicit within philosophy because of the upsetting character of the questions it raises. Crisis is not foreign to its essence but rather constitutive of it. Our self-preservative instincts may make us want to recoil from philosophy's ownmost possibility in order to save both it and ourselves from deconstruction. But there is an alternative to such a recoil: to allow the experience of horror, and specifically horror in the face of death, to shatter the accepted understanding of ourselves both as selves and as philosophers.

Indeed, if an encounter with death is constitutive of the philosophical act itself, we should not try to help philosophy recover from the contemporary crisis which has so radically undermined much of its traditional self-understanding. For if we were to recover (from) it, the very point of the crisis, and perhaps the deepest point of philosophy itself, would have been missed. The point, it seems to me, is not to save philosophy from its own radical undoing but to be receptive to its death by opening ourselves to what horrifies instead of pulling back from it. One way to practice such openness is to philosophize about the experience of horror itself— not in the sense of trying to master that experience by bringing it under philosophical control, but in the sense of surrendering our thought to its sway, even if this means allowing it to undermine our understanding of philosophy. In the previous chapters I have broached this topic; in this chapter I would like to thematize it and explore its ontological implications. That it is our very vocation as philosophers that calls us to this exploration of horror is suggested not just by Heidegger but by the Socratic injunction to which I have previously referred—the injunction to practice dying not once but over and over again, not in order to make death familiar but to let it repeatedly shatter our bond to the ordinary.

THE HORROR OF DECONSTRUCTION
AND THE DREAM OF TOTALITY

The fact that horror is not a perception, an insight, an opinion, a theory or a judgment, and thus is not easily assimilatable into any traditional epistemological category, tempts us to relegate it to the status of a subjective, emotional reaction which we have when something upsetting happens to us. But the view that horror is simply a subjective feeling with no cognitive import is inseparably connected with the presumption that there is no more to the events which provoke this feeling than our "objective" common sense perceives in them. By reducing horror to the status of an instinctual reaction, this view relieves us of the need to consider its intentional character and, at the same time, it allows us to dismiss the possibility that we experience horror because we are becoming aware of realities which our common-sense way of thinking represses. It is this repressed possibility—that horror is a disclosure of the extraordinary, not a reaction to the ordinary—that I would like to explore here.[3]

I can think of any number of events that would be likely to have a devastating impact on me—the failure of a project to which I had devoted my life, a diagnosis of cancer in my child, my wife's death in an automobile accident. But, in fact, even such traumatic events as these will not devastate me if I manage to deal with them as events that happen in my world. For if an event happens *in* my world, it does not happen *to* my world but rather leaves it intact. The genius of the therapeutic mentality[4] lies in its capacity for generating one psychological technique after another to help us handle, cope with, manage, deal with, any crisis that happens so that we will not be devastated by it. The underlying purpose of such therapy, no matter what methodology or theoretical framework it employs, is to prevent the fundamental structures of one's world as a whole from being ruptured.

But just as it is possible to disarm the most traumatic events by reducing them to the status of events that happen within one's world, so too it is possible for even the most insignificant interruptions in one's life to awaken horrifying intimations. Perhaps my wife is forty-five minutes late coming home on a winter evening and, as I stand musing by the window, watching the snow wrap everything in an eerie silence, I find myself suddenly visited by an inexplicable inkling of horror, a hint of some unspeakable possibility. My wife's lateness, although it seems to be only an event in my world, awakens in me an intimation of a radical disruption of it. Other people might be able to view the accident I imagine happening to her, even her death itself, as one occurence among many. But by virtue of her primacy in my life, by virtue of the fact that she is not simply another person in it but the center in terms of which it is structured and focused, my wife's death would be the end of my world.[5] What makes the thought of such an occurence horrifying to me is the fact that it opens up my world to a possibility that, instead of belonging within it, would rupture it at its core.

The world which the horrifying possibility threatens to breach gets its integrity, and thus its very character as a world, from the center in terms of which I live and move and have my being. This center is the axis on which the meaning of everything turns, the structural principle on which the existence of my world as a whole depends. Events which happen to me are perceived, examined, interpreted, and judged in terms of how they fit into the context of meaning that is organized around this center. This world and the language I use to talk about it are intimately related; the outer reaches of my vocabulary define the orbit inside which I move, round and round the center inscribed by the precious name of the one who means the world to me.

Now it is precisely the existence of this world as a whole, whose solidity I ordinarily never question, that momentarily trembles when horror awakens in me. Horror presupposes that the person experiencing it is accustomed to operating inside a universe of meaning whose existence is taken for granted prior to horror's breach of it. Only a being capable of language, capable of operating in terms of a context of meaning, can be horrified.[6] The instinctual fear of danger which animals experience has nothing to do with a horrifying intimation of the end of one's world.[7] In those situations where we are terrified of being killed and act solely on the basis of survival instinct, our participation in the world of meaning is temporarily suspended; we regress back to the kind of inarticulate biological immediacy which would govern us if we did not operate within the universe mediated by language.[8] Horror, on the other hand, acquires its horrifying import precisely from the fact that it awakens us to the possibility of losing the center which holds our lives together and makes them coherent wholes. Instead of causing us to revert *back* to pre-lingual immediacy, it gives us an intimation of a possibility that lies *beyond* our universe, a possibility of which we are ordinarily oblivious.

How are we to deal with these intimations, these inklings whose meaning we cannot imagine or describe but which fill us with such a deep sense of foreboding? This question is itself motivated by the desire to assimilate what is horrifying into the very universe of meaning whose existence it threatens. When we try to "deal with" or "cope with" the threatened loss of our world as a whole, we are attempting to treat it as if it were simply another event within it. But any success we have in assimilating our dreadful intimations into the universe of meaning inside which we ordinarily operate necessarily constitutes a betrayal of their import. For this way of interpreting intimations smothers their radical impact by subordinating them to the very principle of meaning whose stability they jeopardize. The possible end of my world, of which horror makes me aware, will not become more real to me by my thinking of it as analogous to, and thus explicable in terms derived from, the kinds of events that happen within my world. Rather, it will become real to me only as I realize that this possibility shatters all metaphors and analogies I am tempted to draw between it and everything that has ever happened to me. The horrifying possibility of the end of one's world horrifies precisely because it cannot be homologized to any ontic experience.

The impossibility of assimilating a horrifying intimation into the universe of meaning in terms of which one lives is not due to any flaw in one's power of assimilation, nor to any flaw in the structure of the particular universe one inhabits. When it comes to intimations of horror, every universe of meaning is just as vulnerable as every other. That is why there is no point in shifting from one universe of meaning to another in the hope of finding one that intimations of horror cannot breach. For no universe of meaning, irrespective of its content, can explain in terms of its parameters what it would mean for those parameters to be shattered and for the world they define to cease existing. Less important than the differences between the different frameworks which structure our lives is the fact that all of them are liable to deconstruction—and the fact that all of us ordinarily try to make them immune to it. The effort to make the universe in which we live impregnable, though it may at first seem to succeed in excluding the horrifying from our world, will in the end only serve to intensify the horror of its deconstruction. For by drawing boundaries and erecting barriers around our universe, we accentuate and rigidify the very distinction between the inside and the outside which makes a disruption of it upsetting. By erecting such barriers we do precisely the opposite of what we intend: we make ourselves all the more vulnerable to the horrifying by the very act of shutting ourselves off from it. The only kind of structure that could achieve the purpose for which an impregnable structure is designed would be one that included the outside within itself—an all-encompassing structure, one that contained everything and left nothing outside itself. This is what Emmanuel Levinas calls a "totality"[9]—it is the dream of a structure that would be immune to deconstruction.

In the Western tradition philosophy has often been conceived of precisely as a search for the undeconstructible, for a totalizing system from which nothing is left out and which nothing can breach, the search for a center that will not just hold but be immovable[10] and immune to dislodgement, so that it will be able to serve as the irrefragible arche, the Archimedean principle for our world as a whole. But a system cannot be complete and thus fulfill its totalizing purpose if it leaves its arche unquestioned, if it lays down certain presuppositions as its defining boundaries and leaves them unexamined. And so philosophy, insofar as it is governed by the totalizing impulse, is driven to examine its own presuppositions in the vain attempt to bring them inside the total system for which they are to serve as the foundation. When practiced in this way, philosophy ends up chasing its own tail; it tries to draw a perfect circle of meaning that includes everything inside its orbit, but the end of the line it draws never coincides with its beginning: it curves just slightly inward and circles again and again into smaller and smaller spirals. There is always a way into and out of what was supposed to have been its wholly self-contained world.

Seen in this light, philosophy, although the most fundamental of all disciplines, is itself only the servant of the totalizing impulse. But that impulse itself originates in the desire to be secure, to be in control, the desire to avoid the horrifying instead of suffering it. The therapeutic motive which seems to be awakened only when there are breaches in our world which need to be dealt with and managed actually underlies our desire to have an impregnable world in the first place. Philosophy itself, as a search for an undeconstructible universe of meaning, is a profoundly therapeutic exercise, motivated, just like more directly practical therapies, by a desire to structure our lives so as to exclude from them vulnerability itself, our susceptibility to possibilities over which we have no control, our liability to death in any form. We try to structure our lives in such a way as to prevent the end of them.

I might mention here parenthetically that if contemporary pragmatists like Richard Rorty are acutely aware of the multiplicity of alternative conceptual frameworks, and if, unlike their predecessors, they no longer dream of creating an un-deconstructible system, they have not, for all that, succeeded in escaping the sway of the therapeutic impulse animating the traditional totalizing project. When Rorty endorses Heidegger's efforts to release thought from the inhibiting constraints of that project, he does so because he thinks that such a release gives us the freedom to stand outside the various conceptual frameworks available to us so that we can choose whichever one we find useful for our practical purposes.[11] But what is our purpose in undertaking our practical projects? Is not practicality, especially as conceived by the contemporary pragmatist, governed by the same desire to control, the same totalizing impulse that governed the philosophical search for a non-deconstructible system? It is true, as Rorty claims, that Heidegger tries to show how theorizing is grounded in practicality, but that is part of his larger purpose—to show that practicality itself, as we ordinarily practice it, is grounded in our desire to silence intimations of horror, instead of listening to them. Post-modern pragmatism, while it purports to be an alternative to philosophical systematizing, is itself governed by the same underlying motive of control.

A philosophy that took our intimations of horror to heart would begin by undermining the whole project of philosophy as a totalizing system of meaning. But, as we have seen, that project is itself self-defeating. Abandoning it, far from being suicidal, frees philosophy by opening it to what an impregnable system of meaning is constructed to exclude: whatever it is that is intimated by the intimations of horror we repress.

INTIMATIONS OF NOTHINGNESS

In describing our initial experience of horror, I have used the word "intimation" in order to emphasize its disclosive character. Far from being an emotional aftershock following an event that upsets our whole world, horror is what first discloses to us the upsetting possibility that our world as a whole can cease to be. And yet horror does not disclose this possibility in the sense of making it fully accessible to us. Even as it opens us up to the horrifying, it keeps it concealed from us; it draws us out to the very edge of our world, where we can glimpse the abyss that is beyond it. To follow its intimations, instead of recoiling from them, would require our taking one step beyond that vertiginous position. Is this possible and, if so, what does it involve?

The fact that horror conceals the horrifying even as it discloses it to us makes it analogous to wonder. Wonder, as we have seen, projects us toward the unknown, and animates our desire to know it. We would not seek to know the unknown if it were wholly unknown to us, nor would we seek to know it if it were already known; we seek to know only because we are aware of the unknown *as* unknown. Wonder, like horror, may seem too lacking in content, too empty and unilluminating, to be called a kind of knowledge, especially when compared to perception and insight, opinion and judgment. And yet what knowing would there be without this primal awareness of the unknown as unknown which makes exploration possible?[12] It is only because the intimations of wonder situate us on the boundary between ignorance and knowledge that we are able to cross it.

But while wonder leads us across this boundary and into the world of meaning, an experience of horror occurs when the center which holds that world together is threatened and we begin to suspect that it is possible for its existence to be undermined. There is operative in this horrifying suspicion the same kind of intimation that is operative in wonder. If what horrifies us were wholly unknown it would be irrelevant to us; if it were already known, already accessible to us, we would be able to include it within our world of meaning, in which case it would lack the deconstructive power which makes it horrifying. But unlike wonder, which leads us from a condition of ignorance toward knowledge not yet achieved, horror leads us from the familiar world of the known toward an unknown that horrifies precisely because it threatens the existence of the known world as a whole. Wonder founds our world. Horror deconstructs it. Wonder and horror are both intimations and as such they disclose and conceal at the same time. And yet the known unknown of which each makes us aware differs radically in the two cases. The toward-which of wonder invites us, beckons us on, awakens longing, animates the desire to know; but the toward-which of horror horrifies—it tends to fill us with nausea, awaken revulsion, and provoke our instinct to turn and flee. Wonder evokes questioning and the long, arduous pursuit of inquiry; from horror there arises a desire to stop thinking before we become more fully aware of what we never want to think about—the unthinkable loss of the center which holds our world together and makes it meaningful.

Thus, to follow an intimation of horror, instead of repressing it, requires a different kind of courage from that involved in overcoming an ontic fear aroused by a dangerous object within one's world; for it requires overcoming an ontological urge to recoil from the possible loss of one's world as a whole.[13] Bound up with that world are all one's practical interests, all one's longings and achievements, all one's beliefs and certainties; a person who receives an intimation of its deconstruction is therefore right to feel that all he has ever sought to attain is in danger of being lost. Nothing could possibly be more contrary to his inclinations than to open himself to this horrifying possibility, instead of trying to prevent it. Indeed, it is no exaggeration to say that this possibility is as horrifying as death itself. For insofar as we are beings whose world is constituted by a universe of meaning, death is not a biological event which happens within the world but rather an ontological event which affects the existence of the world as a whole. It is not just that we possess an ability to anticipate death which animals lack; we are subject to an entirely different kind of death, one which we would not have to suffer if we did not structure our lives around a center which means the world to us.

Now because the known unknown which horror discloses is not an object within one's world but the possible end of the world as a whole, the process of exploring our intimations of it must be profoundly different from every other kind of knowing. Indeed, from the point of view of the epistemology which tacitly governs all of our ordinary inquiries, such intimations are themselves unintelligible and therefore incapable of being further understood. For under the influence of the metaphysics of presence, we ordinarily presume that the known unknown toward which our inquiries are directed is a being that will become intelligible to us when it is fully and directly present. Inquiry, as so conceived and practiced, tries to assimilate the unknown to the known by finding a way to include it within our world as something present-at-hand. Knowledge in this sense can only be achieved by transforming the other into the same, the possible into the actual, the absent into the present, the "not" in the not-yet into being conceived of as the purely now.

But the known unknown disclosed by horror horrifies precisely because it is an other not assimilatable into the same, a possibility that can undermine all actualities, an absence so different from presence that it cannot be construed simply as a presence that has not yet arrived. Are we forced then to conclude that, since it cannot be presenced, it cannot be known? How are intimations of it to be followed if it lies outside our world, whose boundaries we take to be the bounds of sense itself? Can such intimations of horror be explored or is the horrifying such that no line of inquiry can bring us closer to it because all such closeness requires construing what is brought close as something present-at-hand?

We do at least know the unknown disclosed to us by intimations of horror well enough to recognize it *as* horrifying; and for us to be horrified by it, it must be disclosed to us precisely as an unknown which jeopardizes the whole universe of meaning that is governed by the totalizing project of being as presence. The toward-which of horror is not directly present to us; nor can any inquiry ever make it present. For any such making present, by enclosing it within our world, would cover up the very negativity which makes it horrifying. The toward-which of horror can never be made fully accessible to the kind of objective observation which is often thought to be a prerequisite for knowing. But it does not follow that it cannot be understood at all; indeed, it can be understood precisely as that which resists objectification, as that which, far from being includable within the universe of meaning as an object present-at-hand, is the undermining of that universe, the rupturing of the present-at-hand by nothingness itself. If by getting closer to nothingness as the toward-which of horror one means making it more accessible to insight as insight is ordinarily conceived,[14] the attempt to get closer to it would only prove that one had failed to have the only kind of insight into nothingness that is true—the kind one has when one understands it as the possible end of one's world as a whole. Only by standing at the edge of the universe that contains everything present-at-hand, and on the verge of an abyss which contains nothing, is one in a position to realize the distinction between them.

Because it can never be understood through objectification, the toward-which of horror cannot be described in terms belonging to the universe of meaning which defines and is defined by the limits of ordinary discourse. Nothingness cannot be articulated or depicted in any of the terms deployed for talking about the present-at-hand. But this does not mean that the word "nothingness" is a mere mark on a page and no word at all. It would be a mere mark only for someone who presumed that we can only operate inside a universe of objects, never on its outer edge—i.e. someone who never allowed himself to follow or be affected by an intimation of horror.[15]

To speak of the possibility of nothingness in such a way as to communicate its reality, and at the same time to prevent it from being reduced to the status of something within the universe of objects as ordinarily conceived is the vocation philosophy would adopt if it renounced the totalizing project. Its practice would then consist in deconstructing all totalizing structures of meaning by finding their faultlines, by locating in each of them the cracks and fractures which have the potential of exposing us to the "abyss from which all dangers announce themselves."[16] Such deconstructive thinking would keep trying to pry the "not" free of any objectifying insight that purported to contain it, so that thought would continuously founder, continuously be breached by what is in principle not objectifiable. Philosophy done in this way would prevent our ever conceiving of nothingness as an actuality analogous to anything present-at-hand; instead, it would help us realize that nothingness must be understood as a possibility, "must be cultivated as a possibility,"[17] indeed, as the possible impossibility of being at all.

ANGUISH AND THE ACKNOWLEDGMENT
OF ONE'S NOTHINGNESS

When Heidegger uses such expressions in *Being and Time,* it is because his thinking there takes place on the very verge that distinguishes the horizon from the abyss. Guarding against the danger that we will construe the toward-which of horror as a possibility comparable to other possibilities actualizable within our world, he writes of it as the possibility that "is as far as possible from anything actual."[18] That is why he describes an authentic acceptance of this possibility in terms of our being-*toward* it as a possibility. Because it is not to be conceived of in terms of presence, this possibility must always be thought of as a future toward which we are projected. According to Heidegger, one cannot get into any closer proximity to nothingness than this being-toward it; for the only way one could get closer to it would be to treat it as an actuality present-at-hand.

And yet precisely because he portrays nothingness as a possibility that cannot be brought inside the universe of what is present-at-hand, Heidegger continues to view the former from the vantage point of the latter. Or, to put it another way, Heidegger approaches the abyss from the perspective of the horizon. His purpose is to convince us that the horizon opens up on the abyss and cannot contain it. It would be wrong to say that the text of *Being and Time* is written from within the horizon; rather, the text has its back to the horizon and its face toward the abyss in order to argue that the abyss cannot be presenced but only approached, with the horizon as its backdrop. We can get no closer to nothingness than to acknowledge it as the future which can never be presenced but toward which we are always projected.

And yet if the end of one's world is not a biological event but the deconstruction of one's universe of meaning, it need not lie in the future in the sense of being something that has not yet happened. When one loses the center that holds one's world together and makes it a world, one does not just foresee its possible annihilation. One actually suffers it. Until that happens one has only intimations of horror, inklings of nothingness, presentiments of total loss. But when one's wife is in a fatal car accident, when the child on whom one lavished one's deepest procreative affection dies of a congenital disease, nothingness ceases to be a future possibility. For then the ground on which one stood, even as one looked over the edge of one's world into the abyss, is pulled out from under one's feet. *Being and Time* enables us to understand why it would be wrong to say that, in such an experience, nothingness ceases to be a mere possibility and becomes an actuality; but what does happen in such an experience is that one's world as a whole, with all its actualities, ceases to exist. Nothingness delivers on all the promises horror made on its behalf not by becoming actual but by swallowing everything real and leaving one destitute. Horror itself, because it is only an anticipatory disclosure of nothingness, gives way to a more devastating disclosure of nothingness that surpasses horror and brings it to completion. In such an experience the distance separating one from nothingness is closed: nothingness is no longer the not-yet, the horrifying possibility which awaits one. For when one's world as a whole ceases to be, the self who inhabited that world can no longer use it to keep nothingness away from himself. When one loses one's world, the horror of anticipating nothingness becomes the anguish of wholly succumbing to and identifying with it. That anguish wrings from the very core of the heart an admission of one's own utter destitution. In the experience of such destitution, nothingness is no longer viewed as other than oneself. And so while horror gives us intimations of nothingness, from anguish there springs something even more radical: the realization of our oneness with it. There is no way to express this realization except to say, "I myself, in and of myself, am nothing."

Such an utterance, and the anguish it utters, is not spoken in the Heideggerian text, but it is, I would suggest, the toward-which of the text, as it is the toward-which of horror itself. Such mortal anguish deconstructs the person who is horrified by bringing him down *into* the abyss instead of allowing him to remain standing on the verge of it. Horror discloses the possibility of nothingness but nothingness becomes fully one's own only as one becomes completely one with it. The process of being devastated leaves nothing of one's world intact; it costs, in Eliot's words, "not less than everything."[19] How are we to understand such an experience phil-

osophically, coming to it, as we do, from that Heideggerian vantage point between the horizon and the abyss which the experience
of anguish takes away from us?

The Heideggerian text itself provides the clue when it speaks of
nothingness as Dasein's "ownmost" possibility. The "I" who experiences horror is not the "they-self" of ordinary existence, for the
nothingness toward which horror projects me "must be taken over
by [me] alone."[20] Horror deconstructs the they-self and indi-
vidualizes the person who experiences it. It teaches us that our
kinship with nothingness is so profound and intimate that we only
begin to realize who we are when we acknowledge our liability to
it. But we have not fully owned up to our kinship with nothingness
if we still think of ourselves only in terms of being-toward it. For
while it does help us to realize that our bond with nothingness is
inescapable, this phrase still allows us to think of ourselves in
terms of being and so to disassociate ourselves, to distance ourselves, from nothingness—even if the distance is no wider than a
preposition. But when we have wholly surrendered to the throe of
anguish, we are not just on the verge of nothingness but held fast in
its mortal embrace. And once our hold on being has been radically
undermined, we can no longer identify with being at all, even
being-toward-nothingness. Aware of our ontological destitution,
we identify ourselves with nothingness and no longer view being as
something that belongs to us.

Clearly, this deep kinship with nothingness is not to be reached
by our somehow making nothingness more present to us, or integrating it more completely within our universe of meaning. The
shift which occurs when one moves from understanding oneself as
being-*toward*-nothingness to understanding oneself *as* nothingness
does not occur because nothingness becomes more understandable; the meaning of nothingness remains as deconstructive and
unreconstructible as before. What shifts is not the meaning of
nothingness but one's relationship to it. Heidegger is right in saying that once one recognizes it as the possible impossibility of
existence, one cannot get any closer to the meaning of nothingness.
But without adding to its meaning, one can let it undermine the
position one has always taken with regard to it. Instead of presuming that we are superior to nothingness and in a position to look

down on it, we can acknowledge that it is closer to us than we are to ourselves.

Such a radical reversal in one's ontological position cannot occur without radically deconstructing our ordinary sense of what it means to be a self. But the hermeneutic of horror and anguish lead us to suspect that we can come to a true understanding of ourselves only in and through such a deconstruction, and only when this deconstruction wrests from us the final acknowledgment that, in and of ourselves, we are nothing. Is this too radical a formulation? Am I exaggerating the negativity of anguish by articulating its ontological import in this way?

In order to address this issue, let me bring to the fore an ambiguity that I have kept in the background until now, although it has been at work throughout this chapter and the preceding ones. I have suggested that horror discloses to me the possibility of my world collapsing if something were to happen to the reality which constitutes its center. If everything in me recoils in horror from this possibility, it is ordinarily because losing the other who is the center of my world would deconstruct it and therefore be devastating for me. But this raises the question as to what is of primal importance to me—the being of the other or the integrity of my world which happens to be critically dependent on the other? It would seem at first that nothing could be of more central importance than the reality which centers one's world. And yet if the world in question is mine, even the reality at the very center of it gets its importance from its relationship to me. Even when another person is the center of my world, I myself occupy what is finally an even more significant position—the position of being its proprietor. What prompts us to assume this proprietory role? Why is it that, even when I am in love with someone, and willing to sacrifice everything on her behalf, I still tend to place her in my world instead of entering hers? For the simple reason that the only alternative to having her as my center is to give up my hold on her and have nothing. I make her the center of my world to avoid that horrifying destitution, even though in doing so I betray the very relationship whose loss I am determined to prevent. My attempt to establish a proprietory relationship with what I love is motivated finally by a desire to prevent my own deconstruction. The arche on which my world as a whole depends is not, ironically, the other at its center but my own will to be an undeconstructible self.

This desire on the part of the self to be immune to deconstruction underlies and sustains the entire metaphysics of presence. Under the influence of that metaphysics, our seeking to know the as yet unknown is construed as trying to presence it so that it will reveal itself fully and leave nothing concealed. Every quest for insight, every attempt to understand the meaning of something, is thought of as an effort to make that meaning wholly present. But what holds up the whole universe of meaning as constituted by such acts of presencing? What Archimedian principle makes all presencing possible? Isn't every act of presencing done in reference to the I? I am the one to whom the toward-which of inquiry is to become wholly accessible.[21] The I is the arche underlying the ideal of presence. Indeed, presence itself is derivative; it gets its importance, its character as presence, from the I by reference to whom the very presence of presence is determined.

In the universe of meaning that is thus constituted, everything is understood in terms of its distance from and proximity to the absolute reference point of the I itself. What is possible is defined in terms of its potentiality for being presenced; what is actual is defined in terms of what is real in the present. And what else is there, after one has accounted for actuality and possibility, except the impossible—defined, according to the metaphysics of presence, as that which cannot be presenced and therefore cannot be at all? From the viewpoint of the I which is the arche of the universe of meaning, to be means precisely to be capable of being presenced. This is what enables the I to conceive of its universe as an all-inclusive totality outside of which there is nothing. And of what consequence is this "nothing" to the I for whom being is equated with presence? It is of no account.[22] But this means that, from its point of view, nothingness is precisely what is impossible—and its own nothingness most of all. According to the metaphysics of presence, *it cannot be that the I is able to not be.*

But no one can continue to believe himself immune to nothingness once he has allowed the intimations of horror to lead him all the way to the bottom of anguish. And the fact that it is possible for the self to not be deprives it of the stature it would have to possess to be able to function as the arche of a metaphysics of presence. Before following intimations of horror, one treats oneself as the absolute reference point, as the very condition for the possibility of presence. But once those intimations lead one to a realization of one's nothingness, one can no longer pretend to occupy the privileged position that would justify one in operating as the arbiter of being. In fact, one's real position is exactly the opposite of that which one ascribes to oneself before horror has its upsetting impact. For the fact that I am liable to deconstruction instead of being immune to it does more than jeopardize my being. It shows that I do not have the propriety hold on being I have always presumed to have. And what does this mean if not that being is not at all the same as myself but precisely what is *other* than me? Indeed, even what I refer to as my own being is not mine insofar as it is never securely in my possession. The possessive adjective I use to describe my relationship to being only testifies to my desire to make it belong to me. But, in fact, I never have even my own being firmly within my grasp. And what does this mean if not that, far from being the arche of being, I am in myself destitute of being and always the recipient of it? Anguish is precisely the heartfelt acceptance of our destitute, ontological condition. In opening ourselves to it, we finally embrace our nothingness, instead of evading it.

Perhaps Heidegger hestiated to affirm that the self is nothing, in and of itself, because he thought the only way to prevent nothingness from being interpreted in terms of entities present-at-hand was to treat it as a possibility that always lies ahead of one. But as long as one treats nothingness as a possibility, one only gets to the edge of the horizon of the metaphysics of presence. Heidegger was right to say that the intimation of nothingness as a possibility is deeper than any insight into beings as actualities present-at-hand. But to go further than intimations of horror, to reach the truth which they intimate, one must go beyond the anticipation of nothingness as a possibility to an open-hearted acknowledgment of one's identity with it. Such an affirmation of one's own nothingness makes no sense from the viewpoint of the metaphysics of presence. But it is precisely for that reason that this affirmation, and this affirmation alone, shatters that metaphysic by bringing to bear on its once immovable arche the full impact of what is disclosed in anguish. The dream of creating such a metaphysic is itself only a symptom of the fundamental project of the I itself: its desire to be perfectly undeconstructible, to be in such complete possession of being as to be immune to the loss of it. We could enjoy such security only if being were dependent on us, instead of our being the recipients of it. In spite of the fact that such a metaphysic is impossible, the dream of it governs our very concept of ourselves as selves. Horror shatters that dream and anguish reveals the truth it was invented to cover up: the kind of self we would have liked to be never existed because being has never been us but is always our other. It is not, strictly speaking, true to say that, at the moment of terminal anguish, when this is acknowledged, the self appropriates nothingness as its ownmost possibility. It is more accurate to say that nothingness appropriates the self and wrings from it an admission of its own radical destitution: I, myself, in and of myself, am nothing.

Seen from the viewpoint of the metaphysics of presence, the affirmation of one's nothingness is as suicidal as leaping into an abyss. For it upends the arche one needs to have firmly in place if one is to construct a system of thought. In affirming the reality of one's nothingness, one inevitably feels like one has gone off the deep end of rational thought itself. But, in fact, it is only by going over what *seems* to be the edge of rationality that one severs the deepest avoidances—those which prevent one from exploring, as rationality itself requires, those horrifying intimations that one would like to repress because they promise to be devastating. The affirmation of one's nothingness alone enables one to be appropriated by the truth one has always wanted to keep covered up because acknowledging it requires losing the arche on which one's world as a whole depends. But the truth which means the end of the metaphysics of presence means the beginning of a thought freed from the arche of avoidance. Only the affirmation of one's nothingness anchors such thought in the abyss, and prevents the thinker from construing himself as the principle of presence and presence as the principle of being. What would be the meaning of being in a thought that *begins* with our nothingness? What intimations lie concealed in the depths of the most upsetting anguish? Such intimations do not lead *back* to the breached horizon of being as presence. They do not lead *down* to the abyss of nothingness for it is only by being down there already that we are able to be affected by them. Do they lead, perhaps, *up*, in the direction of a known unknown which evokes neither wonder nor horror but something like awe?

CHAPTER 7

Temporality as Rupture

When Jacques Derrida describes death, "or rather the anguished anticipation of death," as "the horizon and source of all determined dangers, the abyss from which all menaces announce themselves,"[1] he is recapitulating a consensus which pervades postmodern thought as a whole. In fact, death seems to have acquired the kind of privileged position in our thinking which used to be occupied by those indisputable first principles which once provided philosophy, and culture itself, an unshakable foundation. As post-moderns, we have no such foundation to secure us against anxiety when we try to erect a structure of meaning for ourselves. Indeed, Nietzsche and Heidegger, Derrida's two most important predecessors in the hermeneutic of deconstruction, have required us to acknowledge that our desire for an immovable arche on which to ground meaning is itself motivated by an effort to circumvent that abyss from which no universe of meaning, however well constructed, will be able to protect us. By displacing the arche on which thinking has always rested, death has become the an-arche which undermines thought instead of providing it a secure ground.

What entitles death to this privileged position is the fact that it is, in Heidegger's terms, our "uttermost possibility" which "cannot be outstripped."[2] The thinker who, instead of trying to build a system which excludes this possibility, tries to expose all systems to its deconstructive irony, apparently philosophizes from the most radical of all perspectives. For the deconstructionist does not occupy and work to defend a position opposed to an-arche, but rather deliberately exposes her own thinking, and everyone else's, to its mortal danger. The thinker who does not try to construct an impregnable universe of meaning but, instead, lets an-arche have its deconstructive impact, has no privileged position she is strug-

143

gling to maintain and for that very reason has a more profound perspective than any arche, however fundamental, could provide.

The hermeneutic that has been worked out from this deconstructive perspective has cast suspicion on our whole metaphysical and philosophical tradition. The radical point of view provided by death has enabled us to recognize for the first time how profoundly the tradition has been grounded in a denial of it. To transcend death, to heal the breach, to close the chasm, to retrieve the kind of time where there is no not-yet, no "not" at all, to exist in the pure presence of the present—this is the dream that has always kept thought under the sway of what we now recognize as a metaphysics of avoidance. The primary arche-type of that dream, according to the hermeneutics of its deconstruction, is the God of traditional onto-theology who enjoys a delight that is not "corrupted by interval, discontinuity, alterity."[3] What is eternity if not the dream of a dreamlike time from which all fissures have been removed, a time innocent of disruption, a now unbroken by any not-yet or having-been, a now that is whole, complete, self-contained, one?[4] God and eternity belong together in the same dream of time without death.

The decoding of that dream has been, I think, the great achievement of post-modern thought from Nietzsche to Derrida. The rupture of our onto-theological tradition which it has caused has undermined our belief in any eternal verities and in philosophy itself as a gnosis that can help us reach an eternal standpoint. We no longer think ourselves different from animals because we transcend death but because we can anticipate it in all its dreadfulness.[5] Philosophy, when practiced as an exercise in such anticipation, becomes truly a-gnostic for the first time; instead of promising us an angelic vision of presence, it teaches us the horrifying truths which heretofore were repressed along with the experience of death. From a metaphysics governed by the dream of presence to a hermeneutic responsive to nothingness, from a perennial philosophy of eternal truths to a philosophy which acknowledges its own vulnerability to the throe of temporality, from uplifting beliefs to suspicions that undermine all saving faiths, from the myth of original fullness to the admission of our irreparable brokenness—this seems to be the arc that describes the curve of post-modern thought. The abbreviated way to describe that arc is to say that it moves from God as arche to death as an-arche.

Situated as we are in an historical condition which is governed by this curve, we find ourselves trying to choose between a conservative return to the privileged position which belief enjoyed before (what the traditionalist describes as) the descent into nihilism, and a radical embrace of an unforeseeable and therefore terrible and terrifying future. Such a choice differs from that posed by the Enlightenment in ways which illuminate just how radical it is. While in the eighteenth century it appeared that one had to choose between an outdated tradition of dogmatic faith and a new rationality purified of superstitious excrescences, now rationality itself, and the metaphysics of presence which has traditionally grounded it, have themselves been deconstructed as a kind of superstition. Whereas, at the time of the Enlightenment, the future was identified with progress and the past with what was antiquated, now the very idea that the future means progress itself belongs to the past. Indeed, we seem required to choose not between conflicting versions of the meaning of history but between meaning itself and an-archy.

Nevertheless, whatever names are given to the terms of this choice, it is still presented to us as a choice between the past and the future. The fact that the Enlightenment also required such a choice, though of a far less radical nature, suggests that our situation is governed by a fundamentally similar experience of temporality. For us too, as for the thinkers of the Enlightenment, it is a question of choosing between a past in which we no longer believe and a future which transcends it—even if, for us, the future portends something as unimaginable, as unthinkable, as nothingness itself. This very unanticipatable character of the future, its heterogeneity from every past which human beings have experienced, this radical incommensurability between the not-yet and the already, was implicitly present in the Enlightenment idea of liberating culture from its past and freeing it for a future which had never been tried before. But precisely because we have lost the sense of confidence which enabled the Enlightenment to construe movement into that future as positive progress, as an ameliorative or even transformative ascent, the future is more radically available to us in its very character as future, as a possibility which is not homologizable to any previous presence.[6] It is no exaggeration to say that we have no idea of where we are going. As long as one construes the beyond in terms of progress, one is still domesticating it, because one is presuming that it will evolve in the direction one desires. Hope of this kind still suppresses the radically unimaginable, and for that reason potentially horrific, character of the future. We have not progressed further than the Enlightenment so much as we have awakened from and moved beyond the consoling dream of progress itself, with the result that we are able to encounter the future in its inconceivable, unimaginable otherness.

But even more fundamental than the past in its very character as past, and the future in its very character as future, is the turn we make from one to the other, in its very character as a turn. No matter what past we turn from, or what future we turn toward, we are always already caught in the throe of the turn, with no way of escaping it. No matter how hard we try to reverse that turn, and return to our always already lost past so as to retrieve a present that never was, we never break free of that throe. If post-modernists such as Nietzsche and Derrida are to be believed, eternity is the term of our flight from the turn, death the term from which we flee; eternity is our always already lost past, death our always inconceivable, unimaginable future. But whether such terms are an appropriate way to describe our being in time can be decided only by understanding the turn of temporality itself, for its from-which and toward-which acquire their very character as terms of movement from the event of the turn. It is no exaggeration to say that absolutely everything hinges on this turn. Our way of conceiving it determines our understanding of all other matters. In that sense it is the arche of thought—though not the kind of stationary arche thought would like to have. To be always already in the throe of a turn, to be *grounded* in a *throe,* this, it would seem, is the only kind of arche our thought will ever have. Throughout these pages we have been seeking to understand the from-which and toward-which of that throe by exploring the experience of the turn itself, and the abyss which we enter when we make it. Let us now turn more explicitly and directly than we have thus far to the temporal character of that turn in the hope that by exploring it we might begin to broach its ultimate import.

DEATH AS THROE

To gain phenomenological access to the throe of temporality, let us reflect on those experiences which open the future up to us, in a way which prevents our thinking of it in terms of presence. I am thinking in particular of the experiences of wonder and horror which, as we have seen, expose us to the unknown in its very character as unknown. Only because we are capable of wondering and being horrified are we able to encounter in what is already wholly present to us a portent of something not present, an intimation of something which beckons or horrifies us by virtue of its radical otherness.

That the unknown, in its very character as unknown, is not inaccessible to us, that we can be conscious of it without in any way homologizing it to what is already given, means that we are not held in the grip of presence. Insofar as we are wonderers, we are always already situated in between the presence of what is present to us in the present, and the unknown of which wonder makes us conscious. We always find ourselves caught between the given and the unknown, between familiarity and mystery, between the same and the other, between the immanence of the now and the transcendence of the future. Instead of convincing us that all there is to know is available to us, our experience of the given awakens a sense of incommensurable strangeness in us. The rupture caused by our awareness of the unknown as unknown creates a fissure in what would otherwise have been a universe of unbroken presence and unmarred plenitude. We might like to be able to draw upon the plenitude of the given in order to repair the breach caused in it by the rupture of wonder. But the given will never provide us the wherewithal for healing the break caused by wonder because it is precisely the given which is mysterious to us, no matter how completely it is given to us. Any addition to the given, far from diminishing wonder, only gives us more to wonder about. The given always provides us with material for our questions, never with the knowledge we would need to answer them.

Nevertheless, precisely because the given is given, is present, is known, we ordinarily think of it as a positive plenitude, as the immediately, unquestionably real, as the very meaning of being itself. On the other hand, that toward which wonder turns us is not given, not present, not known, does not present itself to us. Indeed, insofar as we presume that the given is being and use it as our ontological standard, we do not view the toward-which of wonder as being at all. And yet, in spite of the fact that, from our ordinary viewpoint it seems to not even exist, we cannot simply dismiss the toward-which of wonder. For it introjects into our experience of the plenitude of the given a void or fissure which is not something given but the not itself. Because of its very lack of substance, we cannot wholly assimilate the void of the not into the plenitude of the given. Rather, it subjects our experience of that plenitude to an irremediable rupture which deprives it of the fullness which it would need to retain if we were to maintain our view of it as being itself.

It is, therefore, this equation of the given with being which the event of wonder requires us to question. The fact that the given cannot prevent us from wondering what it is, and so cannot prevent a disruption of its plenitude by the unknown, makes it impossible for us to continue identifying the given with what it is in its givenness. If we know that we do not know what the given is, we know there is more to it than it gives itself out to be. This more, this surplus, this supplement, this fact that the given exceeds itself, and is not reducible to itself[7]—this is accessible to us only in and through the lack, the not, the fissure, the gap which wonder enables us to recognize in the plenitude of the given. Wonder eviscerates that plenitude; it requires us to affirm that there is more to be known by finding out what is *not* given than could ever be known by simply accepting the given. That is why the turn which wonder requires us to make must lead to an overturning of our very sense of being itself. We are always in the process of being revolutionized by this overturning. There was never a time when wonder was not undermining our original metaphysics of presence. Wonder does not merely make us aware of something more that might be added to the plenitude of the present; the more of which it makes us aware cannot be treated as an addition, an amendment, or an excrescence. For, from the point of view of the given, this more is precisely nothing; and so we cannot take seriously its claim to be more unless we radically question and finally reject the equation of being with the given. We cannot bridge the gap separating the given and the toward-which of wonder by using some metaphor, some similarity, some homologizing or commensurating principle, to liken them to each other. For the toward-which of wonder calls the given into question and disputes its claim to ultimacy. Between them there can be no bridge at all, no reconciling sameness, only irreconcilable difference and the rupture of a throe.

To mitigate that difference would be comparable to treating death itself as an event within one's world. But just as death is not integratable within one's world because it ruptures one's world as a whole and thus deprives one of the only context which one could have used as a principle of integration, so wonder eviscerates the plenitude of the given and takes from it that fullness, that intactness it would have to retain to be able to absorb the toward-which of wonder within itself. Indeed, there are good reasons for thinking that the rupture of the given by the not which wonder introjects into it is itself the original event of death, the original radical disruption of presence. For the irreconcilability of the from-which and toward-which of wonder makes the turn from one to the other an irreparable break, an experience of irretrievable loss (even though, in undergoing it, we forfeit what we never really possessed). This break, this loss, would not involve a mortal breach if it only disturbed one's equilibrium without shattering one's underlying sense of being. But it is precisely the very status of the given as being which the not of wonder undermines. Everything that is is shattered when the meaning of "is" itself is revolutionized. Insofar as the sense of being which is constitutive of our being is always already being radically altered, we are always already in the throe of death, always already caught in between life as presence and its radical other. We do not have to wait for death, as for an event that lies in the future, at the end of our lives. Insofar as the turn from the given to the toward-which of wonder is an irrevocable and mortal breach in our being, we are always already dying. And, indeed, it is only because of the fact that we are always dying in this sense that the future, in its very character as future, is accessible to us.

The interpretation of temporality developed by Heidegger in *Being and Time* is the starting point for the line of thought we are exploring here. Heidegger focuses on our encounter with the "possible impossibility" of existing at all because it provides him the best possible way of demonstrating the irreducibility of the future to the present, the not-yet to the now. Death is the paradigm of the future in its very character as future insofar as it lies ahead of us, but not as a possibility that will sometime be transformed into a present actuality. Our capacity for anticipating this possibility, the fact that we are capable of horror, of being dumbfounded by the not itself—by nothingness—proves that we are not bound by the parameters of presence. Indeed, we are capable of explicitly thematizing the possibility of our own nothingness only because we are always already projected toward the future in its radical otherness from the present. Our being-toward-death is simply the consummate illustration of the human experience of temporality.

However, the inseparability of death and wonder which I have been trying to describe requires rethinking the treatment of our being-toward-death in *Being and Time*. Because he always speaks of death as that *toward* which we are projected, Heidegger situates it in the future, and makes it, in fact, the toward-which of our being. But in doing this he fails to take into account the full import of the very interpretation of temporality which his phenomenology of our encounter with death has enabled him to develop. For we can experience death as our future, as the toward-which of our anticipation, only because we are already caught in the throe which orients us toward the toward-which as such; and that throe, as we have seen, is itself a radical disruption, an evisceration of the given, an introjection of the not into being—in short, a death. Death is not that toward which we are projected, is not the *destination* of the turn, because the *turn itself* is the original event of dying. Wonder, when it ruptures the given, brings about the end of the world as presence, even though the world thus terminated was never our home but only the universe we would have lived in if we were not born to be wonderers. We are always already the sufferers of that primal loss. Death is our end but our end happens at the very beginning, as the beginning of our being as inquirers. Death does not lie in wait for us as the concluding event of our time; death is always already happening as the event constitutive of temporality itself. Without it, our kind of time could never begin. Time itself is, for us, the mortal rupture which situates us in between the from-which and toward-which of wonder; to be caught in the throe of that between means to be always already dying.

This is why, as Derrida helps us realize, there was no original, primal time, no pure beginning undisturbed by rupture, fissure, loss. For such a time could only have existed before time, before the rupture constitutive of temporality itself. If we have always dreamed of such a timeless time, it is precisely because it would release us from our dying throe, and restore us to the plenitude we have never had. All our golden ages are images by means of which we try to re-present the original presence of the present as it was before any future happened to it. Indeed, all our images, insofar as they seek to be re-presentative images of the given, harken backward, try to return us to the original which would make all images unnecessary. If they perfectly performed the purpose we want them to serve, such images would make possible and be effaced by a pure experience of immediate presence. That immediacy would be so perfect, so saturated with presence, that nothing at all—and especially not nothingness itself—would come between us and what was present. Indeed, the between itself would evaporate, and with it the distinction between ourselves and any other, the distance separating noesis from noema, subject from object, the fallen many from the original One. In that original plenitude, without time, without otherness, without the not, being would be what it has never been for us—unbroken oneness.

The deconstructionist hermeneutic of our desire for presence thus leads directly to a deconstructionist dia-gnosis of religious consciousness. For religious consciousness is governed by the myth of presence insofar as it tries to find some way of returning to or retrieving a pre-lapsarian metaphysical condition conceived in terms of an ineffable mystical gnosis. In our dream of that supreme mode of knowing, the distinction between the Original and its image, the One and the other, is effaced in an unmediated experience of presence. This explains why the quest for mystical gnosis has typically been wedded to a henological metaphysic. In order for being to be experienced as pure presence, it must be identical with the One as it is prior to all differentiation. For only the One that is prior to differentiation excludes that otherness which is disruptive of presence. Even the tiniest splinter of otherness would be sufficient to deprive the One of its primal plenitude and timeless impassivity. In its original state, before it becomes other than itself, the One fulfills the deepest of all our dreams—the dream from which religious longing itself seems to be born: we would like there to have been no difference, no otherness, introduced into the oneness of simple presence. We would like there to never have been anything but the pure presence which we think existed once, before the rupture of temporality happened. Where do we locate the One? Always in the past, always already behind us, always as that from which we have fallen—even though what lies back there is a timeless present. In always thinking of that pure present as back in our past, we testify to the fact that we have always already lost it.

Spiritualities of retrieval try to carve out a path that will lead one back to that original oneness where the distinction between the experiencer and the experienced vanishes. Fundamental to any such spirituality is an ascetic withdrawal from the throe of temporality, and whatever might cause one to be caught up in it. That means, of course, a detachment from everything—not just everything toward which wonder draws us but also everything which might serve as wonder's starting point. Thus, a return to oneness is not to be achieved by merely returning to the empirically given, because it is our exposure to the given which makes us vulnerable to wonder's throe. To retrieve an invulnerable presence, one that is not susceptible to the not, one must break through the entire context of the throe, the web of temporality itself. And one can do this only by an unconditional abnegation, a renunciation of everything, a total metaphysical askesis.

Such a transcendence of temporality, such a break through its confining skin, is itself construed as a death. To leave everything behind, to renounce all the things one is tempted to love, to sever all the bonds of kinship and affection by which one is bound to the world—such an achievement surely requires an excruciating surgery, a severing of one's very self from its being-in-the-world. And yet to construe it as a death is to overlook the peculiar character of both that from which and that toward which such asceticism turns. For in turning one from the world, and from the temporality constitutive of our experience of it, this asceticism proposes to release us from the very condition of vulnerability, which makes an experience of death possible. Precisely what eternity understood as the retrieval of presence, promises, is an escape from this vulnerability. It is true that, in order for that promise to be delivered, one must break whatever hold temporality has on one; but such a breakthrough, far from constituting a death experience, enables one to free oneself from the experience of death which the throe of temporality always requires one to suffer. What we are cut off from, by the asceticism of withdrawal, is the very experience of dying which is constitutive of our being. In trying to turn from time to eternity we really turn our backs on the event of turning itself in the hope of releasing ourselves from the dreadful situation of being in between its from-which and toward-which. We deaden ourselves in order to not suffer the dying which living in the throe of wonder requires us to undergo.

Given our original situation of existing always already between the from-which and toward-which of wonder, we can only choose to move in either of two diametrically opposed directions: either back from the toward or toward it. When we make the former choice, we transform our from-which into our toward-which (which suggests that, no matter what, the toward-which is inescapable). A henological metaphysics enables us to articulate the objective of that choice as the One prior to its own fatal self-othering; a spirituality of withdrawal describes the path that must be retraced to find our way back to it. But whether such a metaphysics gives us a true insight into being, whether such a spirituality returns us to our true selves, depends on the wisdom of the fundamental option from which they derive—the choice to escape from the throe of wonder instead of entering and suffering it. It is to the other alternative—the alternative of otherness itself—that I now turn.

THE TOWARD-WHICH OF TEMPORALITY

I have suggested that it is not appropriate to describe this other alternative as our being-toward-death. For being-toward-death, like any intentional act, itself presupposes that breach of the present by the future which alone makes it possible for us to be beings in between the from and the toward. We are not projected *toward* that breach, that fissure, that unbridgeable abyss; we live *in* it as in an abyss which causes simultaneously our primal lapse from plenitude and our primal projection toward the future. The future in its radical otherness from the present is accessible to us only because we have always already fallen helplessly into the gap which separates it from the present.

There is, nevertheless, profound truth in Heidegger's description of death as our toward-which. For we do not ordinarily realize that we are always already in the throe of death, and for that reason we must come *to* this realization *from* our avoidance of it. That we do not want to be nothing, that we recoil in horror from that abyss which is the "source of all determined dangers," means that we try to turn our back on the turn which is constitutive of our being as being-in-nothingness. Avoidance always takes the form of holding onto that from which we are being wrenched so as to prevent the wrenching experience of its loss. Though we are always already in the throe of death, we ordinarily spend our lives trying to get the ground back under our feet. We live trying not to turn, with our backs to the turn, heading toward that to which we can never return because the turn itself never allows us to escape its mortal and mortifying grip. Dying is, as Heidegger claims, that toward which we would be projected if we reversed our avoidances, but not because it is the toward-which of that primal turn which is constitutive of us; dying is that primal turn, is temporality itself.

What then is involved in making that turn—in undergoing the anguish of time instead of trying to evade it? I have suggested that the nature of the turn does not turn on the nature of its terms; rather, the terms can be properly understood only by understanding the ontology of the turn. But ordinarily we interpret the turn from the vantage point of our avoidance of it. Consequently, we view the given, that from which the turn is made, as a positive plenitude, as presence, as being, and the turn as a rupturing of this plenitude, an evisceration of its fullness, a void introjected into presence, the not which nihilates being. Is the not which poses this threat a mere not? Since it cannot be assimilated to presence, is it really nothing at all? If so, it could be dismissed and the on-tological integrity of being as presence could continue undisturbed. But wonder and horror do occur and nothing is more real than the disruption they introduce. These experiences require us to say that the not is not a mere nothing, that it really does introject into the plenitude of the given a void which cannot be filled, a fissure which cannot be sealed over. And this means that the undefiled presence of the present simply is not, simply does not exist, but has always already been fractured. We would like the given to have been being without otherness but, because the not is inextricable from the given, such a metaphysic of oneness has never been more than a dream motivated by the desire to succeed in our deepest avoid-ances.

To turn from that metaphysics means precisely to cease view-ing the turn from the perspective of its from-which and, instead, to start viewing its from-which from the perspective of the turn. The more seriously one takes the not, the more completely one surren-ders to its throe, the less one is governed by the equation of being with presence. Indeed, the crucial point in one's turn away from this dream will be precisely one's recognition that being construed as pure presence does not exist. As long as one continues to view the from-which of the turn as being, one has not completely surren-dered to the throe of it. The break with presence is complete only when one recognizes that it was never being at all but only one's dream of what one would have liked being to be. What being really is is discoverable only by allowing oneself to be completely carried away by the throe of dying which ruptures that dream. Being is to be found not by recoiling from the throe but by entering into it, not by retreating in the direction of its from-which but by advancing in the direction of its toward-which. Being is found in and through that dying which is constitutive of the turn of temporality. To make that turn, instead of fleeing it, to die, means precisely to start understanding the toward-which of the turn as being.

What then can be said of the toward-which, precisely insofar as it is the toward-which of the turn of temporality? First of all, we need to overcome the tendency to think of the toward-which as something which is lying inertly in the future, waiting for us to reach it. Such a view is mistaken on two counts. In the first place, it leads us to conceive of the future as another now that will become real when it becomes present to us, and so fails to take seriously its heterogeneity from the present. Moreover, this way of viewing the future treats it as something separable from and essentially unconnected with the present and so presupposes that the present is an unbreached plenitude. But, in fact, there is no such presence, except in the kind of time operative in our dreams. For us, the present is always already ruptured by a future which is irrevocably other than any future present. This rupture of the present is not caused by the present; it is caused by the future which has always already intervened and created that void in the present which prevents our identifying it with being. And this requires us to say that the toward-which of the turn, far from lying inertly in the distance, actively uproots the present and wrenches it away from itself; it is its intervention into the present that makes the radical turn of temporality possible.

What must the character of the toward-which be, if it is able to create such a radical and irrevocable disruption? It must be, at the same time, radically other than presence, and yet be being itself. Were we to construe it as analogous to presence, or to refuse to call it being because of the breakdown of such analogies, we would not yet have allowed our equation of being with presence to be shattered by it. To allow that break to occur cleanly, irreparably, we must identify that which brings the break about as being itself and as the radical other of presence. Far from being absorbable into the kind of pure union, unbreached by the slightest hint of otherness, which the metaphysics of presence idealizes, this other is what shatters our dream of such a union, and makes it impossible. Precisely what makes it capable of rupturing us is the fact that it cannot ever be rendered present but rather always transcends us. There is no hope that in the future its absolute difference will be effaced in some reconciling sameness because its difference is constitutive of the future as such.

In short, if that toward which our being is projected is to be capable of creating the rupture which is constitutive of our temporality, it must be being itself, it must be radically other than and disruptive of presence, and its heterogeneity from the present must be irreducible. But if temporality is the turn, the rupture, the crux itself, and if this turn can occur only by virtue of the disruptive intervention of something radically other, does this not require us to say that temporality is not self-constituting—that its existence depends on, and is made possible by, a toward-which that is immanent within temporality as a transcendent disruption of it? That toward which we are projected and by which we are ruptured must be wholly other than the crux of temporality in order to be able to effect the irreparable fracture which is constitutive of that crux. It cannot be nothingness, as Heidegger argued, because nothingness is introjected into the plenitude of the present by what is radically other than presence; and it cannot be simply a future "now" which has not yet arrived because, if it were, it would only add to the present instead of irreparably breaching it. The toward-which of temporality must, then, be being, but being so wholly other than presence that it subjects presence to a not from which it never recovers. It must, in short, be other than temporality, if by temporality we mean the crux in which we live. We might call it the non-temporal but this negative way of speaking of it, while emphasizing its otherness, would not express our acknowledgment of it as being. Perhaps, then, we should call it eternity—but eternity understood not as the apotheosis of the now but as the power which contravenes the now and overturns its primacy. If we were to ask where eternity as so understood is to be found, we could only say *within time;* but it is found within time as the toward-which that turns time inside out and thus constitutes it as an irreparable rupture.

Eternity in this sense, I would suggest, must exist because without it time itself, as the rupturing of the present by the radically other would not be possible. As thus conceived, eternity does not lie behind us, as the pure presence we have lost, nor does it await us as a distant future to be reached only when time ceases; rather, eternity is the radical future whose heterogenity pries time open and makes what would otherwise have been a closed womb an open wound. The fact that time and eternity are radically other than each other does not at all mean that each is closed in upon itself and shut off from the other, as our ordinary conception of their irreconcilable difference presupposes. Indeed, if eternity, as time's radical other, were wholly external to it, if eternity transcended time in such a way that time had no relationship to it, time itself would be the same undisturbed, motionless now, the same unbroken, placid presence, which we imagine eternity to be. Without a toward-which, time could not turn. Without a toward-which radically other than itself, it could only turn toward a future that would ultimately prove to be the same as itself. Only because it is projected toward a future wholly and radically other than itself is it possible for time to be that radical, heart-breaking, life-shattering turn which it is. Eternity is the crisis which happens to time in time, as the radical rupture which is constitutive of it.

Temporality, we might then say, has the same structure as wonder and dread. Or, rather, wonder and dread, which enable us to know the unknown as unknown, are themselves possible only because our temporality is not closed in upon itself but is always already broken open by an eternity which it can never contain. Just as there could be no wonder or dread if the unknown were wholly unknown or wholly known, so there could be no throe of temporality if eternity were separate from time or if time were self-contained and self-constituted. The transcendent is not separate and detached from what it transcends but, rather, is immanent within it as the disruption of it.

We might say then that eternity is always already happening to us—but it always happens as the irreparable disruption of the present by an unpresenceable future, never as an "eternal present." The "eternal present" is precisely our dream of time closed completely in upon itself and wholly insulated from any disrupting other. But were time closed in upon itself, its very temporality would be shut down; for there would be no other whose upsetting intervention into the present could make the throe of temporality possible. Such a time, a time without an other, would provide us the perfect escape from time as throe. In fleeing that throe, we really flee the disruption of time by eternity which is constitutive of it; we flee toward a "time" which, immune to disruption, would be nothing but the present forever. The alternative to such flight is to fully enter into time, without holding anything in reserve. And to enter fully into time's temporalizing throe means to suffer that radical rupture by virtue of which eternity creates time by irreparably upsetting the present.

But how then is eternity in itself to be conceived, if we are not to think of it as unaltered presence? That question can never be answered except recursively[8] because, as the toward-which of the turn constitutive of our being, eternity is never accessible to us except as a rupturing, a shattering of what we have already understood. But as the toward-which of our radical turning it must be radically other than that from which we are turned when we are wrenched out of the present we never had by the throe of temporality. We conceive of that lost from-which as a serene and changeless perfection in comparison with which time as we know it, with its incessant motion, is thought of as a fallen condition. But if being is to be equated not with the from-which but with the toward-which of wonder, the real eternity, far from being such a changeless present, is precisely that which introduces crisis into time and prevents us from realizing our dream of imperturbable homeostasis. Whatever this real eternity is, it is that from which we flee when we turn away from the toward-which of time and back toward that motionless present we would like eternity to be. Eternity is precisely the mortally dangerous other we try to escape by returning to undefiled presence. We can know it only as that totally devastating danger.

But in knowing it as that, we also know that it can never promise or present to us an undefiled experience of presence. Whatever the eternal other is, it is not the One. Indeed, the disruption it causes is constitutive of radical difference. It is precisely the dream of oneness which is terminated when eternity intervenes into presence and thus creates temporality. If the turn from the from-which of wonder toward its toward-which is so radical as to be a death experience, it can only be because the terms of that turn are radically other than each other. One is the One, the other is the Other. The Other is the death of the One.[9]

Seen from the perspective of this distinction, an ascetic renunciation of the world and a gnostic spirituality of detachment and withdrawal, far from leading us toward the eternal other, point us in exactly the opposite direction. For if eternity creates the rupture which is constitutive of temporality, it is accessible to us in no other way except in and through time itself. To expose ourselves to this rupture requires an entirely different kind of asceticism from that which is practiced when one conceives of eternity as an eternal presence radically disconnected from time. Instead of encouraging us to sever our bond with time, such an asceticism would ask us to sever all the avoidances we employ to escape that bond; it would not inspire us to reject our vulnerabilities but to embrace them openheartedly; it would not promote indifference to temporality but an unrestrained, and for that reason heartbreaking, surrender to it. The hermeneutic of suspicion is right to suggest that the ascetic withdrawal from temporality is motivated by the desire to escape the experience of death one would have to undergo if one allowed oneself to be caught irrevocably in its throe. Far more demanding than any ascetic withdrawal from that throe is the willingness to suffer it. To be completely in time, to hold no part of oneself back from the rupture which is constitutive of it, to suffer its breach without employing any defense, to enter, without any hope of ever escaping it, the abyss from which all menaces announce themselves—this calls for a willingness to be vulnerable which, as the hermeneutic of suspicion rightly argues, differs profoundly from ascetic self-denial as traditionally conceived. But, if the foregoing account of time is true, it is precisely this willingness to fully enter into temporality which leads one to the eternal other. For eternity in its radical otherness is not that toward which we flee when we turn back from the turn of temporality but that from which we flee since it alone makes the radical turn of temporality happen. When we try to escape time we are in fact trying to avoid the eternity which makes time disruptive. Surrendering to time, while it may seem like losing eternity, is in fact our only access to it. Because the eternal other is that which sets the throe of dying in motion, we reach it only in and through our deaths. The God who would protect us from that abyss, whose timeless present would offer us a refuge from its nothingness, is precisely the God who does not exist. The death of that kind of God is the return, the rebirth, of the Eternal in its genuine otherness.

That other, though it is the toward-which of temporality itself, is not all the time the focus of our (temporally constituted) intentionality. Indeed, it cannot become accessible to us unless and until the breach constitutive of the turn of temporality is thematized. For it is only, so to speak, at the very breaking point of time, at the very crux of its fracture, that the other which creates the fracture can be experienced. The fracture itself is our only opening to eternity. Or, to put it in terms of the experiences which have preoccupied us throughout these reflections, the fracture which is implicit in wonder becomes explicit in horror; but it is only when we follow horror all the way into the abyss of anguish that the eternity which is always the toward-which of time becomes open to us. A spirituality grounded in this ontology could therefore lead us up to the eternal other only by helping us find our way down into time—all the way down to the mortal anguish at the bottom of it.[10]

TIME'S OTHER

The radical successors of the Enlightenment, from Nietzsche to Derrida, thought they could be faithful to the wisest of their predecessors only by taking one step beyond them in the direction of disbelief. Those of us who think of ourselves as the practitioners of radical hermeneutics tend to think that belief in an eternal order and an eternal other is a symptom of a regressive recoil from our unimaginable future. Consequently, we tend to think that the further we advance into that future, the further behind we will leave the whole religious way of configuring our lives and thought. That questions about God continue to recur, in spite of the post-modernist's wish that people would just stop talking about the topic,[11] that we seem unable to extricate ourselves finally and decisively from the very systems of belief against which we have directed our deconstructive energies, only reveals, we think, how deep a hold the past has on the future. This can lead us to believe that one last step, or one final leap, still has to be made before the ultimately decisive break with the religious point of view can occur.[12]

But the more radical a leap we make, the more irrevocable our break with the past, the deeper will be our experience of death, and the more we will surrender ourselves to that future which creates the throe of temporality by fracturing time itself. No matter how completely philosophy tries to transcend its past, it will never be able to take a step that will lead it beyond that eternal other which is constitutive of the future in its very difference from the present.

Every leap into the future leads *to* that other, not *away* from it. It is, in fact, only its intervention that creates a gap, a fissure, an abyss, in time and so makes a leap into the future possible. All the time we have thought of that other as the from-which we were leaving behind, it has been the toward-which whose upsetting disruption of the present is constitutive of our temporality. The fact that there is no way to step out of time, the fact that its throe is inescapable, leads one to suspect that eternity is no more than the impossible dream of a presence that has never been and can never be. But the inescapability of time means exactly the opposite: its abyss has no bottom precisely because the other toward which it projects us will never arrive as a present. The inescapable throe of temporality makes eternity accessible to us. It is and will always be the death of us.

I have said that there would be no abyss for us to leap if eternity did not create in time the irreparable fracture constitutive of temporality itself. But I do not mean to imply that we gain access to eternity by leaping *across* that abyss and getting to the other side of it. That would be to conceive of eternity as another present and thus to deprive it of that very otherness which makes it deconstructive of presence. We do not get to the future by jumping across the little separation which exists between now and it. Death is not a gap to be traversed. One does not reach eternity by finding a way to leap *over* the abyss of death but only by leaping *into* it without holding on or hoping to get out. It is only by entering into one's death, not by getting through and past it, that one gains access to that otherness which makes dying possible.

The deepest of all metaphysical ironies is that for us whose very being is constituted by the throe of temporality, to be fully ourselves and thus fully alive, we must be fully engaged in dying. In holding ourselves back from it, in clinging to presence, in dreaming a metaphysics of oneness, we aspire to a life protected from all mortal vicissitudes. But such a life, for a being whose very being is constituted by turning, would be death, precisely because it would make dying impossible. By making us die, eternity brings time to life. And if this will always be true, if philosophy will never be able to take a step that leads beyond this truth, it is not because it is a timeless verity but because every step philosophy takes into time will bring it under the sway of that other which makes every step possible by being the future. Time is the wound by which eternity afflicts us. We experience eternity not by healing this wound but by keeping it open and suffering it.

CHAPTER 8

In the Throe of the Absolute Other

Here in the final chapter of these explorations I would like to explicitly address the issue which the throe of wonder and horror finally lead us to raise if we do not try to reverse their momentum or inhibit the process of thinking which they naturally set in motion: the question regarding the existence of the absolute Other. This question lies at the very center of our onto-theological tradition and, for that reason, it is very difficult even to ask it in a way that does not commit one to a conceptual framework which the hermeneutic of deconstruction has rendered suspect. But the fact that the traditional way of raising and answering the question of God's existence was hermeneutically naive is not, in my judgment, a sufficient reason for dismissing the question itself as unintelligent. To take the hermeneutical imperative seriously does not necessitate rejecting the questions inherited from the metaphysical tradition; it requires recasting them in a way that liberates their deepest meaning by freeing them from the hermeneutically inadequate framework which shaped our traditional understanding of them. My purpose here, hesitant as I am to attempt it, is to try to recast the question of God in just this way.[1]

Consequently, with regard to the traditional arguments for and against God's existence, my purpose will be to discover whether there is a deeper meaning in them which the traditional way of formulating them does not bring to the surface. Ordinarily no such excavation of deeper meaning is considered necessary because the arguments themselves are thought to present us with all the relevant issues in a clear and direct way. Once we conceive of the question of God's existence as an issue to be resolved through rational demonstrations, we tend to focus our attention exclusively on the vicissitudes of particular proofs. In such a context, the way to be fully reasonable about the question is to become expert in philosophical argumentation, and to objectively assess the logical merits of each chain of reasoning. But this whole process of rational argumentation tends to overlook or ignore the deeply personal bearing which the question of God's existence has on the life of the persons who ask it. Both Kierkegaard and Freud, opposed as they were on the issue itself, understood the crucial importance of this deeper meaning and, as a consequence, viewed belief in God as a matter of the heart which has little or nothing to do with the purportedly rational arguments devised by metaphysicians and logicians. Freud wanted to replace what he thought were philosophy's groundless speculations with a scientific explanation of the motives which lead the heart to embrace its most consoling illusions.[2] Kierkegaard enjoined us to be suspicious of the entire project of rational theology because, in his view, it transforms what ought to be a matter of the heart, an existential decision, into a merely intellectual exercise.[3] No profound commerce exists, according to either of these thinkers, between the rationality of the philosopher and the deep religious passions which animate the believer.

But in the process of criticizing philosophical theology, as traditionally practiced, and emphasizing the primacy of the heart in religious belief, Kierkegaard and Freud actually reinforced the very divorce between reason and the heart which is characteristic of rational theology and the philosophical tradition. Their critique, in fact, has made the differences between these estranged principles of the self seem unreconcilable. But must the philosophical mind and the passionate heart necessarily work at cross-purposes, as both the critics and practitioners of rational theology often presuppose? The heart, Pascal said, has reasons which reason cannot understand. But perhaps we cause reason to be incompetent in such matters by artificially limiting it to the specific set of rational operations used in arguing the logical merit of objective proofs. Perhaps intelligence, when released from such narrow confinement, can actually help us appreciate and articulate the insights hidden in our feelings, and find in them the repressed import of its own bloodless propositions. And, on the other hand, while it may be true, as Freud and Kierkegaard imply, that one becomes a religious believer or disbeliever not as a result of rational arguments but only as a result of a change of heart, there is no reason to think that a change of heart has to be unreasonable. Indeed, perhaps it is our narrow conception of reason, and our artificial dichotomy between reason and the heart, which prevent our appreciating the profound role which insight and rationality can play in a conversion which happens in the very core of our being.

It is precisely this narrow concept of reason which our phenomenological reflections on knowing have led us to question. These reflections suggest that to be reasonable does not only mean to be logically consistent, to be rigorous in argumentation, or to conform to the canons of scientific method in any of its many guises. For prior to all argumentation and presupposed by all method are the experiences of wonder and horror which awaken questioning and provoke the whole process of inquiry. Rationality itself originates in these prior experiences, although all we gain knowledge of, in and through them, is the unknown itself. From this perspective, taking up the question of God's existence in a fully rational way does not only involve evaluating arguments; it requires retrieving the original experience of wonder or horror out of which the question originally emerges. Although this question has been inherited from our tradition, a retrieval of it in its original form is not to be achieved by a return to the past, not even by a return to that point in the past when it was originally asked. For the only way to inherit a question is, paradoxically, to raise it anew, and one cannot raise it anew by going back to any previous versions of it but only by subjecting the whole past history of the question to the future that becomes accessible to us by asking it. The only appropriate way for us to inherit a question is to let it lead us into the territory not yet explored by the tradition which left it to us. Only then does it become questionable in a way that has never occured before, so that, instead of being our past, it becomes the unknown future into whose throe we are drawn by our very being as questioners.

On the other hand, the ordinary way of continuing the traditional debate about God's existence allows us to take the question for granted by concentrating on the various arguments that can be used to support different answers to it. Such a procedure, however sophisticated the reasoning employed by it, tends to leave unthematized the profound personal experience which generates the issue and gives it its gravity. By treating the question as a given—as a question which has already been asked, and therefore does not need to be asked again but only answered, philosophy fails to appreciate its deepest meaning. For when we use reason to answer a question without first surrendering to the throe which inspires it, we artifically separate the process of reasoning from its own source, and thus make Kierkegaard's suspicion of its abstractness justifiable. But to return to the source of reasoning, to immerse ourselves in that font from which questions spring, does not at all require, as Kierkegaard sometimes implied, leaving our reason behind. To discontinue philosophizing about the question of God on the grounds that rational inquiry is irrelevant to those deeply personal feelings which affect our response to it would be warranted only if it could be demonstrated that the heart itself is never seized by wonder or horror, is never affected by a devastating question, is never filled with a longing for insight. That this is not the case is proven by the fact that we are never more upset, never more deeply troubled, than when someone finds a way to express, in words we can understand with our reason, the very things we have kept locked away in our hearts, on the pretext that reason is not able to comprehend them. Perhaps we want to believe that reason cannot understand the heart because we have an inkling of how overwhelming it would be to break the heart open and acknowledge the truths we have secreted away in it.

To create a dialogue between reason and the heart by raising heartbreaking questions seems to me to be one way to describe the special vocation of philosophy. To philosophize in this manner about the question of God's existence means trying to let that question emerge in its original awfulness, instead of either dismissing it or taking it for granted. This is my purpose in this chapter.

THE OBJECTIVIST FRAMEWORK OF THE TRADITIONAL ARGUMENT

The arguments for God's existence typically begin with the familiar things of this world, whose existence we ordinarily presuppose and leave unquestioned.[4] The arguments point out that the existence of these familiar things needs to be accounted for, since nothing can be the cause of itself. Then arguments are advanced which try to prove that, if we explain the things which exist now as effects of things which existed previously—our customary causal reasoning—we will really only be multiplying the number of things whose existence remains ultimately unexplained. No ultimate explanation for the existence of all the things that exist and have existed can be provided except by affirming a being whose existence did not have to be caused by a being other than itself. This being exists "outside" the whole ensemble of caused beings, and is the uncaused cause of all of them. Because it is not like any other being, special ways of thinking and speaking about it have to be devised if we are not to make the mistake of treating it like one of the beings with which we are familiar.

Prescinding from the merits or flaws of this argument, I would like to consider the underlying perspective in terms of which it and its many variations are typically formed. While the argument begins by calling our attention to the fact that the existence of the familiar things which occupy our world cannot be taken for granted, it does not in any way challenge our ordinary conception of the world as a collection of objects. Indeed, the persuasive force of the argument entirely depends on our accepting the unquestionable reality of the world as it is ordinarily conceived since, without it, there would be no need to inquire about its cause. Although the argument concludes by affirming that all effects depend on God as their uncaused cause, it makes our knowledge of this cause dependent on and derivative from our knowledge of its effects. In that sense, the world of objects constitutes the arche on which the entire edifice of natural theology is ordinarily built.

This world of objects, though it functions here as the basis for what can become an extremely sophisticated philosophical argument, is the familiar, everyday world of common sense. We need no special intellectual training, no theoretical expertise, to familiarize ourselves with the objects that belong to it, for they are directly accessible to our observation. Or, rather, their direct accessibility is presupposed both by the argument and by common sense itself. That objects are given, and that we accept them as real because they are given, is the given on the basis of which our ordinary sense of the world is developed. And while science may radically transform our sense of what these objects are so that our common sense no longer recognizes them, the scientific description of them is itself ordinarily considered an improvement on common sense because of the fact that it seems to give us a more accurate knowledge of objects or a more effective way to handle them. In this sense, science and common sense, as ordinarily understood and practiced, share a common horizon within the context of which the differences between them can emerge without becoming fundamental. The specialized objects of science, as ordinarily understood, do not differ in their essential character as objects from the familiar things which populate our everyday world.

What *is* the essential character of these objects which are the foci of both science and common sense? One crucial feature of them is that they are always thought of as existing outside of us in the real, objective world. We are able to study objects objectively precisely because they are already out there for us, waiting to be known. It is true, of course, that ordinarily we are too busy using these things to be objective observers of them; indeed, in our ordinary commerce with them, we are too busy using them (or dealing with the problems they pose) to even conceive of them as objects. Objects only become objects for us when we interrupt our practical projects long enough to look at them as things which exist apart from us. But even though the practical person may not take time to look at trees, no practical person doubts that they are there, that wood must be a tree before it can be lumber, and that trees can be cut down only because they are always already out there in their givenness before we decide to use them. What makes an object an object is precisely the fact that it is objectively out there and, as such, can be the terminus of a look we direct toward it, whether such looking is taken literally or figuratively. The object qua object is conceived of as lying outside the knower, as being out there in the world; and knowing, in order to be objective, is supposed to correspond to and be in conformity with it.

Now if it is the very nature of objects to be out there, if what we mean by an object is that which is to be known by taking a look, and if the givenness of objects is the unquestioned presupposition of both science and common sense as ordinarily understood, why are we ever prompted to ask for an explanation of their existence? If objects are given, why do we not simply accept them in their givenness as givens, rather than asking why they are? Why, in short, does the "why" spring to our lips?[5] We wonder why things exist only because we are aware of the fact that they *could* not exist. They are, in fact, right here now in front of us, but they do not have to be; they are present but the fact that they are present does not exclude the possibility of their absence, and this possibility of not being is real enough to make it necessary for us to seek an explanation of why they are.

Given the context of objectivity in which it occurs, this quest for an explanation of the existence of objects tends to take the form of a search for another object which is capable of functioning as an explanatory principle of the given. But any object which we might posit as an explanatory principle would itself be in need of an explanation if it too suffered from the same possibility of not being present which afflicts the objects with which we are already familiar. Therefore, we have to keep looking for an explanation until we find some object that does not need to be explained; and the only object that does not need to be explained is an object that cannot possibly be absent, an object that is pure presence itself. Any other kind of object would only renew the need for an explanation instead of providing one. Only a being that is completely coincident with itself, completely identical with its own presence, possesses such unconditional givenness that its existence is not open to question and therefore not in need of explanation. Though it may not be spoken of as *an* object or *a* being, this is not because it lacks objectivity but because it is seen as *the* principle of presence, as the ultimately real object, the one which constitutes the ground of objectivity itself. Not only is it "out there," distinct from and external to our knowing minds; it is the object which cannot not be out there because its very essence is to be there, in its consummate, uncaused presence. It is the sustaining arche on which the reality of the given in its entirety depends. Without it, in its pure presence, there would be no given, no being distinct from and external to us, and therefore, if we equate being with presence, no being at all.

This way of restating the traditional argument for God's existence brings into the foreground the metaphysics of presence and the objectivist epistemology which tends to influence our understanding of it.[6] As so stated, the argument does not require that we hold a literal, pre-philosophical picture of God as being "out there" in a physical sense. But it does presuppose a theory of knowledge according to which the ideas in the mind are supposed to be conform to the given objects which exist outside it. The search for objective knowledge as traditionally understood rests on this presupposition that objects are given to the knower, and constitute the criterion by reference to which our ideas are to be judged. The arguments for God's existence are ordinarily developed within the framework of this project, but, at the same time, they stabilize it by providing it an immovable ground. For the supreme being whose existence they prove is the principle of presence itself, thematized and objectified as an ultimate given which is "out there" prior to our thought of it, and which cannot not exist.

Now this means that it is possible to undermine the argument not just be detecting deficiencies in its chain of reasoning, but also by calling into question the entire project of objectivity itself on which it depends. Hume, who suggested the possibility of such a challenge, Kant, who explicitly formulated it, and Heidegger, who fully radicalized it, all rejected the traditional arguments for God's existence not so much because of any particular demerits to be found in them but because they presupposed the very framework of objectivity which these thinkers were moving to deconstruct. In this book, I have been arguing, in large part under their influence, that the nature of wonder itself requires us to deconstruct the metaphysics of presence and the understanding of objectivity which is inextricably bound up with it. But this metaphysics cannot be challenged and rejected without undermining the affirmation of God which has been traditionally couched in its terms. In fact, if Nietzsche's diagnosis of it is right, belief in God has not just been influenced by the metaphysics of presence but has played a crucial role in sustaining it because a God who is presence itself provides that metaphysics an unshakable foundation. This is one reason why those trying to undermine presence have tended to think that deconstructing belief in God is an indispensable part of their project.

In these pages I have argued that our very experience as wonderers necessitates our calling the equation of being with presence into question. While the traditional argument for God seems to lead us back from the immediately given to the ultimately given whose being needs no explanation because it is presence itself, wonder leads us in exactly the opposite direction—not back to an original presence but ahead toward what is not given, not present, what is not even presenceable. If we yield to its throe it will lead us in the end to radically rethink our understanding of being itself. What is the religious significance of this reversal of direction? And what does it bode for the question of God? Granting the fact that it would turn us away from God understood as pure presence, toward what would it turn us? Might this turn, though it seems at first to turn us *away* from the ultimately sacred, actually turn us *toward* it?

WONDER AS THE ORIGINAL CONVERSION

That this is not an entirely implausible possibility is indicated by the fact that, in the religious literature of every culture and every historical period, the process of discovering God, or more generally, the ultimately sacred, is itself depicted as a radical reversal which turns one's whole life upside down.[7] Whether one studies the initiation rites of so-called primitive cultures, the conversion stories of Christian saints, or the ascetic practices of the mystics, the process of becoming attuned to the ultimately sacred is described as a revolutionary personal transformation. The change of heart which one must undergo to reach such rapport is said to leave no part of one's old life intact. That is why it is invariably compared with dying, with the actual ending of one's life; for without this death, no new beginning is possible.

Now this is precisely the kind of reversal, the kind of radical shift in the whole direction of one's thinking and living which the argument for God's existence, as traditionally formulated, does not require us to make. Not only can we intellectually understand the argument and even be persuaded by it without being existentially affected by it; we can also be persuaded by it without having it disturb in any fundamental way the principles which ordinarily govern our thinking. Far from inviting us to radically transform our whole sense of being, the traditional argument appeals to our ordinary sense of being and, indeed, provides us a way to explain its most troubling aspects. For, as we have seen, what gives rise to the argument in the first place is the realization that what is present could be absent; and the whole purpose of the argument is to locate a presence which is exempt from this possibility. How then are we to interpret it except as a remedy designed to close up the breaches we find in the given so as to make the world of the given a total, airtight system? The traditional argument for God's exis- tence has the (not consciously intended) effect of providing our ordinary understanding of the world with precisely the kind of immovable foundation which it needs to have if it is to be perfectly secure from the possibility of being undermined. As the argument itself makes clear, this is a kind of security which ordinary beings themselves are not able to provide us because their presence is liable to absence. But by assuring us that there exists a being which is presence itself, the argument helps put to rest any insecurity which we may have started to feel because of the frailty of the beings that are present to us. If we were to explore the depths of that frailty, we would be led to question our most basic ontological assumptions. But the traditional argument for God, instead of en- couraging that radically disruptive possibility, actually helps to seal us off from it by explaining the frailty of beings in terms of the very principle of presence which the fact of their frailty threatened to jeopardize. In that sense, the move from beings liable to absence to a being which is pure presence, far from requiring an irreparable rupture in our fundamental sense of being, is precisely a flight from such a rupture. And if by a conversion one means a reversal so radical that it is comparable only to dying itself, the move from the contingently present to the absolutely present points one in exactly the opposite direction—not into the throe of conversion but back away from it toward a security that promises to protect one from it.

On the other hand, a primal reversal in our whole sense of being can occur if we allow the full import of our frailty to emerge, instead of trying to secure ourselves against the danger it poses. But we cannot plumb the depths of our frailty simply by taking the possibility of absence more seriously than it is taken in traditional metaphysics. For however seriously one takes it, absence always means the lack of presence; even if it is understood as the negation of presence, it acquires its meaning from what it negates, and therefore leaves the latter intact as the arche on which the meaning of being is grounded. In this sense, absence still belongs to the system of presence, and taking it seriously does not jeopardize the traditional metaphysical equation of being and the given.

What does jeopardize that equation, as I have repeatedly argued, is the event of wonder. For while the experience of absence causes one to think of the absent object as lacking that fullness of being which we associate with what is present to us, wonder causes one to realize that the unknown is *more* than can ever be present to us, and thus leads us to treat what is present to us in the present as *less* real than the unknown in its transcendence. Because absence is negative only in the sense that it is the privation of presence, it leaves presence intact as the principle of being. But when wonder makes us aware of an unknown that cannot be known by being made present, it calls presence itself into question and raises the possibility that presence is not to be equated with being. The status of presence as metaphysical arche is jeopardized not by the negation of presence but by the possibility that presence is itself a negation, a lack. This is precisely the possibility to which wonder awakens us when it directs us away from the given and toward that which is accessible to us only in and through its throe. The event of wonder is the original conversion.

What we experience, in the throe of that conversion, is in a real sense the end of our (ordinary) world, for it undermines the whole world of objects in the midst of which we ordinarily locate ourselves. When we are in the grip of this simple, childlike experience, we know that what lies right out there now in front of us as the term of our ocular attention cannot be equated with itself because it gives rise to questions about itself and thus prevents our identifying it with what is given to us. That toward which wonder directs us is not an object *in* the world, but a world unto itself, and we discover it *as* a world not by observing it but only by surrendering to the throe of wonder which gives us access to it.

But that the world of the other into which wonder beckons us is not accessible to us as an object present-at-hand, and in that sense cannot be known "objectively," should not be construed to mean that to explore it we must suspend the exercise of rationality. On the contrary, what must be suspended and deconstructed is the metaphysics of presence and the ocular epistemology which causes us to equate rationality with objective observation and the study of something present-at-hand. To be intelligent does not mean to look at what is present but to ask questions about it, and to let those questions lead one toward that unknown other which is not accessible to us in any other way except through our intelligent exploration of them. To be rational we must be engaged in the whole process of asking the relevant questions, thinking through all the possible answers, and judging which of them best satisfies the exigencies of our desire to know; to be fully rational we must trust this whole process of inquiry, insight, and judgment so completely that we allow it, and it alone, to determine what we accept as being. It is only because we have grown so accustomed to identifying rationality with "objective" conformity to what is present-at-hand, that we think rejecting objectivity as so defined entails abolishing rationality. But, in fact, it is only by rejecting such objectivity that we release rationality from the obligation to approximate an intuition of what is present-at-hand, and thus allow it to become our way of access to the being of the other which is never present to us.

Anyone who has been stung by this eros of inquiry knows that it can be as transformative as the experience of love itself. Once one starts to question, one's life is never the same again. For there is literally nothing that must be accepted as it is in its givenness, nothing we cannot ask about, nothing which can justify its claim to be exempt from the scope of our questioning. Once wonder is allowed free rein, there is literally nothing that will remain what it was before we realized we could ask what it is. The process of questioning transforms the ordinary world of objects into a million universes none of which is given and all of which invite exploration. So upsetting is that explosion, so disorienting are the confusion and uncertainty it engenders, it is not surprising that we sometimes regret the loss of the world as it was before we became questioners. But it is only by letting that old world die that the world of any other, in its otherness, can be born. And is there anyone who has fallen in love who would not prefer the mortally upsetting world of the other to the everyday world which reduces the other to the status of being an observable object within it?

No matter which of the worlds opened up by wonder we happen to enter, no matter which other becomes the compelling focus of our fascination, we recognize in it a sacral importance which no mere object *within* the ordinary world can ever possess. Between the other seen as an object within the ordinary world and the other recognized as the radiating center of its own world, there is an absolute incommensurability, an irreconcilable difference, as radical as that which distinguishes the profane from the sacred, the trivial from the important, the merely apparent from being itself. To discover the world of the other is already a metaphysical conversion which revolutionizes one's whole sense of being, for it undermines the ordinary equation of being with objects present-at-hand. It is precisely the being of these objects which we cannot take seriously, once wonder awakens in us a passion to know that other which, under the sway of wonder, we begin to think of as being itself. If by becoming religious one means awakening to the sacred as a reality which deserves to be treated as radically other than, and more significant than, the things we ordinarily experience, as we ordinarily experience them, then we become religious only when we cease using as our criterion of what is real that sense of the present-at-hand which governs us in our ordinary world. A religious conversion cannot be brought about by a philosophical argument that proves the existence of a being which epitomizes the present-at-hand because such an argument belongs inside the very metaphysics of objectivity which is irreparably undermined by an awakening to the reality of the sacred. To take the sacred in its otherness from the profane seriously means precisely to recognize that it, and not the present-at-hand, is constitutive of being.

In short, the primal religious experience does not consist in our adding another being (even if it is the paradigmatic being) to those we already accept as present-at-hand. It consists in an undermining of the principle of presence itself, and an awakening to the reality of an unpresenceable other. By virtue of such an awakening, nothing any longer seems ordinary. For, viewed in the light shed by the radiating brilliance of the other which has become the centrifugal principle of one's universe, even the most mundane objects can become amazing, and so cease to be mere objects. By entering the world of the other, we do not close ourselves off from all others but put ourselves in a position where they can be discovered for the first time. Our discovery of the other makes it possible for the universe as a whole to astonish us in so profound a way that we are never again able to equate anything in it with the given in its mere givenness.

NOTHINGNESS AND ITS DIFFERENCE FROM ABSENCE

I have tried to contrast the world as ordinarily conceived, the world as an ensemble of objects present-at-hand, with the world of the other in its otherness as it becomes accessible to us through wonder and the eros of exploration it sets in motion. As we have seen, these worlds are so radically different that the shift from one to the other is not a smooth transition but precisely the kind of revolutionary recentering of one's life which is characteristic of religious conversion. Given the radical character of such a transformation, it is understandable that those who have undergone it view their life, as they lived it before, as a kind of death, and their life, as they live it now, as comparable to being born anew.[8] The last thing they would ever want to do is go back. Indeed, I do not think it is an exaggeration to say that, once we have discovered an other and allowed it to become the centrifugal and centripetal center of our world, we cannot bear the thought of something happening that would cause the loss of it. The sacred other is that which, once found, it would be the death of us to lose. That is why we would do almost anything to make it impregnable, inviolable, impervious to every possible threat of deconstruction. For just as the other, in its otherness, is radically different from an object present-at-hand, so the mortal loss of the other, its ceasing to be, is radically different from the absence of something that was once present. It is this radical difference I would now like to explore.

The loss of an object whose being is understood in terms of its being present and thus directly accessible to my ocular or intellectual gaze can only be understood in terms of absence. When someone whom I did not know (except as a being once present-at-hand) "passes away," I know that the corpse which is present for my viewing at the funeral home is no longer the one who died. It is nothing but her "remains," what is left of her since her "departure." All I can say about the departed, as I gaze at her corpse, is that she is not here now in front of me, nor is she in any of the other places occupiable by objects whose being consists in being present-at-hand to some viewer. She is utterly absent from the universe of objects, and therefore is not anymore (since being is defined in terms of presence). The corpse has taken over the place she has vacated. And with regard to the occurrence of death itself, the objective point of view understands it as a biological event which medical science can more or less factually explain. Such an explanation must focus, of course, on the causes of death that can be objectively studied, not on the absence itself, since what is absent, precisely insofar as it is absent, is not accessible to objective scrutiny. Because absence itself cannot be studied, even though it is, from the objective point of view, constitutive of death, it inevitably disappears from the objective account of what has happened. In this way, death comes to be equated with the biological details which are objectively accessible and thus becomes completely indistinguishable from any other event that occurs in the world.

Now, as Heidegger has explained, while death may be indistinguishable from any other event for the objective observer, it is certainly not just another event for the person who dies.[9] For her, death is not something that happens *in* the world but something that happens *to* her world. And something similar would have to be said for the person whose life is centered on the one who is dying because she has come to mean the world to him and so, for him, her death is no objective event but rather the end of his world as a whole. For the person who is dying and for the person who loves her, death cannot be understood as an event occurring within any kind of wider context, for such an interpretation would presuppose that the wider context is going to remain fundamentally undisturbed. But what the dying person faces, and her beloved with her, is precisely the discontinuation of the wider context and the impossibility of going on at all.

How, then, are we to articulate and evaluate the radical difference between these two ways of interpreting death, one of which treats it as an ontic event, the other as a shattering of the world as a whole? To lose an object that once was present within one's world is to experience absence; but to lose the other which constituted the center of one's world as a whole is to experience nothingness. *Nothingness is as different from absence as being is different from presence.* Just as being becomes accessible to us only because wonder draws us away from the present-at-hand toward an unknown other, so nothingness becomes accessible to us only through those intimations of horror from which we would like to recoil because they expose us to the horrifying possibility of losing what has come to mean the world to us. Nothingness to no mere absence because it is not the loss of an object that was merely present. It does not remove an object; it deconstructs a world. For that reason it is not experienceable by, and will not be understandable to, someone for whom nothing matters ultimately, someone whose life is not centered on any being—someone who has no world to lose because he treats everything, even himself, as something merely present-at-hand.

The fact that nothingness is not an object, and is therefore not accessible to the kind of objective inquiry we associate with science, might lead us to conclude that it is only meaningful to use the term to describe a subjective emotional experience. But that conclusion would be justifiable only if being were equatable with the present-at-hand, nothingness with absence, and knowing with (physically or intellectually) looking at things. But I have tried to suggest throughout this book that we cling to this metaphysic of presence and ocular epistemology precisely for the purpose of avoiding the upsetting import of our deepest intimations. Once we adopt such a metaphysic, we can justify our avoidance by dismissing the experiences which generate these intimations as merely subjective and emotive. We would like to think that the joy and the anguish secreted away in our hearts have no truths to teach us, no knowledge of reality to convey to us. Technical philosophy, we tend to think, is no place for expressing those heartfelt realizations which might mean the world to us personally but have doubtful value when introduced into an intellectual discussion which is supposed to be governed by objective standards of argument and proof. But how rational is the objectivity philosophy achieves, how profound are the insights it generates, if its objectivity is purchased by repressing intimations? To be fully rational we must take such intimations seriously, and explore them even when we are most desperate to hide from what they portend; we must ask the questions which our intimations evoke, even when these questions upset the presumptions we hold most dear; we must consider every possible answer to these questions, even those which run counter to everything we have ever thought to be true; and we must make the best judgment we can about the possible answers, even if it means radically revising our most fundamental convictions about reality. We dismiss our most upsetting intimations precisely because we do not want this whole ordeal of radical inquiry to be set in motion.

The feeling of dread which insinuates itself into the heart, the sense of emptiness which creates a hole in the pit of one's stomach—these are no merely "subjective" experiences, even though it is impossible to locate an object present-at-hand in our world which causes them. Nothingness cannot be known "objectively" because all such knowing focuses on objects within the world, and an intimation of nothingness is brought on only when one's world as a whole (not any object within it) is in jeopardy. This means that we cannot become familiar with nothingness by studying it as an objective observer but only by personally participating in an experience of it. Such an experience has overwhelming emotional reverberations precisely because it affects us wholly, precisely because it is our suffering the end of our world. But that does not make it any less a knowing, if by knowing we mean first and primarily our awakening to the unknown, and our discovery of it as unknown to us. It does mean that we know nothingness only by opening ourselves to it and in that sense participating in it, rather than by trying to be "objective" about it. On the other hand, such participation—which must inevitably take the form of suffering, of being devastated—would not be participation in, receptivity to, the unknown if it did not include the willingness to let the unknown become known through the (in this case horrifying) process of asking questions and thinking about it. We fully suffer the end of

our world, instead of avoiding it, only if we thoughtfully explore
the dreadful intimations it evokes in us, even though they lead us
straight down to our nothingness. For those willing to do this,
dying itself becomes a way of knowing, and suffering a way of
inquiry. To allow nothingness to cut all the way through to the core
of one's being as a subject—this, surely, is no "subjective emo-
tionalizing" but rather the ultimate surrender of the self to a truth
that cannot be known objectively because it deprives the knower of
that secure position in the world which objectivity presupposes.

The nothingness which becomes accessible through such an
experience differs radically from the mere absence of an object
once present-at-hand because, unlike the latter, it cannot be integrated into one's world. Whereas absence is understandable as and
reducible to a privation of presence, and therefore does not prompt
us to call the universe constituted by presence into question, nothingness undermines what means the world to us and thus deprives
us of any context into which our experience of it might otherwise
have been integrated. As the absolutely unimaginable other, nothingness spells the end of all possible worlds—for there is no world
which can integrate within itself the possibility of its own deconstruction.

The discovery of nothingness, therefore, and the realization
that our world is liable to it, no matter what it is centered on, is an
entirely different matter from an objective recognition of an object's absence. The traditional argument for God's existence points
to contingency understood as absence for the purpose of convincing us that a being incapable of absence exists; but, as it is ordinarily understood, it leaves our ordinary sense of being as presence undisturbed, and is therefore incapable of giving even the
person persuaded by it the kind of revolutionary insight that would
transform one's understanding of reality as a whole, as religious
conversion requires. On the other hand, the experience of nothingness as not integratable into any world evokes in the one who is
open to it precisely that radical sense of contingency and fragility,
that devastating sense of an irreparable and mortal liability, which
the traditional argument, for all its discussion of contingency, fails
to provoke. If contingency is taken as seriously as the experience of
nothingness requires, it undermines the secure world we think we
belong to when we think in objectivist terms.

We cannot know, when we first respond to our intimations of nothingness, what insights they might lead us to—only that they must be devastating because they will require us to suffer with an open mind the end of our world. For someone who has entered the world of an other, and allowed that other to become the radiant center of his own life—for someone who is religious in the sense I have described above—the encounter with nothingness necessarily precipitates a religious crisis. For to realize that the other which I have come to recognize as inexhaustibly precious is caught irretrievably in the throe of nothingness, can only mean that nothingness is more ultimate than the other, and that all we will ever love is fated to be swallowed up in a nameless abyss. No being that wonder ever leads us to discover, no world we enter, however radiant its center, will be exempt from the liability to nothingness of which horror gives us an intimation. Nothingness, in this sense, is deeper than being, horror deeper than wonder, the loss of life deeper than the celebration of it. The end of all worlds is more ultimate than the genesis of any of them. Whatever might begin again from nothingness would still be liable to it and unable to contain it. We would like to think, in the face of nothingness, that life goes on, but this would be true only if being were presence and nothingness a mere absence. Life can go on as before only for those who lost what did not mean the world to them. On the other hand, what does the person have left who has lost what meant everything to him? Simply nothing, simply nothingness itself. There is no being on this side of nothingness that can hold out against it. All the beings toward which wonder draws us are themselves drawn irretrievably toward nothingness. Is nothingness itself, then, the final, ultimate, most radical other? This question can be answered only if nothingness can be known, and nothingness can be known only if we follow our most devastating intimations of it. Toward what truths can we be brought by that dreadful exploration? To what insights are we opened by the eros of suffering?

RADICAL CONVERSION

There are any number of possible responses to the intrusion of nothingness into our world, anger, resentment, and depression among them. It is tempting to think that the diversity of human response to this experience is the consequence of differences in temperment, background, and character, in which case it would be a mistake to think that any one feeling is more appropriate than any other. But such a view presupposes that feelings are the products of causal forces and denies their intentional character. That this view is inaccurate is suggested by the very fact that when we express our feelings we do so by articulating a judgment[10] because only such a judgment adequately says what we feel. That I curse my flat tire, that only a curse expresses my feeling, proves that I am not merely venting an unintelligible emotive energy—for any gutteral utterance would suffice if that were my purpose. The curse does not attach a meaning to a feeling but renders articulate the meaning already implicit in it; it makes explicit the judgment I have already made about what has happened to me, even if that judgment was made without my thinking it out before I rendered it. I become angry because I have already decided that the flat tire ought not to have interfered with my plans.

Now if it is true that feelings are inseparable from judgments, then it may be that they are more or less appropriate, depending on the appropriateness of the judgments which underlie them. That there are widely different responses to the experience of nothingness does not mean that they are all equally appropriate responses to that experience or to what becomes accessible to us through it. Indeed, all of the feelings I mentioned above—anger, resentment, and depression—are grounded in a fundamental recoil from nothingness as from a possibility to which I ought not be liable. Whether any of them are ultimately appropriate depends, therefore, on whether I can justify the claim that I deserve such a metaphysical exemption. Is such a claim defensible?

That, in fact, I *am* liable to nothingness is the realization which is presupposed by the various ways of recoiling from it. I would not have the impulse to recoil from this realization if it did not evoke in me a sense of horrified surprise. That I am liable to nothingness is the last thing I would have ever expected. For ordinarily, I think of myself as a being whose being can be taken for granted. Such a presumption becomes understandable when we remember that, ordinarily, we think of being in terms of presence, and nothingness in terms of absence. For I am the one being whose absence I can never experience; my presence is, in fact, the precondition for the possibility of anything being present, and in that sense is the foundation without which nothing could exist as presence. This is why, in the metaphysics of presence, the existence of the I cannot be doubted without the doubt being undermined by the very performance of it.[11] The "I" which functions as the reference point of presence is, by virtue of that very status, more fundamental than any being which comes into presence by reference to it. That which is presenced always defers to that which presences—even if what is presenced is a being which is supposed to be identical with presence itself. In a metaphysics of presence, God can only be the ultimate being that is presenced and, as such, lacks that ultimacy which belongs to the I itself as the principle of presencing. When the hermeneutical presuppositions underlying the metaphysics of presence are exposed, the I turns out to be the primary being who anchors the whole system, including the God who is present within it.

If, then, I recoil from the realization that I am liable to nothingness, it is because this liability radically calls into question the indubitable givenness of the I itself. When wonder leads me into the world of the other, and I orient myself by reference to her, the status of the I is jeopardized but not necessarily undermined in a radical way. For even when I make the world of the other my own so that she becomes the central reality to me, I may still not have entered *her* world but only made her the focus of mine. Even when my life is centered on the other, it can continue to be oriented in terms of my self. The primacy of the self is radically called into question not by my discovering the other, or my making the other my center, but by my having to *give up* the other and *not* have her as my center. For having to give up what means the world to me leads me explicitly and directly to an experience of nothingness.

That I who have always been in the position of being the very principle of presence, and whose absence is therefore inconceivable, can nevertheless not be—this is no mere fact to be added to what I already know about my self. For my self is not a being within my world but the principle constitutive of its very mineness. That I can not be means that I cannot be what I have always assumed I was: the very principle of presence and, therefore, being itself. Discovering my liability to nothingness shatters the fundamental presumption on which my world as a whole depends. Little wonder then that I recoil from it as if it were a horrific violation. But for me to be liable to nothingness would be a *violation* only if I deserved to be exempt from it. Which is inappropriate, my liability to nothingness, or my treating such a liability as a violation?

I would have to have an absolute right to being, indeed, I would have to deserve to be being itself, for my liability to nothingness to be an injustice. Is there anything that could possibly justify my claiming such a right? Or does my wishing to claim it reveal an underlying presumption concerning my own importance which I do not want to be exposed or challenged? The view that nothingness is an intruder trespassing into my world is not an innocent one; it is inspired by my underlying assumption that I deserve to be exempt from it. But the very fact that I am liable to nothingness makes that assumption indefensible. For I could only show that I deserve to be exempt from nothingness if I could demonstrate that there is something special about me that entitles me to be being itself. But the fact that I am liable to nothingness is itself the proof that there is nothing about me that can support my claim to this privileged status. I would be justified in treating nothingness as an intruder only if a liability to it were not intrinsic to me. I view nothingness as a trespasser only because I presume that I deserve to be being.

We can continue in this presumption only by repressing the truths which horror intimates to us. Were we to open ourselves to these intimations, instead of repressing them, they would radically undermine our very sense of ourselves as being. For it is not enough for me to say that I am a being which is liable to nothingness. When I acknowledge my relationship with nothingness in this way, my being retains its priority over it, my liability is relegated to the status of an adjectival phrase which does no more than modify the substance of the self. But if I am liable to not be, I cannot be being itself. And if I am but am not being itself, being must accrue to me. What, then, am I, in and of myself, apart from the being which accrues to me? Precisely not being, precisely not at all: precisely nothingness. Nothingness, then, is no intruder, no trespasser, no other. It is what I am, in and of myself.

But, if this is the case, then being itself is neither me nor mine; none of us who are liable to nothingness can be identical with it or the proprietor of it. Since, in and of ourselves, we are nothing, being itself must transcend us and be radically other than us. Underlying all our efforts to dissociate ourselves from nothingness and repress it is our desire to avoid the revolutionary acknowledgment of our identity with it, and the transcendent otherness of being itself. For such an acknowledgment requires us to relinquish that presumption of our own importance which, as we have seen, sustains our ordinary sense of ourselves. The conversion from this presumption to this acknowledgment is a turn than which none more radical can be conceived, for in making it we turn from assuming that we are being and deserve to be exempt from nothingness to realizing that, in and of ourselves, we are nothing and so do not deserve to be. To turn from the ultimate presumption (the equation of oneself with being) to an acknowledgment of one's ultimate destitution, to not just revise but reverse one's fundamental attitude toward being and nothingness, is to undergo a change that changes everything about everything. It is the total breach, the complete rupture, the definitive deconstruction. We cannot suffer it without being wrung with anguish.

But suffering that breach cannot be only anguish. For the acknowledgment of our nothingness, which wrings us with anguish, cannot occur without intimating to us that being itself is absolutely other than us and wholly transcends us. And we cannot receive an intimation of such otherness except in a state of awe that fills us simultaneously with reverent dread and holy joy: dread because the thought of its transcendent otherness is overwhelming, joy because we have an inkling that the reality to which we are awakening surpasses every sacred being we have ever known, and is transcendently lovable. Such an other, if it is real, is Otherness itself and the ultimate source of all our other intimations. For all the beings which wonder has enabled us to discover are analogues of it, since they are nothing in and of themselves; and all the intimations of nothingness which horror has given us come to fruition when we discover our poverty in relation to it. Wonder and horror can thus be viewed as anticipations of this speechless awe which is at the same time more upsetting than any other dread, and more joyful

than any other ec-stasis. In this sense, all of our experiences lead us
to intimations of being itself as the ultimately sacred, the absolute
Other.

AWE AS THE TOWARD-WHICH OF
WONDER AND HORROR

Such an intimation of the transcendent Other is not ordinarily our
first or only acquaintance with the experience of awe. We feel awe
whenever we are dumbstruck by something sublime in character—
whether it be an artistic masterpiece such as a Beethoven symphony or some magnificence in nature such as the Grand Tetons.[12]
On the surface such experiences do not seem to have the profound
ontological import which I have ascribed to awe in its most radical
form. And yet, whenever we encounter something sublime, its
grandeur evokes in us an awareness of our smallness, its majesty a
sense of our poverty. And so there is at work in such experiences,
even if it remains implicit and appears to have no lasting importance, an anticipation of, and perhaps in a small way a preparation
for, the kind of revolutionary transformation which radical awe
can initiate. Awe in the face of the sublime can become astonishment that being is the wholly Other; our awareness of our poverty
can become our confession that, in and of ourselves, we are nothing.

But whether its ontological import is consciously appreciated
or not, awe always exposes us, as do wonder and horror, to the
unknown in its very character as unknown and beyond us. If the
sublime were so far beyond us that we were incapable of being
aware of it, it would not be able to overwhelm us; if we could
understand it, it would by virtue of that very fact lack the superior
stature it must have to make us aware of our inferiority. Awe is
possible only because we can be aware of what is beyond us *as*
beyond us. In this regard it is similar to wonder and horror.

What, then, distinguishes awe from wonder if, as we have
claimed, the experience of wonder itself inspires us to make the
other our center, and to spend ourselves on it in a way that is
analogous to worship? Precisely because it has such a capacity to

provoke our awareness of the irreducible otherness of the other, wonder can lead us to think we have awakened to the absolute other itself. And to the degree that this is so, wonder does include awe within it, and can even be indistinguishable from it. Indeed, no profound distinction between wonder and awe can emerge as long as the beings which awaken wonder are experienced as, and identified with, being itself. For if we make that identification, we will worship what we love as ultimately sacred—until we begin to realize that it is liable to nothingness. The horror of that recognition drains the awe out of our wonder because it makes us realize that what we love is liable to nothingness, and that nothingness is, for that very reason, more ultimate and more devastating than it.

This realization turns us away from being entirely by making us face the nothingness to which all beings are liable, even the being which came to mean the world to us. Insofar as awe also includes an awareness of nothingness, it can be said to have something in common with horror, but the difference between them is profound and fundamental. For even when horror exposes us to nothingness, it allows us to keep on thinking of ourselves as beings who are superior to it. Awe, on the other hand, instead of allowing us to look down at nothingness from an elevated perspective, puts us in a radically inferior position and requires us to turn toward what is above us. But this implies that we cannot experience awe, in its fully differentiated form, until we are in that destitute condition to which horror itself leads us. We cannot experience awe fully until we are devastated by the loss of the being which wonder led us to love as being itself. For only in that loss do we experience the nothingness intrinsic to beings, and thus their absolute difference from being itself. In wonder that difference is effaced—and there is no way for it to emerge except by our giving up what means the world to us. But if we open ourselves wholeheartedly to it, the anguish of losing everything is itself the awful breakthrough to being itself.

Awe, in its fully differentiated form, is thus more profound than either wonder or horror. Like wonder, it gives us an intimation of being, but it radically differentiates being from beings and it does so by requiring of us a confession of our nothingness which even the experience of horror does not ask of us. Wonder inspires us, horror devastates us; but only awe can radically humble us. And while humility is the attitude toward oneself which is developed from a confession of one's nothingness, worship is the attitude toward the Other which develops from the affirmation of its transcendent Otherness. Humility and worship are conceived together in the crux of the conversion that turns on anguish and awe.

But while humility and worship begin to emerge in the experience of awe, that experience alone cannot sustain them or help them develop. For neither humility nor worship can mature until a conclusion is reached and a position taken on the question of whether the reality of the absolute Other should be affirmed. An intimation is not an affirmation, and should not be used as a substitute for one. While the experience of awe involves our feeling overwhelmed by a reality wholly Other than us, this in itself does not justify our immediately drawing the conclusion that this Other is real. For, in spite of the fact that nothing can have a more deconstructive impact on us, this experience, like the wonder and horror which are anticipations of it, does not terminate inquiry but initiates it. It is not supposed to take the place of careful thinking but to provoke it. If we are to take our awful intimations of the wholly Other seriously, we should not blindly prostrate ourselves before it but address as rigorously as we can the radical question it inspires us to raise: is the wholly Other real?

Certainly none of what awe opens up to us is real—if one equates the real with what is given, or with what is to be known through analogies to the given. If we try to determine the validity of awe by checking to see whether there is anything in the given that corresponds to its intimations, we will find no evidence that supports it. But no more than wonder or horror does awe pretend to be a copy of what is already available to us in a more direct way. To dismiss awe as an emotive episode lacking cognitional import, on the grounds that there is nothing present-at-hand corresponding to it, would require our dismissing wonder and horror as well, and our equating reality with whatever is directly given to us. But how can awe and horror and wonder be noncognitional when all the questions we ask, and all the inquiries we pursue, originate in the breakthrough to the unknown as unknown which they make possible? The intimations of awe are more revolutionary than those of wonder or horror because they do not just surprise or devastate us: they call upon us to humbly acknowledge our nothingness and to worship being itself as our radical Other. But we can dismiss its intimations, as we can dismiss those of wonder and horror, only by repressing our own intelligence and refusing to be questioners.

To be intelligent, then, requires us to be open to the possibility that being is our absolute Other and, as such, deserves our worship. But once we are open to the possibility of such an Other, intelligence moves us to ask the further question: should the reality of it be affirmed? This question, as it emerges within the context of radical awe, does not ask us to judge whether an object conceived of as pure presence is actually "out there." It asks us whether we should affirm as real, and as really Other than us, the transcendent Other which we do not find outside our experience of awe but only within its throe. Awe itself can do no more than expose us to the *possibility* of this transcendent Other; it is up to us to judge whether there are good reasons for affirming the reality of it.

I have tried to explain, in a previous chapter, why I think there are good reasons for affirming not just that our being is liable to nothingness but that, in and of ourselves, we are not being at all but rather nothing. Even with regard to our own being, we cannot rightfully claim to *be* it or to be the possessor of it; our own being is itself other than us. This, in my judgment, is the only way to state the ontological truth which is implicit in the deepest experience of anguish. But if, in and of ourselves, we are nothing, then "our" being must be derivative from a reality Other than us and Other than everything like us; for, otherwise, there could be no being at all. If beings which, in and of themselves, are nothing, nevertheless exist, they can do so only by virtue of an Other—indeed, only by virtue of an Other which, in and of itself, is being. For what can being mean for someone who, in and of himself, is nothing, if it does not mean to participate in some way in what is Other than himself? And how could such participation occur if the Other were not real? If the Other were not real, we could only be what we are in and of ourselves—which is nothing. If we exist, it is only as the derivatives of a reality radically other than us—being itself.

In my judgment, this is the conclusion to which we are led when we use reason to address the questions which emerge from anguish and the experience of awe to which it leads.[13] Only reason enables us to appreciate the reasons for making this judgment. But only the experience of anguish sets in motion the deeply personal question which requires this affirmation; and only awe provides the context in which its full import can be realized.

When the argument for the existence of the absolute Other is removed from this context, the meaning of its most important terms comes under the influence of the very ontological presumptions which anguish and awe upset. Contingency then tends to be reduced to the status of an attribute belonging to beings which are present-at-hand. The existence of beings continues to be taken for granted, even when the fact that they could not exist prompts the mind to ask for an explanation of them. And the search for an explanation, when undertaken in this context, presupposes the metaphysics implicit in ordinary thinking, instead of jeopardizing it. Consequently, even if such a search leads to an affirmation of transcendent being, that affirmation has little in common with the realizations which are brought about by the process of conversion. For there is absent from it the humility and worship to which reason leads us when anguish and awe are animating it.

What makes conversion a radical process is precisely the fact that it deconstructs the ontological presumptions which govern both our ordinary way of thinking and the "proofs for God" that are based on it. But it is for that very reason not less but more profoundly rational than the kind of thinking which rests on those presumptions. As long as they remain intact, our contingency, our liability to nothingness, can be interpreted as an attribute of our being which, because it is only an attribute, does not affect in a fundamental way our stature *as* beings. But if we allow nothingness to upset our basic presumptions, instead of interpreting it in terms of them, it can lead us to realize that we are nothing, in and of ourselves, and that our being is derivative from the wholly Other. Thus, the discovery of the wholly Other does not derive, as the traditional argument implies, from our knowledge of ourselves as beings; it derives from a knowledge of our nothingness which overturns our deepest presumptions about ourselves as beings.

This overturning, this conversion, at the crux of which we find an anguish more devastating than horror and an awe more uplifting than wonder, is the toward-which of all our other turnings. It is the worst of all possible fractures and, for that reason, the most radical of all breakthroughs. All the intimations we receive, all the questions they provoke, all the realizations we reach, lead us finally to the position of prostration. From the beginning, without realizing it, we are in the throe of the absolute Other.

THE OPENING TO OTHERNESS

What then of the absolute Other? What can we know of the toward-which of all our longing—what knowledge is implicit in our knowing it as the unknown Other toward which all our questions are directed? More specifically, should we equate it with that principle of presence posited by the traditional arguments for the existence of God?

What may make such an equation initially plausible is the fact that I have identified the absolute Other with being itself—with being which, unlike us, is being in and of itself. If the absolute Other is being in and of itself, it is not liable to nothingness. If it enjoys immunity to nothingness, is it not appropriate to think of the absolute Other as presence itself—as the very principle of presence which ordinarily we try to be ourselves?

If this were the case, it would legitimate the very metaphysics of presence which the process of discovering the absolute Other undermines. The principle of presence and the absolute Other lie, so to speak, at opposite ends of this entire process, and we ourselves lie in between them, stretched between presence as that from which we are disrupted by the throe of inquiry, and the absolute Other as that toward which the throe of inquiry carries us. Insofar as we seek to escape that throe, we are not searching for the absolute Other but, rather, trying to repress all Otherness so that there will be nothing Other than the self, the very principle of presence. The very idea of presence is generated by our desire to be invulnerable to the throe of the Other—it is nothing else but the dream of such invulnerability, the dream of there being no Other that is not ultimately reducible to the self.

That the absolute Other is not such a self, not such an apotheosis of presence, is indicated precisely by the reality of our otherness from it. I have suggested that the full import of anguish and awe only becomes accessible to us when we affirm that our being is given to us in our nothingness. But while dependent on it, and derivative from it, our being is nevertheless other than the absolute Other which is being itself. For only if it were other than being itself could it be liable to nothingness. Indeed, this very otherness from the absolute Other, this very difference from it, can only originate in the absolute Other, in the very event of its distinguishing us from itself. Far from being closed off to otherness, the absolute Other gives us, in this event, an intimation of its radical openness to there being others other than it.[14] The absolute Other does not guard itself from the other, is not possessive of its being, but is rather like a profligate generosity which is creative of differences and calls into being all the universes which wonder explores. Such openness does not merely let others be but gives them the very being which enables them to be as others. It does not simply permit otherness but is constitutive of it.

That is why the worship of the absolute Other—the wholehearted prostration of oneself to it—does not require anything like a withdrawal from all other others or a retraction of the reverence they evoke from us. It requires, in fact, just the opposite—our turning to every other and discovering in it just that otherness which the absolute Other gives it to be. For what we worship, when we worship the absolute Other, is Openness itself, and what can worshipping it mean if it does not mean opening ourselves to it, surrendering to its throe, and thus becoming open to that Openness to all others which is the Absolute Other?

Toward what are we led when we open ourselves to this Absolute Openness? To enter that opening does not mean getting answers to all one's questions; it means becoming at last the absolute, total questioner. It means breaking through a barrier that had prevented one from being wholly consumed by wonder, wholly penetrated by horror, wholly converted by awe. It would be the absolute surrender, the throe from which nothing was held back. Toward that turn everything turns us, as toward the consummation of both our being and our nothingness. We cannot say, as long as we are on this side of it, what it would turn us toward, only that there is nothing beyond it because it turns us toward the beyond itself. This, I believe, is what is meant by God.

EPILOGUE

From the given to the throe of the other, from the world of the other to its deconstruction and the throe of nothingness, from the confession of one's own nothingness to the throe of the absolute Other— this, in my judgment, is the path down which our hearts would lead us if we were willing to follow their most unsettling intimations. In each case, the shift involved is not an expansion of our horizons but a breach, a fissure, a rupture that can become a breakthrough but only if we allow it to break us irreparably. To make such breakthroughs requires the willingness to be so broken by them that we never recover—never return to what we were before the rupture, never retrieve our original wholeness. We cannot help but experience such an irrevocable loss as a death which we would like to be able to prevent. But, in fact, the cost of preventing such a death is only death of another sort. For we can keep our lives intact, and preserve their wholeness, only by closing them up, and erecting inviolable boundaries to keep every other out. Our fundamental human predicament is that we must choose between these radically different kinds of death; we cannot live except by dying in one way or the other.

That choice is crystallized for us at those critical junctures in our lives when we are seized with wonder, or arrested by horror, or struck dumb with awe. For in each of these primal experiences we are on the verge of discovering something so wonderful, or so horrible, or so awe-full, that it will change our lives irrevocably. But for that very reason, these experiences tear us apart, with one half of us wanting to hold onto the known and present, and one half of us in thrall to the future in its unknowable otherness. We would not have to make a choice between these halves if the unknown other had not already broken through to us, had not already breached our homeostatic enjoyment of the same. The very fact that we have the choice means that we are always already torn, always already caught in the throe of the other. To choose to hold onto the known and the present would be, therefore, to seek an escape from our very being as choosers, would be attempting to return to a condition of wholeness that we have always already lost. To hold onto the from-which of wonder, or horror, or awe, to recoil from that toward which they would lead us, is to choose against the very future which makes the act of choosing possible. To choose to live that kind of death is the suicidal option.

To choose ourselves as choosers, on the other hand, means to embrace what makes choice possible—the rupture created in our lives by the other which only becomes accessible to us through wonder and horror and awe. In making such a choice we cannot possibly know ahead of time what we are opening ourselves to— for it is precisely the unknown itself that beckons and horrifies and fills us with awe. But we can know that if we were to close off this opening instead of entering it, we would be repressing that awareness of the unknown which makes all exploration and discovery possible. The question we face in choosing between the from-which and toward-which of wonder and horror and awe is also a choice we face regarding our very being as questioners: whether to let the process of questioning set in motion by these experiences become our way of life, even though doing so requires losing everything we have accepted as given and thus suffering a kind of death. The only alternative to suffering such a death is to deaden one's capacity to question.

In short, everything is at stake in the decision we make at those critical junctures when wonder or horror or awe require us to choose between that from which they uproot us so radically and that toward which they direct us. These are the supreme turning points of our lives, even though, when we are in the process of making such a turn, it is impossible for us to say what is happening to us. At the critical moment of the turn on which everything hinges, we cannot know where we are headed or what we are doing; all we can know is that, by undergoing the turn instead of recoiling from it, by surrendering to its throe instead of trying to escape it, we are giving ourselves over to the unknown itself. To give up everything, instead of holding onto it, must seem to us, even as we do it, a kind of suicide since it goes counter to our instinct for self-preservation, and a kind of madness since it goes counter to all prudent calculation. But in fact it is the eros of intelligence itself which counsels us to surrender ourselves to the throe of the unknown and to become complete questioners. Can we be intelligent if we do not trust it?

This is a question each must answer for herself since it involves nothing less than deciding whether to be oneself. In my judgment, no one can take seriously the whole process of intelligent inquiry and rational reflection which culminates in making judgments and not take seriously those primal experiences in which all inquiry originates. To be fully intelligent, fully rational, we must side with wonder and against the self-evidence of the present-at-hand, with horror and against the recoil that wants to flee from nothingness, with awe and against the self-importance that refuses to acknowledge the possibility of there being a reality greater than ourselves. The decision to trust these experiences as the primal sources of knowing is more crucial than our commitment to any theory, more fundamental than our affirmation of any proposition. For theories and propositions themselves owe their existence to the creative eros of intelligence which is itself set in motion by the unknown which these experiences alone make accessible to us. None of the specific realizations to which inquiry leads us, no matter how important they may be, can rival the transformative effect of our primal decision to turn from the given to the eros of questioning. That turn is our fundamental conversion.

But the distinguishing characteristic of this conversion is that instead of providing us with an unshakable foundation or an unquestionable truth on which to base all we think and do, it pulls all foundation out from under us and throws what we thought were our certainties into question. It requires our giving up all the hope we ever had of grounding our thought on an arche that can be known directly, without having to trust ourselves to the uncontrollable, unpredictable throe of inquiry. To make this conversion is not to acquire a dogma but to become a questioner.

But we cannot enter fully into the ordeal of questioning unless we allow ourselves to be bound by its own immanent imperatives. If we leave our safe harbor and venture into the unknown which both fascinates and horrifies, we cannot possibly know where we are going. But exploring is different from pointless drifting—not because the explorer has a destination but because her movement is governed by the throe of the unknown itself. The fact that the given does not provide us with an immovable truth on which to erect the edifice of our thought does not mean, as the pragmatists of postmodern culture claim, that the idea of truth itself has to be jettisoned. Indeed, it is only our habit of equating truth with the given which would lead us to jump to that conclusion. But if being is not the given, is not the from-which of wonder, horror, or awe, if, rather, being is the unknown toward-which of all our questions, then the knowledge of being becomes possible only when we relinquish our hold on the given and open ourselves to those truths which cannot be reached except by trusting the eros of inquiry. The post-modern dismisal of truth as a philosophical objective, far from demonstrating a radically deconstructive approach to traditional foundationalism, only confirms that the post-modern pragmatist remains wedded to its presuppositions. He has simply despaired of achieving what the foundationalist still hopes to accomplish.

The underlying cause of such despair is our refusal to give up the dream of having the truth given to us. To relinquish that dream is a kind of death, and requires a willingness to suffer nothingness. Such suffering is intrinsic to the very nature of the turn—we cannot make the turn unless we experience it. In the experience of wonder, nothingness remains implicit; in horror it becomes conscious and is explicitly addressed; in awe it is fully acknowledged and finally embraced. Immanent within each of these experiences is an imperative to let go of that from which they wrench us. Thus we can become explorers only to the degree that we are willing to surrender our hold on life. That we can live fully only by letting go of life—only by letting go of everything and becoming destitute, that our enthusiasm for life can be heartfelt only if our hearts are broken open—this is the paradox which lies at the crux of that turn which is constitutive of our very being, the turn which, when we make it, engages us in the throe of questioning and so converts us into lovers of wisdom. To surrender to that throe unconditionally, to be willing to follow it wherever it leads is not an imperative just for the philosopher. It is the only way to be fully human.

NOTES

PROLOGUE

1. Henry David Thoreau, *Walden and Other Writings* (New York: Bantam Books, 1981), p. 115–116.

2. This is the conception of philosophy in general and metaphysics in particular which Bernard Lonergan develops in *Insight* (New York: Philosophical Library, 1958).

3. One could argue that the dread of such a misstep is the governing principle of Descartes's philosophy, and that through his influence it became a dominant concern throughout modern thought. In the process of Socratic dialogue, on the other hand, where philosophizing is always conceived as a dialogue with an Other, there is no such thing as a beginning without missteps; indeed, if such a beginning had been required, no Socratic dialogue would ever have gotten under way.

4. See especially Plato's *Phaedrus,* and Josef Pieper's commentary on it in *Enthusiasm and Divine Madness,* trans. by Richard and Clara Winston (New York: Harcourt Brace and World, Inc., 1964).

5. See Lonergan, *Insight,* pp. 207–244.

6. I certainly do not mean to imply that every philosopher who calls her way of practicing philosophy a "method" conceives of knowledge as a goal to be reached through certain strategic procedures. But Heidegger's critique of methodical rationality and his explanation of its connection with the economy of control, makes it necessary to scrutinize our philosophical "use" of "methods" so as to determine whether we are, to some degree, allowing the desire to know to come under the influence of the drive to control. Bernard Lonergan, whose affinity with Heidegger I discuss in chapter 3 and whose theory of insight has profoundly influenced everything I say in this book, "used" "transcendental method" in *Insight* and wrote a book called *Method in Theology.* Lonergan was not profoundly influenced by Heidegger and so did not feel compelled to compare his conception of method and Heidegger's conception of a "way." In the present work I am trying to find my "way" (in Heidegger's sense of the word) to the insights Lonergan reaches through his "method." That the latter is not a method in the pejorative sense Heidegger gives it is indicated by the fact that Lonergan takes pains to emphasize that "method," as he praises and practices it, is a profoundly personal exercise in self-reflection, not a mechanical device for producing true propositions. Cf. *Insight,* p. 328; *Method in Theology* (New York: Herder and Herder, 1972), pp. 3–25.

7. I am influenced here and throughout this book by Emmanuel Levinas, *Totality and Infinity* (Pittsburgh: Duquesne University Press, 1969). While I agree with Levinas that our relationship with the Face, with the Other who is a person, is our deepest and most important experience of otherness, I think our relationship with *everything* other than us can properly be understood as analogous to it. I suspect that Levinas would object that my unthematized dependence on this analogy throughout this book demonstrates my failure to take seriously the radical difference between the Face and everything else. While I believe that Levinas overlooks the reverence due to things which are not persons, I think he would be right to say that in this book I have failed to take into account the suggestion which emerges from his work, namely, that our experience of the Face is not just the prime analogue of all otherness but a kind of transcendental condition for the possibility of all experience of otherness.

CHAPTER 1

1. Aristotle, *Nicomachean Ethics*, 114a, 17–19, trans. by W. D. Ross, in *The Basic Works of Aristotle*, ed. by Richard McKeon (New York: Random House, 1941).

2. See Richard Rorty, *Consequences of Pragmatism, Essays: 1972–1980*, (Minneapolis: University of Minnesota Press, 1982), pp. xiii–xlv, 211–230.

3. Aristotle, *Nichomachean Ethics*, 1141a, 19. In the *Metaphysics* (1006a, 13–28) Aristotle does not appeal to intuition to establish the principle of non-contradiction but instead develops an argument to convince us that the denial of it is self-refuting. An appeal to argument differs from an appeal to intuition insofar as the former is addressed to the judgment of the interlocutor whereas the latter attempts to bypass judgment. I am suggesting in this chapter that such an attempt to short-circuit judgment is unwise and, in fact, a flight from the upsetting process of seeking wisdom. Aristotle's method in the *Metaphysics* suggests that he does not think wisdom must necessarily derive from "intuition" as that term is understood throughout this book.

4. *Nichomachean Ethics*, 1141a, 9–15.

5. I am using the masculine pronoun in this section because it is the one Aristotle would have used in discussing "the wise man" but also because, in our culture, the quest for mastery has traditionally been a masculine aspiration and perogative. Similar considerations influence my pronoun usage throughout this book. Many of the themes to be discussed in the book—e.g. our attitude toward vulnerability and our concern for control—are profoundly and intimated related to gender questions, but I have not attempted to thematize or explore the connection.

6. On the question of whether first principles are internal or external to a conceptual framework, see Rudolf Carnap, "Empiricism, Semantics and Ontology," in *The Linguistic Turn*, ed. by Richard Rorty (Chicago: University of Chicago Press, 1967). On the whole matter of the relationship between the "inside" and the "outside" of the structures which deconstruction undermines, cf. Jacques Derrida, *Of Grammatology*, trans. by Gayatri Chakravorty Spivak (Baltimore: Johns Hopkins Press, 1976), especially pp. 30–65.

7. See Paul Ricoeur, *Freud and Philosophy*, trans. by Denis Savage (New Haven: Yale University Press, 1977). One of the first practitioners of this hermeneutic was Thrasymachus in book 1 of the *Republic*. This suggests that it is not exclusively a post-modern phenomenon, but a recurring effort to deconstruct culture, an effort which spawns, and is spawned by, cultural crisis.

8. See Richard Rorty, *Consequences of Pragmatism*, passim.

9. John Sallis, *Delimitations; Phenomenology and the End of Metaphysics*, (Bloomington: Indiana University Press, 1986), pp. 139–151.

10. See Martin Heidegger, *Being and Time*, trans. by John Macquarrie and Edward Robinson (New York: Harper and Row, 1962), H2–H15, H235–H311 (German pagination).

11. See Jacques Derrida, *Of Grammatology*, passim.

12. It seems to me that this is the difficulty which besets many responses to deconstruction. Someone who tries to take deconstruction seriously, while still seeking to preserve some sense of being and objective truth from its critique, can agree to indefinitely defer our attainment of truth and our breakthrough to being, and thus avoid abandoning the entire pursuit of them. But this attempt to steer a middle course between deconstruction and the tradition it undermines requires us to keep hoping in the possibility of (a perhaps eschatological) intuition of presence.

13. Rorty, *Consequences of Pragmatism*, passim but especially xiii–xlv.

14. Throughout this book, when I speak of the "pragmatic" alternative, I have in mind the kind of post-modern pragmatism articulated by thinkers such as the later Carnap, Thomas Kuhn, and Richard Rorty, not the "classical" pragmatism of James and Dewey. However, I suspect it would be possible to develop a convincing case that the post-modern kind of pragmatism is what emerges from a classical pragmatism when the latter is stripped of all the vestiges of the traditional metaphysics and epistemology it critiques.

15. Rorty's pragmatism seems to me to be symptomatic of, and profoundly influenced by, the therapeutic mentality which Philip Rieff diagnoses in *The Triumph of the Therapeutic* (New York: Harper and Row, 1966).

16. See *Insight*, 348–374 and passim.

17. See Lonergan, *Insight*, pp. 279–318 and 375–384.

18. See Aristotle, *Metaphysics*, 1006a, 13–28.

19. Cf. Joseph Boyle, Jr., "The Argument from Self-Referential Inconsistency: The Current Discussion." Unpublished Ph.D. dissertation, Georgetown University, 1969, and "Self-Referential Inconsistency, Inevitable Falsity and Metaphysical Argumentation," *Metaphilosophy*, 3 (1972), 25–42.

In *Insight* Lonergan claims that the self-referential arguments he employs there yield non-revisable judgments (see especially p. 335). Insofar as this can be construed as an attempt to establish a set of non-revisable propositions it remains under the influence of the modernist drive to secure indisputable first principles. But, in the first place, *Insight* insists that "judgment" is not to be equated with a proposition but with a profoundly personal act of the subject, one that brings the whole ordeal of inquiry to its culmination. Secondly, while Lonergan does not explicitly say that entering into that ordeal requires acknowledging fallibility, one of the main points of his book is that we do not have the kind of intuition that would provide us the direct access to being which, I have argued, we would need to avoid fallibility. And thirdly, a personal act of insight and judgment can be both non-revisable and fallible in the sense that I have given to the latter term. For the non-revisable character of the insight "It is always possible for me to be wrong" is not due to the infallibility of the speaker but to the inescapability of the throe of inquiry to which the speaker is subject.

20. I am grateful to my friend and colleague Tony Whall for suggesting the title of this chapter, and for our many fruitful conversations about its topic.

CHAPTER 2

1. Martin Heidegger, "What is Metaphysics?" trans. by R. F. C. Hull and Alan Crick in *Existence and Being*, Gateway edition (Chicago: Henry Regnery Company, 1949), p. 348. I have also been influenced by Josef Pieper's *Leisure: The Basis of Culture*, trans. by Alexander Dru (New York: New American Library, 1963) which beautifully describes the experience of wonder as the root of human culture (see especially pp. 97–111), but does not take into account the critique of the metaphysics of presence.

2. Jacques Derrida, *Of Grammatology*, p. 65. As will quickly become apparent, the works with which I am principally preoccupied throughout this chapter are Heidegger's *Being and Time* and *Of Grammatology*. The perspective from which I approach these texts has been profoundly influenced by Lonergan's *Insight*.

3. Reported by Thomas Sheehan in "Derrida and Heidegger" in *Hermeneutics and Deconstruction*, ed. by Hugh J. Silverman and Don Ihde (Albany: State University of New York, 1985), p. 217.

4. I am borrowing words here from Mircea Eliade's phenomenology of religious experience. See *The Sacred and the Profane*, trans. by Willard Trask, (New York: Harcourt Brace and Jovanovich, 1959), p. 20 and passim.

5. Cf. *Of Grammatology*, p. 30 and passim.

6. Our relationship to any reality that transcends us is analogous to, and in fact made possible by, this capacity to be aware of the unknown as unknown. If we lacked this capacity, we would either know the transcendent (and so it would not transcend us) or be utterly oblivious of it. I think a main reason why thinkers such as Hume (see *Dialogues Concerning Natural Religion*) and Feuerbach (see *The Essence of Christianity*) become stuck on the horns of this false dilemma is because they do not take the experience of wonder sufficiently into account.

7. I am suggesting that wonder exhibits the same structure of thrownness and projection which Heidegger uncovers in his analysis of environmentality in the first half of *Being and Time;* the crucial question for the phenomenology of wonder is whether one can say of it what Heidegger says of anxiety in the second half of *Being and Time:* that, unlike fear, it projects us toward a not-yet which is not homologizable to any present.

8. See Lonergan, *Insight*, pp. 250–254, 322–326. One might say that Lonergan's whole cognitional theory is an attempt to draw out all the implications that follow from the basic insight that data never answer any questions; rather, data require an explanation but do not provide one.

9. Just as Heidegger argues that the ocular theory of knowing arises from and reinforces a metaphysics of presence, Lonergan argues that it causes us to

equate being with what is right here now in front of us. See *Insight,* especially pp. 250–254 and chapter 11.

10. Knowing the other, therefore, is not, as Levinas implies, a matter of integrating the other into the economy of the same but rather requires a decisive and irreparable breach in that economy. Cf. *Totality and Infinity,* passim.

11. Thomas Merton, "Song: If You Seek . . . ," in *Emblems of a Season of Fury* (New York: New Directions, 1963), p. 38.

12. Richard Rorty moves in this direction in "The World Well Lost" in *Consequences of Pragmatism, Essays: 1972–1980,* pp. 3–18.

13. *Of Grammatology,* passim—but especially pp. 195–229 and 269–316.

14. *Ibid.,* pp. 6–26.

15. *Ibid.,* pp. 195–229.

16. Heidegger, "What is Metaphysics?," pp. 337–349. However, in many of our experiences of wonder the dreadful aspect of our encounter with the unknown remains implicit and can be almost entirely effaced.

17. See Edmund Burke, *A Philosophical Inquiry into the Origin of Our Ideas of the Sublime and the Beautiful,* ed. by James Boulton (Notre Dame: University of Notre Dame Press, 1968), pp. 58–64.

18. Gaston Bachelard, *The Poetics of Space,* trans. by Maria Jolas (Boston: Beacon Press, 1969).

19. Dylan Thomas, "Fern Hill."

20. I am responding here to the discussion of metaphor in *Of Grammatology,* pp. 270–279.

21. Cf. Martin Heidegger, *Poetry, Language, Thought,* trans. by Albert Hofstadter (New York: Harper and Row, 1971), pp. 57–78.

22. See, e.g., Shelley's *Defence of Poetry.*

23. There are thinkers who emphasize the role of the creative imagination in generating scientific theories, thinkers such as Michael Polanyi from whose work (e.g. *The Tacit Dimension,* [Garden City: Doubleday and Company, Inc., 1967]) I have borrowed much of my imagery of exploration. Lonergan emphasizes the importance of the heuristic image in generating insights. Cf. *Insight,* pp. 8–9, 18, 439–440.

24. Bachelard, *The Poetics of Space,* pp. 3–73, especially p. 16.

25. *Of Grammatology,* pp. 10–26.

26. See *Insight,* pp. 348–374.

27. *Of Grammatology,* pp. 49–50, and passim.

28. I am thinking of, among others, Edmund Burke, Rudolf Otto (*The Idea of the Holy* [London: Oxford University Press, 1958]), G. Van der Leeuw (*Religion in Essence and Manifestation* [New York: Harper and Row, 1963]), Abraham Heschel (*Man Is Not Alone* [New York: Harper and Row, 1966]), and Mircea Eliade. Of the innumerable religious writers who have emphasized the importance of wonder and awe in their conversions or religious evolution, I might mention two who differ enormously in mentality and temperment: C. S. Lewis (cf. *Surprised by Joy* [New York: Harcourt Brace and World, 1955]) and Jonathan Edwards, ("Personal Narrative," in *Selected Writings of Jonathan Edwards,* ed. by Harold Simonson [New York: Frederick Ungar Publishing Co., 1970]).

29. Cf. Franz Kafka, *The Trial,* trans. by Willa and Edwin Muir (New York: Alfred A. Knopf, 1960), pp. 267–269.

CHAPTER 3

1. While the later writings of Heidegger and Lonergan have influenced my understanding of their thought, my reflections in this essay come out of the attempt to think my way into the relationship between *Being and Time* and *Insight*.

As this chapter essays a rethinking of what is at stake in these texts, rather than a scholarly exegesis of them, I will place my more technical observations and comparisons in the notes.

2. According to Heidegger, Dasein's un-covering of what-is becomes sedimented into assertions which are construed as something present-at-hand (Cf. *Being and Time*, section 44). In Lonergan's terms, insights are typically reduced to and wrongly equated with ideas that are generated from them; the conceptualist then makes ideas instead of insights the focus of epistemology.

3. *Being and Time* is a phenomenological essay on the limits of phenomenology and in a profound way aims at undermining itself. When Heidegger calls into question the possibility of any pure intuition of essences (see e.g., section 63, esp. H315), he means us to understand that his own text, indeed his own statement of this fact, cannot be definitive. Consequently, one might be tempted to argue that *Being and Time* is not just self-referential but self-referentially inconsistent. The thesis which emerges from it about the impossibility of reaching any definitive point of view seems to undercut by its own logic its own claim to truth. If the statement "This text does not contain the final truth about anything" is finally true, is it self-defeating and therefore false? This question is, I believe, not answerable on its own terms. One must first distinguish between (1) saying that a statement is the final truth (with the implication that no further insights are possible) and (2) saying that a statement is finally true (in the sense that a rational person can give it unqualified assent). This distinction in turn requires distinguishing, as Lonergan does, between insight and assent. See section 4 of this chapter.

Insight becomes explicitly self-referential when Lonergan invites the reader to affirm herself as a knower (chapter XI). Lonergan thinks the self-referential inconsistency of other epistemological theories makes them mortally vulnerable to criticism. While *Insight* is, I believe, as rigorously self-critical as *Being and Time*, it intends to lead the reader to make a self-referentially consistent judgment of self-affirmation. *Being and Time*, on the other hand, invites the reader to undergo a dialectical reversal which undermines her ordinary sense of herself.

4. Both *Being and Time* and *Insight* invite the reader to participate in what Lonergan calls an exercise in rational self-consciousness by virtue of which one's understanding of oneself is radically transformed. But such an exercise has, to use Heidegger's phrase, both an existential and an existentiell dimension: it has the capacity to revolutionize not just one's theoretical self-understanding but also to uproot one from one's whole way of living. Self-appropriation is fully achieved not by a theoretical grasp of what it means to be Dasein but through a conversion to authenticity. Because *Insight* is written from the point of view of cognitional theory, the existentiell dimension of the intellectual conversion it invites one to undergo remains largely hidden and to some degree masked, although Lonergan does advert to it explicitly, especially in the chapter on ethics. The existentiell dimension is emphasized much more strongly in Lonergan's later writings.

5. Neither Heidegger nor Lonergan think there can be an absolute beginning to philosophy. According to Lonergan, metaphysics only thematizes the orientation toward being in terms of which we are always operating, though we do so for the most part unconsciously (see pp. 390–401). And according to Heidegger, we are always already inside the hermeneutical circle and so cannot pretend our thinking begins with a presuppositionless first step into it (see H315).

6. Hermeneutics in the narrow sense of understanding a text or any product of human history is made possible by hermeneutics in the wide sense of that projective understanding which is constitutive of Dasein. (See *Being and Time,* sections 18, 32, 76). According to Lonergan, understanding a text requires the same process of experience, inquiry, insight, and judgment as any other kind of knowing. (See *Insight,* chapter 17, section 3.)

7. The story is told by Vasari in *The Lives of the Artists* (Baltimore: Penguin Books, 1965), p. 163.

8. *Insight,* p. 9.

9. *Being and Time,* sections 40 and 53.

10. *Insight,* p. 251.

11. *Ibid.* Convincing arguments have been advanced by many philosophers to show that we never operate purely and simply at the strictly experiential level: we are always interpreting or on our way toward interpreting. But this does not mean that we cannot distinguish between the experiential and the interpretative, even as we admit that they never exist in isolation from each other.

12. The unknown which wonder knows as unknown is not reducible to the "already out there now", just as the not-yet of the future is not merely another present that has not yet arrived. Only a being subject to ecstatic temporality in Heidegger's sense can experience the peculiar eros of the unrestricted desire to know as Lonergan explains this eros.

13. Heidegger rarely uses this term. Lonergan identifies it with the objective of the unrestricted desire to know in section 1 of chapter XVII.

14. If someone objects that Lonergan would not be so radical as to say that wonder makes the world happen, I would point out that, insofar as being is what is to be known through rational reflection, one cannot say, strictly speaking, that the already out there now *is.* The only real world there is, according to Lonergan, is the one known through intelligent inquiry and rational reflection, just as for Heidegger the only real world is that which appears in the clearing opened up by Dasein's disclosedness. (See *Being and Time,* sections 43, 44; *Insight,* chapters VIII, XIII.)

15. See *Being and Time,* section 44.

16. So as to emphasize that he is not an idealist, in spite of his insistence that, without Dasein, there would "be" no "world" at all, Heidegger insists that Dasein does not exist except as Being-in-the-world. To emphasize that he is not an empiricist, in spite of his insistence that Dasein is not a worldless subject, Heidegger insists there would be no world without Dasein. Lonergan balances himself on a similar tightrope: being is what is known through intelligent inquiry and rational reflection—a statement which, taken by itself, could be interpreted as idealism; but inquiry and reflection always point beyond themselves toward being—a statement which, taken by itself, could be interpreted as naive realism.

17. I do not at all mean to suggest that the fundamental judgment which grounds the meaning of one's world as a whole is arbitrary simply because it

cannot be justified by a fixed and already adopted horizon of meaning. Heidegger and Lonergan differ from the pragmatists and nihilists precisely because as they think our fundamental choices should be grounded in our authentic responsiveness to what Heidegger calls the call of being and what Lonergan calls the transcendental imperatives. For both of them, the primordial human option is between exercising primordial choice in a responsible way or an irresponsible way. (The flight from this choice is itself irresponsible.)

18. Heidegger argues against Husserl that pure intuition is incompatible with Dasein's ecstatical temporality (H147). Lonergan argues that insights only enable us to grasp possibilities, what might be the case, and that only judgment enables us to know being. But insofar as judgment is mediated, it lacks the directness and therefore the kind of inerrancy associated with intuition. That there is a relationship between temporality as understood by Heidegger and judgment as understood by Lonergan is the burden of the argument in the final section of this chapter.

19. The best fictional portrayal of this post-modern experience which I am familiar with is John Barth's *End of the Road* (New York: Bantam Books, 1969) where man's power as world-maker is governed by nothing except his own (arbitrarily chosen) pragmatic purposes. Barth rightly recognizes, I think, that such pragmatism leads to murder and/or suicide (i.e. the end of the road), a conclusion which Richard Rorty, among others, fails to draw. Rorty's pragmatic reading of Heidegger is, in my judgment, profoundly erroneous, for reasons I will try to explain in the next section of this chapter. (See Richard Rorty, *Consequences of Pragmatism,* Essays: 1972–1980, pp. 3–18, 37–59.) Rorty's thought does help to clarify our situation insofar as it shows that, once the picture theory is rejected, there are only two options: pragmatism and the kind of responsiveness to being practised by thinkers such as Heidegger and Lonergan.

20. Dread is discussed at greater length in chapter 6 where I refer to it as horror.

21. Such a calling into question of the basic presuppositions of a theoretical framework causes the disruption of what Kuhn calls normal science and the beginning of what he calls scientific revolution. (See Thomas Kuhn, *The Structure of Scientific Revolutions* [Chicago: University of Chicago Press, 1962].) The argument as to whether paradigm shifts are theoretically or only pragmatically justifiable reflected the wider controversy that had been brewing since Wittgenstein's *Philosophical Investigations* as to whether disputes between alternative universes of discourse (language games) can be somehow arbitrated by an appeal to reality. Since the discrediting of logical positivism, with its empiricist version of the picture theory of knowing, philosophy has shifted steadily toward pragmatism. For an early version of this shift, see Rudolf Carnap, "Empiricism, Semantics and Ontology," in *The Linguistic Turn,* ed. by Richard Rorty (Chicago: University of Chicago Press, 1967).

22. Scotosis in Lonergan's sense of the term becomes existentiell inauthenticity in Heidegger's sense when we repress the questions we would be led to ask about our lives if we allowed angst to hold us in its sway. We repress the unrestricted desire to know whenever it would lead us to ask ourselves worldshattering questions. The pragmatist's account of knowing is, I think, fatally flawed because it does not take into account the fact that such questions, while typically repressed, can be allowed to emerge and can be intelligently addressed.

Questions about the meaning of alternative universes of meaning can be asked; in asking them one does not reside within one particular frame of meaning but within the throe of inquiry which originates all meaning. Pragmatists cannot make sense of this conundrum because, for them, nothing lies outside our alternative conceptual frameworks except desire, and in particular the desire for control. For Heidegger and Lonergan there runs through and beyond all our frameworks the call of being.

23. Deconstruction as a way of reading texts seeks to locate the fissures, cracks, faults, in the world of meaning constituted by them. The nature of such worlds is discussed at length in the next chapter.

24. *Being and Time,* sections 46–53.

25. Neither Lonergan nor Heidegger equates being with "everything about everything" but both would agree that how we think about being affects our understanding of everything. When Lonergan says that to know being would be to know everything about everything (*Insight,* pp. 348–352), he is seeking to clarify the unrestricted nature of the notion of being, i.e. the fact that being is, in Heidegger's words, "no class or genus of entities; yet it pertains to every entity . . . Being is the transcendens pure and simple" (H38).

26. Because *Insight* is written from a pedagogical point of view which appeals to the reader's unrestricted desire to understand, it gradually draws one on, like wonder itself does, from one insight to another, from lower viewpoints to higher viewpoints, in a gradual, cumulative unfolding. *Being and Time,* on the other hand, is constantly trying to overcome the reader's "flight from understanding" (*Insight,* p. xi), the tendency to recoil from what horrifies so as to avoid being shattered by it. Because *Being and Time* as a whole has principally in view an undoing of avoidances, it is not just about dying but is itself an exercise in dying. While each text is an argument on behalf of being, in the one being beckons, in the other it horrifies. Lonergan's thought precipitates a crisis in the reader's self-understanding though the reader is beckoned into experiencing it; Heidegger's thought beckons one to a new understanding of being, though the reader recoils from it in horror.

27. *Phaedo,* 67e.

28. If the remote source is Socrates, the proximate source is Kierkegaard.

29. This belief that we are held in the grip of being and that, to be authentically, we must surrender to it in a radical way, removes Heidegger's thought about as far from pragmatism as it is possible to go. Indeed, one might say that the whole burden of Heidegger's thought is to argue on behalf of dread and its power to undermine our will to be in control of everything. Inauthentic everydayness is governed through and through by the pragmatic cast of mind.

30. I am struggling here to rethink what Heidegger says in section 44b.

31. I am struggling here to rethink what Lonergan says in chapter IX.

32. See *Insight,* chapter X. According to Lonergan, we should evaluate a theory by judging how well it explains the data which we are trying to understand. Thus, judgment is the third stage in the dynamic process of cognition; it presupposes that there are data to be explained, and a theory (or competing theories) whose attempt to provide an explanation must be evaluated. The process of making a judgment thus requires bringing together the two previous stages of knowing (the experience of the data and the insight which purports to explain them) for the purpose of judging whether the purported insight is a real one. There

is, then, at the level of judgment, a kind of return to the data. But it is crucial to note why this recursion to the data is necessary. Its purpose is not to "check" the insight against the data to see if the insight "conforms" to them. For, in that case, the data as directly experienced would be the determining factor in the process of knowing; the given would then be the criterion against which the validity of insight is measured. But the data are crucial because they are what are to be explained, not because they determine whether purported explanations are true. Only judgment can perform this latter function and it does so by returning to the data (what-is-to-be-explained) for the purposed of determining whether the purported explanation succeeds in accounting for the data.

In my description of Lonergan's cognitional theory, and in my effort to explore the ramifications of that theory throughout this book, I emphasize the way it undermines the primacy of the given (the data) in a way that comes dangerously close to implying that the given can be dismissed—as if it were a kind of starting point that can quickly be left behind. Given the Platonic cast of my thinking, it is not surprising that I would have a tendency to push a profoundly Aristotelean thinker like Lonergan in this direction. Although I know they have influenced it, I hope that my Platonic prejudices have not caused me to misunderstand or misrepresent the substance of Lonergan's thought.

33. See chapter 7.

CHAPTER 4

1. That the world is not a collection of things but a context of meaning in terms of which entities are interpreted is argued persuasively by Heidegger in *Being and Time*, pp. H91–H148.

2. This chapter in its entirety may be read as an effort to think through some of the questions raised in my mind by reading Jacques Derrida, especially "Structure, Sign and Play in the Discourse of the Human Sciences," in *Writing and Difference*, trans. by Alan Bass (Chicago: University of Chicago Press, 1978).

3. My description of the heterogeneity of the other and its importance for the constitution of our worlds has been influenced by Eliade's *The Sacred and the Profane* and by Levinas's *Totality and Infinity*. However, I am attributing to the non-human a heterogeneity which Levinas would attribute only to the face.

4. When Thoreau appeals to the genius in each of us (*Walden and Other Writings*, p. 171), he means our natural (but profoundly repressed) capacity to be "awake," i.e., to see each thing "as it was in the beginning, when it came fresh from the Creator's hands" (Eliade, *The Sacred and the Profane*, p. 65).

5. The concept of virtual space is used by Suzanne Langer in *Feeling and Form* (New York: Charles Scribner's Sons, 1953).

6. For an especially effective evocation of how we can be radically and permanently affected by the discovery of a world other than the ordinary, see the fictions of Willa Cather, especially *The Song of the Lark* (Boston: Houghton Mifflin and Co., 1943).

7. I am thinking here, of course, of eros as described by Plato in the *Symposium* and the *Phaedrus*. Also, see Josef Pieper, *Leisure, the Basis of Culture*, pp. 57–64, and *Enthusiasm and Divine Madness*, trans. by Richard and Clara Winston (New York: Harcourt, Brace and World, Inc., 1964).

8. See Eliade, *The Sacred and the Profane,* p. 12 and passim. See also Heschel, *Man Is Not Alone,* pp. 3–4.

9. See Eliade, *The Sacred and The Profane,* p. 57.

10. On the nature of insight and its relation to meaning, see Lonergan, *Insight,* passim. Lonergan's distinction between insight and data corresponds to the distinction I am making here between the "elements" within a world and the order which is constitutive of its very character as a world. There are similarities which connect Lonergan's theory of insight, Langer's aesthetic theory (see *Feeling and Form*) and the theory of worlds which I am trying to explore here.

11. On insight as constitutive of the world, see Lonergan, *Insight,* passim, and *Method in Theology,* pp. 57–99.

12. See Jacques Derrida, "Structure, Sign and Play in the Discourse of the Human Sciences": "By orienting and organizing the coherence of the system the center of a structure permits the play of its elements inside the total form. And even today the notion of a structure lacking any center represents the unthinkable itself" (pp. 278–279). That an order requires a unifying principle and that Western philosophy has been dominated by the search for such a principle is one of Reiner Schurmann's theses in *Heidegger on Being and Acting: From Principles to Anarchy,* trans. by Christine-Marie Gros (Bloomington: Indiana University Press, 1987). In my judgment, Schurmann fails to adequately distinguish between what I am calling a world and what Levinas call a totality.

13. Eliade, *The Sacred and the Profane,* pp. 20–65.

14. Ibid., p. 43.

15. I am influenced here, and throughout this section, by Aquinas's aesthetics which identifies radiance, integrity and harmony as the distinguishing traits of the beautiful. See *Summa Theologica,* I, 39, 8, and Jacques Maritain, *Art and Scholasticism and the Frontiers of Poetry,* trans. by Joseph W. Evans (New York: Charles Scribner's Sons, 1962), pp. 23–37.

16. See Derrida, "Structure, Sign and Play in the Discourse of the Human Sciences": "Nevertheless, the center also closes off the play which it opens up and makes possible. As center, it is the point at which the substitution of contents, elements, or terms is no longer possible" (p. 279).

17. See Heidegger, *Being and Time,* H279–H311.

18. I am borrowing here from Jacques Derrida, *Of Grammatology,* pp. 30–65 and passim.

19. I am using the term with the meaning given it by Levinas in *Totality and Infinity.*

20. In Robert Frost's words, we would like to keep "her heart in a case of gold / And pinned with a silver pin." See "Love and a Question," in the *Poetry of Robert Frost,* ed. by E. C. Lathem (New York: Holt Rinehart and Winston, 1969), p. 7.

21. I have in mind here not only the kind of rationalism generated by Descartes's *Discourse on Method* and the kind of empiricism exemplified by Ayer's *Language, Truth and Logic,* but more generally the impulse to totalize which every attempt at philosophical systemization has to struggle to resist, and to which philosophy itself, because of the unrestricted character of its questions, is always in danger of falling prey.

22. The distinction I am making between the open world of insight and the closed world of intuition is derived from Lonergan's distinction between an "in-

tellectualist" theory of cognition which acknowledges the pivotal importance of insight and a conceptualist theory of cognition which identifies knowing with a direct vision-like grasp of ideas. To use the language of the phenomenologists, ideas are insights that have become "sedimented"—i.e., detached from their animating context, and reified into abstractions. Lonergan's distinction between the intellectualist and the conceptualist theory of cognition is itself derived from the pivotal distinction in his work—that between insight and intuition.

23. In *Thus Spake Zarathustra*, Nietzsche seems to me to be approaching this kind of view of the world. The inseparability of being and nothingness, the world and its deconstruction, life and death, and therefore celebration and anguish, seem to me to be the central theme of that great text. And yet I think Nietzsche is prevented from appreciating the full import of this inseparability by the fact that he tends to view all our worlds as creations of the will and as lacking any intrinsically sacred character. My reasons for thinking that this vitiates his synthesis of celebration and anguish are explained in section 4 of the present chapter.

24. See the *Symposium*, trans. by Benjamin Jowett (New York: The Macmillan Company, 1956), 210e. But to give up one's world, to allow it to be deconstructed, is, I think, a much more devastating ordeal than Diotoma's speech suggests. The path Diotoma describes, dialectical as it is, leads upward to Beauty without venturing down into nothingness.

25. See Jacques Derrida, "Structure, Sign and Play in the Discourse of the Human Sciences," p. 292.

26. See Philip Rieff, "The Impossible Culture: Oscar Wilde and the Charism of the Artist," *Encounter*, Vol. xxxv, 3 (Sept., 1970) and *The Triumph of the Therapeutic* (New York: Harper and Row, 1968).

27. See Richard Rorty, *Consequences of Pragmatism, Essays: 1972–1980*, pp. xiii–18 and passim.

28. That something ultimately matters means, I think, that it is of central, fundamental, essential importance. Insofar as Derrida's deconstructive critique tries to undermine the distinction between the fundamental and the derived, the essential and accidental, it undermines the idea of ultimacy as well. But once that idea is deconstructed, it is difficult to understand what is to prevent both life and death from losing that seriousness which gives both our joy and our horror their depth and intensity. In "Structure, Sign and Play in the Discourse of the Human Sciences," Derrida equates a Nietzschean affirmation of the world with the kind of play that is made possible by decentering. If by decentering he means an upsetting of what, following Levinas, I have called a totality, this would lead to an ultimate experience of (life and) death. But if by decentering he means ceasing to treat any matter as ultimate, this would lead precisely to the kind of pragmatism I am discussing here. One can distinguish these two kinds of decentering only if one distinguishes the open world of the sacred from both the closed world of a totality and the "open world" where nothing is taken seriously. I have not yet found this distinction in Derrida.

This same ambiguity is found in Nietzsche himself. For, on the one hand, he says that nothing has ultimate importance apart from our decision to treat it as important, and on the other hand, he is contemptuous of the utilitarian for whom nothing matters ultimately except getting what he wants.

CHAPTER 5

1. See Henry David Thoreau, *Walden and Other Writings*, pp. 165–166 and passim.

2. "We believe . . . that the course of [mental] events is invariably set in motion by an unpleasurable tension, and that it takes a direction such that its final outcome coincides with a lowering of that tension—that is, with an avoidance of unpleasure or a production of pleasure." Sigmund Freud, *Beyond the Pleasure Principle*, Standard Edition (London: Hogarth Press, 1955), p. 7.

3. "Psycho-analysis is an instrument to enable the ego to achieve a progressive conquest of the id." Sigmund Freud, *The Ego and the Id*, Standard Edition (London: Hogarth Press, 1955), p. 56. See also Philip Rieff, *Freud: The Mind of the Moralist* (Garden City: Doubleday Anchor Books, 1961), pp. 67–69, 76.

4. Freud, *Beyond the Pleasure Principle*, p. 10.

5. Freud, *The Ego and the Id*, p. 40; see also *Beyond the Pleasure Principle*, p. 57.

6. I am influenced here by Derrida, *Of Grammatology*, part II.

7. The phrase is C. S. Lewis's. See *Surprised by Joy*, the memoir of his religious conversion.

8. See Josef Pieper, *About Love*, trans. by Richard and Clara Winston (Chicago: Franciscan Herald Press, 1974), p. 27.

9. See Diotoma's speech in the *Symposium*. Even Josef Pieper, whose discussion of these matters is rich and nuanced, says that ". . . the reason for joy . . . is always the same: possessing or receiving what one loves. . ." (*In Tune With the World: A Theory of Festivity*, trans. by Richard and Clara Winston [Chicago: Franciscan Herald Press, 1973]), p. 17.

10. Cf. Josef Pieper, *Leisure: the Basis of Culture*, pp. 56–74.

11. Kierkegaard tends to equate the romantic experience of love with the "aesthetic" and the renunciation of the beloved with the "ethical." (Cf. *Fear and Trembling*.) But if one is authentically in love with the beloved (and not in love with the experience of being in love, as is the case with Kierkegaard's aesthetic individual), one already knows that it would be a betrayal of the beloved to be possessive toward her. Romantic love is dialectical in its very essence; one remains faithful to its inspiration only if one's longing for the beloved leads to a renunciation of her, not a possession of her.

12. See Michel Meslin, "Heart," trans. by Kristine Anderson, *The Encyclopedia of Religion*, 1987, vol. 6, pp. 234–237.

CHAPTER 6

1. I find this term a more evocative translation of "angst" than "anxiety," a word too suggestive of neurotic worry. In the final section of this essay I will introduce a distinction between "horror" and "anguish" which Heidegger, for reasons which I will try to elucidate, does not thematize in his treatment of angst in *Being and Time*.

2. But the deconstructive experience of nothingness (which is to be explored in this chapter) is radically different from a suicidal pursuit of death which, I would argue, is motivated by the kind of regressive recoil from the experience of nothingness discussed in chapter 5.

3. On states of mind as disclosive, see Heidegger, *Being and Time*, H134–H140. For a discussion of the disclosive character of feeling, see Cheshire Calhoun, "Cognitive Emotions?" in *What is an Emotion*, ed. by Calhoun and Robert Solomon (New York: Oxford University Press, 1984), pp. 327–342.

4. I am using the term "therapeutic" in the sense given it by Philip Rieff in *The Triumph of the Therapeutic.*

5. In saying that my wife's death can mean the end of my world, I do not mean to disagree with Heidegger when he argues (*Being and Time*, H237–H241) that we cannot get close to our own death by experiencing the death of others. But a literal reading of Heidegger can mislead one into thinking that an encounter with death occurs only when one faces one's own physical demise. *Being and Time* is, among other things, an argument against just such literality; the encounter with death it describes occurs whenever one's world is shattered, irrespective of the event that triggers it. The death of my wife, insofar as it means the end of the world to me, opens up to me my *own* ownmost possibility.

6. See Heidegger, *Being and Time*, pp. H184–H191.

7. See Derrida, *Of Grammatology*, p. 184.

8. See Lonergan, *Insight*, pp. 182–184, 250–254.

9. See Levinas, *Totality and Infinity*, passim.

10. See Derrida, *Writing and Difference*, pp. 278–293.

11. See Rorty, *Consequences of Pragmatism, Essays: 1972–1980*, pp. xiii–xlvii.

12. See Lonergan, *Insight*, pp. 9–10, and passim.

13. See Heidegger, *Being and Time*, pp. H236–H267.

14. By "insight as ordinarily conceived" I mean insight construed as a direct objective knowing of something present-at-hand. See chapter 1.

15. See Heidegger, "What is Metaphysics."

16. Derrida, *Of Grammatology*, p. 183.

17. Heidegger, *Being and Time*, p. H261.

18. *Ibid.*, p. H262.

19. T. S. Eliot, "The Four Quartets," in *The Complete Poems and Plays* (New York: Harcourt Brace and Company, 1952), p. 145.

20. Heidegger, *Being and Time*, p. H263.

21. See, for example, Descartes's *Discourse on Method*, trans. by Laurence J. LaFleur (New York: Bobbs-Merrill Company, Inc., 1956):

> The first rule was never to accept anything as true unless *I* recognized it to be evidently such: that is, carefully to avoid precipitation and prejudgment, and to include nothing in my conclusions unless it *presented* itself so clearly and distinctly to *my* mind that there was no occasion to doubt it. (Emphasis added.)

22. See Heidegger, "What is Metaphysics," pp. 329–337.

CHAPTER 7

1. Jacques Derrida, *Of Grammatology*, p. 183.
2. Martin Heidegger, *Being and Time*, p. H262.
3. Derrida, *Of Grammatology*, p. 247.
4. See, e.g., Plato's description of being as eternity at the end of Book 5 of the *Republic*.
5. See Derrida, *Of Grammatology*, pp. 183–186.
6. And this is why a distinguishing theme of post-modern, as contrasted with Enlightenment, thought is the topic of heterogeneity itself which is thematized in works as different as Levinas's *Totality and Infinity* and Kuhn's *The Structure of Scientific Revolutions*.
7. See Derrida, *Of Grammatology*, passim.
8. See Bernard Lonergan, *Insight*, pp. 348–374.
9. I would therefore argue that the Heideggerian and deconstructionist critique of the metaphysics of presence are actually critiques of henology and of the persuasive influence of henological thinking on our thinging about being. The ultimate impact and benefit of such critiques is that they can help us release being from the influence of the One, where the One is conceived as the effacement of difference.
10. See William Lynch, *Christ and Apollo* (Notre Dame: University of Notre Dame Press, 1975) for a remarkable, if skeletal, description of the kind of spirituality for which I am arguing here.
11. See Richard Rorty, *Consequences of Pragmatism*, pp. 97–98.
12. See Soren Kierkegaard, *Fear and Trembling*, trans. by Alastair Hannay (New York: Penguin Books, 1985), pp. 145–147. Because Kierkegaard works out his conception of the relationship between eternity and time in the context of his effort to understand Christianity, he is not so much interested in developing an ontology of temporality as in reappraising our way of valorizing our historicity. The view of time and eternity which I am trying to develop here, while profoundly influenced by Christian theology and spirituality, is not, in my judgment, distinctively Christian in its essence.

CHAPTER 8

1. Heidegger's "On the Origin of the Work of Art," in *Poetry, Language, Thought,* trans. by Albert Hofstadter (New York: Harper and Row, 1975), pp. 15–88, which neither accepts nor rejects but radically transforms the traditional understanding of the work of art, is the model I have in mind for the type of "recasting" I am attempting here.
2. See, e.g. *The Future of an Illusion*, chapters 5 and 6.
3. See, e.g. *Concluding Unscientific Postscript*, passim.
4. There are, of course, many different arguments by many different philosophers. In my synopsis and throughout the ensuing discussion, I focus on the contingency argument not because I think all other kinds of argument are reducible to it but because I think to some degree the other arguments imply it, and

because it is the argument most directly relevant to the issues involved in my effort to recast the argument in ontological terms.

5. Heidegger, "What is Metaphysics," pp. 347–348.

6. I do not mean to imply that the argument for God's existence has never been formulated in a way which minimizes or even subverts the influence of the metaphysics of presence. Indeed, insofar as Aquinas identifies being with what is known through judgment and not with "the already out there now," his metaphysics, and the arguments for God's existence which are part of it, are *not* under the sway of the metaphysics of presence or an objectivist, ocular epistemology. Aquinas's profound insight into contingency is most revealing in this regard. As I will try to argue in the next section of this chapter, the metaphysics of presence leads us to interpret contingency as absence and prevents our appreciating the liability to nothingness which contingency in the deepest sense involves. I would say not only that Aquinas takes this liability to nothingness seriously but that he makes it philosophically significant for the first time. Insofar as this is the case, Aquinas's discussion of God's existence should be viewed not as the paradigm case of what I am calling the "traditional argument" but as the original effort to address the question in an ontologically appropriate way.

On the other hand, it seems to me that the Aristotelean framework which Aquinas uses to develop and articulate his ontology does not allow the ontological significance of his thought to emerge in all its radical originality. This leads me to think that, just as Lonergan had to make Aquinas's thought pass through Kant in order to fully develop the cognitional theory implicit in it, so too we have to make Aquinas's thought pass through Heidegger in order to fully develop the alternative to ontic metaphysics which Aquinas anticipates and begins to explore. This book as a whole, and this chapter in particular, are devoted to this latter project, which Karl Rahner initiated. (Rahner's influence on these pages is less pervasive than Lonergan's because I have found Lonergan's cognitional theory indispensable in trying to make sense of Heidegger's critique of traditional metaphysics.)

Finally, I should say a brief word about Lonergan's own argument for the existence of God. In *Insight* Lonergan rejected ocular epistemology and the metaphysics of presence associated with it, as did Heidegger in *Being and Time;* but, unlike Heidegger, Lonergan used his own understanding of being to develop arguments for God similar to Aquinas's but couched in terms of his own cognitional theory. In his later work Lonergan did not so much repudiate such arguments as acknowledge that discovering God is a matter of conversion involving existential realizations, not just a matter of arguments involving intellectual insights. (See *Method in Theology,* especially chapter 10. For a discussion of Lonergan on conversion, see Robert Doran, *Psychic Conversion and Theological Foundations* [Atlanta: Scholars Press, 1981].)

I will be arguing that these existential realizations principally have to do with our asking ourselves the questions we would most like to avoid, and letting that process lead us to an awareness of our own nothingness. Thus I will be trying to couple Lonergan's cognitional theory with Heidegger's account of our encounter with nothingness in such a way that together they might provide a way to understand the experience of contingency which Aquinas, though operating under the influence of an ontic metaphysic, argued is our only access to the absolutely Other.

7. See Mircea Eliade, *The Sacred and the Profane,* and *Rites and Symbols of Initiation,* trans. by Willard Trask (New York: Harper and Row, 1965), and Joseph Campbell, *The Hero with a Thousand Faces,* Meridian Books (New York: World Publishing Company, 1956). In *The Way of Suffering: A Geography of Crisis* (Washington, D.C.: Georgetown University Press, 1989), I attempt to develop a phenomenological account of the dialectical process involved in undergoing such a reversal.

8. The most accessible description of such a transformation with which I am familiar is Tolstoy's *The Death of Ivan Ilyich.*

9. See Heidegger, *Being and Time,* H235–H266.

10. The relationship between emotion and judgment is discussed at length in *What is an Emotion?,* ed. by Calhoun and Solomon, but I know no more subtly perceptive treatment of the issue than that developed by N. J. H. Dent in *The Moral Psychology of the Virtues* (New York: Oxford University Press, 1984) pp. 64–93.

11. See Descartes, the first of the *Meditations.*

12. My reflections here have been influenced by Burke's *A Philosophical Inquiry into the Origin of our Ideas of the Sublime and Beautiful.* ed. by James Boulton (Notre Dame: University of Notre Dame Press, 1968).

13. In my judgment, Heidegger never makes this affirmation. I have been struggling for years now with the question of what prevents him from doing so. While he speaks of sheparding Being, and develops a way of thought which is profoundly reverent toward what he calls Being, he does not approach it in a spirit of worship or radical humility. I have tried to discuss, in chapters 3 and 7, what I have come to think of as the sources of this failure. There is, first, Heidegger's tendency to understand judgment, and the whole intellectual process involved in making judgments, not just as a derivative mode of knowing but as a mode of knowing bound up with the metaphysics of presence and ocular epistemology. I have tried to argue in this book, under Lonergan's influence, that the rejection of this metaphysics and epistemology, far from requiring us to abstain from intelligent inquiry and rational reflection, actually enables us to take them more seriously than was ever done while philosophy was under the sway of objectivism.

Secondly, there is Heidegger's failure to follow our intimations of nothingness all the way to the point where they wring from us the confession of our identity with it. In *Being and Time,* nothingness is never more than a possibility to which I am liable and so its capacity for radically undermining my very status as a being is not fully explored.

I am arguing here that if we let horror carry us all the way down to the bottom of our nothingness, and if we intelligently think through the questions which such an experience provokes, we will be rationally led to affirm the reality of being itself as our radical Other—though the entire meaning of such a judgment would be misconstrued if it were interpreted in terms of the metaphysics of presence.

14. This is why, though I spoke earlier of our participation in being which is radically Other than us, I would argue against understanding such participation in an emanationist sense. While the source of emanationist theology is, in my judgment, the religious experience of our nothingness in and of ourselves, emanation theory concludes from this experience that our being must, in and of itself, be divine. But if this were true, our very being would not be liable to nothingness.

And it is the liability of our being to nothingness that proves we are nothingness in and of ourselves.

According to the creation theory which I am struggling to articulate here, our being is finite through and through, and in no sense divine, but it is radically Other than us who, in and of ourselves, are nothing. In distinguishing itself from emanation theory, creation theory came to speak of the ontological relationship between the absolute Other and created being as a causal one, for the language of causality emphasizes the distinction between the creator (cause) and the creature (effect) in a way that the language of participation does not. But the language of causality has encouraged the kind of "objectivist" thinking associated with the metaphysics of presence and ocular epistemology. To create a language that avoids this pitfall and that expresses the insights which become accessible when we reflect on our deepest intimations is, I would argue, the specific vocation of a religious philosophy.

INDEX

217